TO
Jim + June
With my very best regards,
Pete Widener

THE
FLY-FISHINGEST
GENTLEMEN

A Fourteen-Rod Book

This is copy number

749

of a limited edition of 1200

Keith C. Russell

Photograph by R. Dugald Pearson

Our host, Mr. Russell

THE FLY-FISHINGEST GENTLEMEN

A choice assemblage of fly-fishing adventures

by

Keith C. Russell
and 69 of his
Brothers and Sisters of the Angle

Foreword by Gardner L. Grant

Illustrated by Joseph C. Fornelli

WINCHESTER PRESS

An Imprint of New Century Publishers, Inc.

Contemporary drawings by Joseph C. Fornelli

Old engravings and woodcuts from the Elman Pictorial Collection

Printing Code
11   12   13   14   15   16

Library of Congress Cataloging-in-Publication Data

The Fly-Fishingest Gentlemen.

A collection of essays by various authors on fly fishing.
1. Fly fishing. I. Russell, Keith C., 1920–
SH456.F586 1986   799.1'2   86–8786
ISBN 0–8329–0403–1
ISBN 0–8329–0430–9 (case)

DEDICATION

This book is dedicated with love to my mother and father, Ruth and Ford Russell, and with thanks for their constant encouragement and support throughout their lives and mine.

And again to my Margie who has, and still, puts up with more than most while I engage in various "labors of love."

Contents

BEAT TWO—*Keith C. Russell*

BEAT THREE

BEAT FOUR—*Keith C. Russell*

BEAT FIVE

BEAT SIX—*Keith C. Russell*

BEAT SEVEN

Preface

Apart from the members of my family, I have had only two other lasting loves in my life: fly fishing and waterfowling. Having put together two books on the latter, *The Duck-Huntingest Gentlemen* and *For Whom the Ducks Toll*, it seemed only fair and proper to do one on the former. Thus, *The Fly-Fishingest Gentlemen* was born.

Whatever measure of success *TFFG* may enjoy will be due in substantial part to the "most memorable" fly-fishing experiences related herein by my good friends: sixty-nine Brothers and Sisters of the Angle. To all of them I should simply like to say, "You are the greatest. I thank you for your participation and hope you are pleased with the result."

I should also like to express my deep appreciation for the excellent services performed in the preparation of this volume by my longtime secretary, Carole West; my longtime assistant in many matters, Michael Wardeiner; and by my longtime wife and helpmate, Margie.

Finally, with respect to the use of the word "gentlemen" in the title, it should be noted that the pages of all my books have been graced by ladies, sportswomen who have demonstrated abilities with a fly rod and/or a shot-gun and are equal to or have surpassed many of their male counterparts. I love it, and them. And I should like to especially thank them for their meritorious literary efforts. Moreover, not one of them has objected to being included in a book that does not give them credit in the title. For that I also thank them.

The fact is we are fly fishers all.

Keith C. Russell
Chagrin Falls, Ohio

Gardner L. Grant

Past president of Theodore Gordon Fly-fishers; former chairman of the New York State Commissioner's Council on Environmental Conservation; past president of the Federation of Fly Fishers; national director of Trout Unlimited; director of the Atlantic Salmon Federation; chairman of the board of the American Museum of Fly Fishing; director of the Catskill Fly Fishing Center; and organizer and co-chairman of Wild Trout Symposia I, II and III. Gardner is the quintessential conservationist. Scarsdale, New York.

Foreword

Somehow, fly rods and shotguns go together, and surely Keith Russell goes exceeding well with both.

A life-long fly fisher and waterfowler, Keith has served as senior vice president and trustee of Ducks Unlimited, Inc., and is currently a national director of Trout Unlimited and a trustee of the American Museum of Fly Fishing. He has given much back to those resources which have meant so much to him, and, in his writing and editing, he contributes much to the pleasure of his fellow devotees.

His earlier and very successful books, *The Duck-Huntingest Gentlemen* and *For Whom the Ducks Toll*, didn't help you shoot ducks, and this one probably won't help you cast a fly or catch a fish. Most readers will already know well how to do both anyhow.

What, then, is *The Fly-Fishingest Gentlemen?* It is a delicious bouilla-baisse of expressions on a sport they love by Keith and his angling friends, few of whom have ever had anything published before. Here is the composite response to Keith's request for a memorable personal vignette, story, philoso-phy, or viewpoint on flyfishing. "Fish" through the seven beats of this book and sample the world of today's fly rodding in fresh water and salt from the perspective of seventy very individual contributors unified by a common dedication to this most engrossing sport of them all. There is something here for everyone.

It has been said that fly fishers, more than participants in any other sport, if they are not actively doing it, like to read about it. I think you'll enjoy *The Fly-Fishingest Gentlemen* as the next best thing to doing it.

"An Atlantic salmon will take when it takes!"

Keith C. Russell, 1984

This cartoon appeared on the program cover of the Centenary Dinner of the Flyfishers' Club of London held on October 25, 1984 at the Savoy Hotel. I am indebted for this delightful bit of whimsy to M. B. (Buck) Franks, M. D., of Jamestown, New York, a member of the club who attended the dinner. It struck me as deserving a place in *TFFG*.

It is reproduced here through Buck's courtesy; the very kind permission of the artist, Mr. Rodger McPhail; The Flyfishers' Club, Commander N. T. Fuller RN (Retd.), Secretary; and the owner of the original, The Honorable Ayhner Tryon.

BEAT ONE

Dixon B. White

*A fly fisherman, waterfowler, outdoor writer,
and conservationist. His business? Why, an
Orvis Shop, quite naturally. Wayland, Massachusetts.*

Half a Four-Leaf Clover

Dr. Charles Mixter plucked a four-leaf clover from the lawn. It was at Carter
Hall Lodge, overlooking the confluence of the Kedgwick and Restigouche
rivers—fifty-six miles above the latter's mouth in northern-western New
Brunswick. The doctor's smile bridged to his ears. "Now we've no excuses,"
he said and laughed. Riverwater burbled assurance.

The trip barely materialized. At the final moment, Charlie was offered
three gratis days on these legendary waters by his friend Baldwin Terry of
Bath, Maine, who owns the lodge. I was invited. It was for the last three days
in June of '77. I had a near conflict. Dad and I had signed up for the week
following to trout in Yellowstone. I would have time for a clothes change.
Wife Sally said: "It'll be a trip to be remembered." That did it.

From Boston to Presque Isle, Maine via Delta Air and then by rental car to
Kedgwick took several hours. As we set up rods, I thought "Poor rehearsal;
good show." First off, my antique Hardy Perfect's reel foot was too thick for
the reel seat of my untried Orvis graphite. Camp guide Adelard Gallant took

the reel and disappeared into the gloaming. He solved the dilemma by grinding down the brass reel foot. I trust he never noticed the tears in my eyes.

Secondly, I couldn't locate my spool of salmon tippet material. Overlooking the possibility of trophy-sized fish in these storied waters, I found a used trout leader and knotted its butt onto my leader for the point. A further catch was my failing eyesight. I had blood-knotted this tippet on the camp porch in the fading light of dusk.

Mist and fog accompanied the hush of dawn. The water was dropping, an optimistic sign. Bright hens tend to make their spawning run now. Grilse later. Fishing for salmon with big high water hairwings, we hook and release half-a-dozen smelt-size trout. Comes the sun.

Charlie and I take turns wading and fishing the drops from the 28-foot canoe with Adelard. Drops are traditional for fishing New Brunswick salmon rivers. The guide successively anchors down through each pool. His angler blankets the water with pie-section casts, abeam to astern. When a salmon is hooked, the fish is played from shore.

The sun becomes intense. Salmon and blue sky arrive together. We each connect. Dix's comes first. It takes a #4 double-iron Black Jack in the Barn Pool at 10 a.m. Twelve pounds of shimmering sunlight. The nine-weight graphite whips her in twelve minutes. A pound a minute.

Charlie ties into his at 11:40 on a featherwing yellow #2 Doctor Special. In twenty-five minutes, a 26-pound Atlantic lies beached at the Pot Hole Pool. She's also a bright and handsome hen—sleek yet deep-bellied. No kype.

Still and heavy the air. Another trout at eventide for Dix. She hooks herself. The fly is almost her own size—a double #1/0 Jock Scott. At 7:30 p.m., the Doctor loses a sparse, hair Silver Rat to a hefty salmon as the sun disappears in a lacy crimson halo. At last light, a 12-pound Atlantic socks a green-butted Conrad for Dix. We enter three salmon in the camp log. Fifty pounds of fish today.

Fair and warm, day two dawns at 4 a.m. The lodge operates on U.S. time. We fish for four hours in an escalating wind. The grilse are moving. We spot half-a-dozen acrobatic fish off Campbell's Beach. Charlie hooks and loses a big salmon. Three deer materialize out of the alders above the beach.

We sense impending rain. By 11 a.m. the wind gusts to twenty knots out of the sou'west. We beach picnic with the Bobby Goodyears of Aiken, South Carolina from Edmund Rogers' lodge across the river. With their party is artist Bob Clem of Ducks Unlimited fame, commissioned by the Goodyears to do an oil of salmon fishing on the family waters.

The Goodyears know something about entertaining. Cocktails and fresh grilled salmon planks with Canadian bacon precede a tour of the Rogers' pools—waters whose names conjure up scenes of angling history: Rogers' Pool (leased by Irving Paper Corporation), Kedgwick Pool (for the river), Bogan Pool (where the salmon are stacked like cordwood), Looking Glass Pool (she of the steep bluffs), Jimmy's Pool (where fishing-the-patent produces best), Moffat's Pool (a low water fishery), Soldier's Pool (the second best pool in the Matapedia River system) and The Government Water (bounded by red stakes). A drenching downpour precludes further fishing. At day's end, a roaring fire at the lodge reknits soul to body.

The rains raise the rivers during the night. They are up several inches as day breaks in the east. We start our drops under a leaden sky. Midmorning finds an elated doctor sinking a #2 Professor into a jumbo 22-pound hen. The fish is netted as the sun burns through. It is a happy omen.

Dix's turn catches him with half an unlit cigar in mouth. In the Barn Pool, two surging eddies meet in a classic feeding lane. Dix casts a #4 Black Jack double to the center of the vee and starts the retrieve. A muted "whump" and the rod tip dips with a solid hit. Salar is on.

Adelard puts me ashore on Campbell's Beach, above where the Kedgwick dumps into the Restigouche. First run takes the backing down to metal. This fish is a crauncher. Two 200-yard surges and she's off on a third. She takes it well into the backing. She's been on for over half an hour, yet still seems green. "Give her full butt!" Charlie yells. The 8-foot 9-inch graphite is bowed double under the strain. The line strums and sings. We muse on the vagaries of ancient tippets and dusk-tied blood knots. We nervously chomp on the unlit cigar.

She has taken me down river and around the corner into the Restigouche. Sounding now, she slackens slightly. Adelard steps out into the river, net at the ready. We watch the unwilling approach of a dark-backed submarine. Adelard slips the four-foot net under the quarry and gasps "Congratulations!" His craggy face is all grin. The fish, hooked in the Kedgwick, is finally netted in the Restigouche. People ask where I caught her and I can't decide which river to name.

She's a bright hen over four feet long and weighs just under 40 pounds. She now resides on the wall of our Orvis Shop in Boston.

We take two more salmon this day for a trip total of seven fish, with an average weight of just over 20 pounds. Yes, it was a trip to be remembered, but only half of Dr. Mixter's four-leaf clover worked. Sure, I caught the fish, but I swallowed the cigar in the process.

Charles H. Leavell

*A gentleman, sportsman, and a fourth gen-
eration Texan, Charles has always paid his
dues and is thus most deserving of his two
beloveds: wife Shirley and the 4UR Ranch.
El Paso, Texas.*

One Infinite Moment

Shirley,

Do you remember our search for the fisherman's Shangri-La? Shirley, I don't think that Shangri-La is so much a place as it is a state of mind.

For I vividly recall sitting in our boat late one evening when the sun had gone behind the divide, and the cliffs were mirrored in the dead calm Lost Lake. We were casting under the half-light and found ourselves afloat in the clearest water I had ever seen. There was no definable horizon line as air and water became one. I remember that a great sense of well-being flowed over us as we felt suspended in time and space.

Suddenly, a tremendous school of bait fish swept under us as though swimming in air, and a school of rainbows was slashing through them, leaving silvery scales to settle from the fury of their attack. Then, mysteriously, underneath it all we saw an immense form, the shape of a trout so huge that he had to have been close to a century old.

But before my fly could settle to him, a second trout hit as I tried to take it away. While I was still hung into this smaller fish, the silver school and the great fish moved off into the mist. It was then you told me, for one infinite moment, together we had seen and felt the mystical Shangri-La!

Editor's note: Lost Lake is a beautiful alpine lake at 10,500 feet altitude and over 90 feet in depth, surrounded by cliffs and black forest.

Frederick C. Pullman

Called "Uncle Fritz the Woodsman" by his nephews and nieces, he caught his first trout on a fly between Upper and Middle Saranac Lakes in the late 1930s. A banker, rancher, land manager, and past president of the Boone and Crockett Club, the oldest conservation organization in North America, he now lives so close to a trout stream that his back cast gets caught in the deck furniture. Lamoille, Nevada.

The Summer of 1942

I was at Pomfret School and 16 years old. My father was out of the country in the Navy. My mother wanted me to come home to Lake Forest for the summer with my younger brother and sister and play tennis at Onwentsia. I wanted to go trout fishing in the West. Ray Bergman was my idol. Every time I finished reading *Trout* I started again at the beginning. I wanted to fish the Firehole with Scottie Chapman.

Somehow, it worked! I do not remember exactly how now—43 years later—but I managed to get myself in with a group of other 16 year olds from

Illinois who were going to work for the government putting up hay for the elk in Jackson Hole and boarding at Weenie Wilson's Teton Valley Ranch up the Gros Ventre.

The hay wasn't ready when we arrived so we spent the first week or two helping local ranchers gather cows and calves for the branding. The West was not new to me. I had been at Los Alamos for two years before the government took it over to develop the atomic bomb, and before that I had been at A Bar A, but the glory of those early summer mornings in Jackson Hole I will never forget. We would be on horseback before dawn riding up the creeks and then the rounded ridge lines to the forest above where we would wait until it was light enough to see a cow and calf, and then we would start down, each of us in our own valley, moving the pairs gently ahead of us. I remember one morning I had a yearling moose for awhile until he decided to go back uphill. It always sort of fascinated me to start in the cool of the early morning with two or three cows and calves in front of me, and then to come out of my own little valley as the sun came over the ridge tops, to join another rider with his little bunch, and then to find ourselves an hour later, three or four of us by then, with fifty or sixty cows and their calves in front of us. As the sun rose, and the day warmed, we would come out of the hills and onto the flat where we would join still other bunches, bigger now, and take the whole bawling, dusty herd to the confusion, and the noise, and the trauma of the branding fires.

When haying started, we were trucked down to the valley and divided into crews of five. The smallest boys got to drive the trucks, the next two in size stacked bales on the trucks and the tallest two stayed on the ground on either side of the truck and lifted the bales to the stackers. It was healthy work day after day, although monotonous, and we relished a day when it rained because that gave us the next day off.

One day when we were eating lunch in the hay meadows, I was leaning against the top rail of a fence which crossed a small stream and looking dreamily into the depths of a pool. The stream was no more than 15 feet wide and the pool on a bend was quite deep for a stream that size, perhaps four or five feet. The current on the surface made the stoney bottom indistinct. You know the way it is when you are looking at something and not seeing it, and then all of a sudden there it is where you had not seen it before. Well, all of a sudden, I realized that I was looking at something in the depths of that pool that had moved and it made the hair stand up on the back of my neck. The more I looked, the more amazed I became because on the bottom of that pool were eight or ten huge trout holding in the current, the great grey shapes moving with respect to each other in such a way that they could not be rocks. Now I needed a day off and finally it rained.

There was not a truck to take me down there on that day, when everybody else was playing softball. I took a horse and rode the 18 miles to the creek which was called Cold, or Spring Creek, or something like that and ran into Jenny Lake. I was in the saddle at dawn with the tubular fly rod case under my left leg where a rifle scabbard belongs and a canvas sack with lunch and fly boxes on a strap over the pommel. It was a good young horse and I rode at a steady sit-down jog, just out of walk but not into a trot. It probably took me about three hours to ride to the stream, but then I was insouciant about time and distance.

I tied the horse to the fence and set up. I would have been using a nine-foot leader tapered to probably no less than 2X. I tied my own flies in those days and I do remember using a multicolored variant, I suppose, on a #14 hook. Carefully I moved into position at the foot of the pool, next to the fence, where I had first seen the trout, and I waited for a long time, watching. A trout moved up to the head of the pool, into shallower water, above which the current came in from the right. It was feeding casually on small floating insects. The cast had to be with the line falling on the water below the trout and the fly landing in the current above and to the right of the trout so that it would float around and to the trout without presenting the leader first. It worked. As the fly came around, the great grey shape lifted slowly to the surface and the fly disappeared. I set the hook, there was an enormous swirl, something big and grey went by me very fast and on under the fence where the leader broke against the bottom rail, it went leaving a great wave from bank to bank and then finally, out of sight around the next bend, there came the sound of a great splash.

It took me quite a while to stop shaking, and as for the rest of trout in the pool, they seemed to have lost their appetites, for none of them moved up to the feeding lie at the head of the pool. I rode home, pondering.

In a week or so it rained again, and I was back. I had planned my strategy. I was afraid it would not work, but I had to try. I could not move up to a heavier leader for fear of putting the fish down, and I did not think the 2X tippet would turn a fish that size, but whatever, I had to keep the trout from going under the bottom rail of the fence. This time when the fish took I set the hook as gently as possible and raced up stream away from the fence. The great trout and I passed each other about mid-pool, both of us going as fast as we could in opposite directions. He must have seen me go by for instead of going for the fence, he went to the security of the bottom of the pool and held there. Now I was in position at the head of the pool with the trout between me and the fence. Three times he went for the fence and the leader held and he turned. After what seemed like a very long time, he turned on his side and I was able to slide him gasping onto the gravel. Later, when I was able to measure and weigh him, he was 23 inches long and a little over five pounds, a spawning cutthroat up from Jenny Lake. An hour later I caught another just like him the same way. After cleaning the two fish, I put them head down into my sack, their great square tails sticking conspicuously out of the top. With the sack over my shoulder, rather than over the saddle to keep from bruising them on the long ride back, I started home. On the way, I passed two older men, they must have been in their middle twenties, fishing unsuccessfully with casting rods and bait. The looks of astonishment on their faces when they saw the two tails hanging out of my sack were enough to keep me smiling all the way back home.

Later that summer, when haying was over and the other boys had gone back to Illinois, I hitchhiked up to Yellowstone. There were not many cars on the road in those days, but the ones that were would invariably pick up a 16-year old with a duffle bag in one hand and a fly rod in the other. I did fish the Firehole with Scottie Chapman and with Ken Reid, then Executive Director of the Izaak Walton League, but that is another story.

Epilogue

I have no recollection of the train trip out from Chicago. I know we got off the train in Idaho Falls and were driven to Jackson, which then really was a cow town. The Cowboy Bar was on the left as you came into town and there was a general merchandise store across the square. I think the arch of elk antlers was there, but the rest of the honky tonk you see now was not.

I do remember the train ride back. I sat at the window and studied every stream we crossed, from Wyoming through Iowa. If they didn't have trout, at least they had bass or bluegills, and you could catch them all on a fly.

James C. Kennedy

An outdoor man by avocation and a news-paperman by profession; he also is the former Chairman of the Colorado Wildlife Commission. As a practical and practicing conservationist, Jim can be counted on to be on the side of our natural resources. Atlanta, Georgia.

Rob Roy

Placing qualitative values on one fly-fishing experience over another is almost impossible. That's why trying to determine one's most memorable fly-fishing experience is no easy task.

When I wade into a river or stream armed with a fly rod, 1 enter another world. Each time I cast a popping bug into the weeds, or try to present a dry fly properly, or fight the wind on the flats, my mind is in a different dimension. The terms "good, better, or best" or, for that matter, "most memorable," are really irrelevant. I'm simply fly fishing, which, in itself, is very special.

As I look back at almost 20 years of fly rodding, however, one experience does continue to surface. It wasn't an instance of landing a gigantic fish after a perfect cast and a long battle, but it was, nevertheless, unique. It was the day I caught my first Atlantic salmon.

It was in August before my junior year of college, and I was in Scotland hunting grouse. In preparation for an earlier grouse hunting trip, I had read everything I could find about hunting and fishing in England and Scotland.

That's when I learned the term "Rob Roy" was more than a drink, that it's also the Scottish term for "Grand Slam." It means killing a deer, bagging a grouse and landing a salmon all in the same day.

As we arrived in Grantown-on-Spey, our host, Sir William Gordon Cumming, advised us that after three days of grouse shooting there would be a "bye-day," or a day of rest. What would we like to do on that day? Some of our group wanted to tour, others wanted to try some rough shooting. In my innocence, I asked about trying for a Rob Roy.

"That, of course, will be extra," replied Sir William, "but if you would like to try I can arrange it." As my trip thus far had been paid for by a relative, I decided to spring for a little extra.

The deer, a roe buck, and the grouse came easy. The Atlantic salmon was to be a real challenge.

My fly-fishing experience had been limited to pestering trout in the streams and rivers of Colorado, where I was enrolled in college. I had become a quite proficient caster, but I was still a long way from being a fly fisherman. My experience on the River Spey would add to my education.

After lunch on the banks of the Spey, Fred Palmer, Alfred Kennedy and I, at the heels of our ghillies, headed off to try our luck with salmon. It was far from the peak salmon season, and my ghillie warned me not to get my expectations too high.

My first surprise was the giant fly rod. It didn't look anything like the trout rods I was used to. It was perhaps 12 feet in length and fitted with a huge two-handed grip. I was even more astonished by the double-hooked fly my ghillie attached to the end of a very stout leader. It looked more like a decoration from a cheap cowboy hat than a trout fly. Little did I know. When I asked my ghillie what this fly was meant to imitate, he regarded me with justified contempt and told me it was an old salmon fly that had killed many a salmon.

Wading into the Spey thus armed, I quickly demonstrated the fine points of casting 20 feet with a rod designed to cast across a river. Repeatedly, my ghillie waded out to demonstrate the proper casting technique for the two-handed monster he had given me. Finally, I mastered it and began to enjoy the casting and to fish seriously.

The cold wind and lack of success drove Alfred and Fred from the Spey to its banks where they could sample other treasures of Scotland and warm themselves at the same time. As they sipped fine Scotch, they offered unsolicited advice on where to cast, where to stand, how to wade, what facial expression should be worn for success, and so on.

I did my best to ignore the comments from what a couple of hours earlier had been two very serious and sober companions. My dogged persistence then did pay off with a short hookup. I was so anxious to silence my advisors that I tried to horse in my fish and I lost it. I had that fish on just long enough to know that I really wanted to hook another.

As the sun began to set, Fred and Alfred left the bank and returned to the warming hut. From that strategic perch, they could watch the constant changing colors as the sun set over the rolling moors. They could also keep an eye on me as the hut warmed their exteriors and the Scotch warmed their interiors.

I fished toward the warming hut, intending to call it quits when I reached the shelter. By now I was really enjoying casting the big rod. I was sure another strike was imminent.

When it came, I was almost reduced to the role of a spectator. The fish hit so hard that I simply raised the tip of the big rod to set the hook. The details of the ensuing fight remain unclear. The commotion aroused Alfred and Fred, who reappeared from the warming hut to now offer advice on how to land my fish. My ghillie simply smiled as he waded to my side and told me to remain calm. I made my way slowly toward shallow water and let my equipment do most of the work. After what seemed an interminable period, my fish began to tire and yield line. When it was finally spent, my ghillie, with little fanfare, reached down and expertly tailed my fish. Then, with proper ceremony, he dispatched it, making the "kill" official. My Rob Roy was complete.

Alfred and Fred clambered down the bank and congratulated me for heeding all their advice. They told me they knew I would catch a fish once I began following their instructions.

Fred Palmer and Alfred Kennedy are not with us any longer to enjoy the fruits of the fly rod and the shotgun. They were both great sportsmen and great friends. Occasionally I think about them and remember a wide-eyed college student still wet behind the ears carrying his 12-pound salmon and trying to control his smile, while Fred and Alfred, each with an arm over my shoulder, walked with me through the heather toward our vehicle. We all laughed and joked and bragged, and the memories of that day continue to grow in a stature.

Maybe that fish was only 10 pounds.

Isn't that what hunting and fishing are all about anyway?

Laurence G. Isard

Nationally known for his dynamic wildlife sculptures, he is the Acting Director at the Cleveland Natural History Museum. As nice as he is talented. He says that a family, mortgage, and job have somehow side-tracked his aspirations of becoming an internationally renowned fly fisherman and wing shot. Cleveland, Ohio.

Losings

In the northern third of Michigan's Lower Peninsula, there are a number of trout rivers which are generally avoided by most fishermen. Dead falls, partially submerged logs, beaver dams, and other natural obstructions occur with enough regularity to totally deter canoeists, make spin casting impractical, and discourage the average fly fisherman.

Lined with alders and occasional stands of white cedar and spruce, these streams are usually no wider than a two-lane country road. They may broaden briefly at right angle bends to three lanes, or at the other extreme become so restricted that overhanging alders on opposite banks form a tunnel of vegetation over a narrow lane of hip-deep water.

I have fished other more spectacular and productive rivers in the far West and East, but I am drawn back year after year to a quiet stretch of a particular Michigan river like the proverbial moth to a flame. There is little to recommend this river to a really avid fly fisherman except its isolation, and the solitude and subtle beauty of its northern forest. There is, however, the remote possibility, but always a possibility, of catching a large brown trout, and the likelihood of success increases greatly if the fisherman savors the unique pleasures of night fishing.

As an urban dweller I am normally indoors at nightfall. However, each summer with the approach of evening I voluntarily enter this river in search of night-feeding trout, and the apprehension can become almost overwhelming when I suddenly find myself alone in an environment which to all outward appearances has been totally altered by the advance of darkness. With visibility reduced to less than 10 feet and the water surface mirroring the sky, I stumble, lurch and blunder over, and into, a variety of submerged and partly submerged objects. Hearing becomes the predominant sense, and all manner of unfamiliar noises seem exaggerated and close.

Under the right circumstances, apprehension can border on panic, and I experienced near panic my first summer on this river. It was past 11 p.m., heavily overcast and particularly dark. I was working a trout which had established a feeding station under an impossible mess of alder foliage entwined with floating branches. The audible slurps of the feeding fish kept me casting long after the trout had me defeated, as he refused to be lured from beneath the mat of floating debris.

As I doubled over in the knee-deep water to avoid hanging the fly in the brush, there was sudden explosion of sound as if a large slab of concrete had been dropped in the water. The next explosion, seconds later and 20 yards away, sent me up the bank where I stood shaking, tangled in a thicket of scrub dogwood.

This was my first encounter with a very agitated beaver that wanted me out of the river and out of his way. His tail slapping succeeded beyond his wildest rodent imaginings, for in the darkness I was totally undone and hastily retreated to the familiar comforts of a brightly lit cabin.

In the quiet black of a Michigan night, the abrupt slap of a beaver tail still puts my nerves on edge, but at least I know the source of the sound. Even more annoying, the resounding thwack instantly puts down the surface feeding trout. There is one particular broad, deep pool located within a hundred yards of a beaver lodge which I have never successfully fished after dark. The beaver so resent my presence they put the trout down and drive me away before my first fly has settled on the surface.

Over the years, I have learned to recognize the external but unrelated natural signals which trigger the nightly feeding of brown trout. They occur at dusk, about 9:30 in this latitude, when the woodcock flutters from the alders, the final gentle call of the white-throat is replaced with the harshness of whippoorwills and the first bat courses the river erratically searching for insects.

This is my personal witching hour. The trout are leaving the protection of the stream side cover in their first tentative search for food. Unless there is a significant hatch, there are few if any rises to mark feeding fish. I cast blindly to random pockets of open water and the dry fly drifts gently past a log or exposed tree root. In the gathering dusk I catch my breath, anticipating the strike I know will come, possibly not on the first cast, but the next, or next, or next. Most of these night-feeding brown trout range from 12 to 16 inches. However, I know much larger ones inhabit this river and the knowing keeps me there often well past midnight.

I have a predilection for large trout and will spend an inordinate amount of time casting a variety of wet and dry flies, streamers, and nymphs at any site which has the remotest possibility of harboring such fish. Although large trout are not commonly taken on this river, the survey records of the Michigan Department of Natural Resources indicate they are more prevalent than most fishermen suspect.

An abundance of natural obstructions are the major obstacles to contend with at any time. Add the factor of darkness and the possibility of successfully landing a large fish is significantly reduced. It was under such circumstances that I had a most unusual and frustrating series of encounters with a large, night-prowling brown trout.

Using a 7½-foot rod for a six weight line, I was fishing a section of stream largely devoid of cover and generally unproductive of trout. Halfheartedly casting near an isolated stand of alders, I saw the fly disappear in a gentle rise the instant it touched the water. When I set the hook there was no give and I knew there was a good fish on. The trout instantly raced for the alder tangle several feet away. The show was over in three seconds flat. Defeated in a context that ended before it started, I stood dumbfounded, mouth agape, as the line slowly drifted downstream—less the fly and several inches of tippet.

Using the same rod the following evening, I approached that particular piece of river with great caution, and like the contender who refused to enter the field of battle until the signs were right, I sat on the river bank watching and listening. When the woodcock, whippoorwills, and bats signaled dusk, I reentered the river.

Considering my lack of fly-casting skills and the anxiety of the moment, I managed to present the fly with considerable delicacy. Again the trout struck on the first cast and again, in complete control, the fish reached the shelter and safety of the alders. My only minor triumph was extending the battle from three seconds to 10. I reeled in the line, again minus the fly, most of the tippet, and much of my self confidence.

Included with the fishing equipment I took to Michigan that summer was a beautiful Orvis bamboo rod, eight-feet long for an eight weight line; a gift from my wife's understanding parents. Using a heavy rod on this small river, the action is slow, but the extra backbone of such a rod would hopefully tip the odds in my favor for my third scheduled assault on this trout.

Wading the stream to within casting distance of the trout's lie, I waited and fidgeted, impatient for the promise of dusk. Tense with anticipation before the first and second casts, I became disheartened after the third, and following the fifth cast quietly retrieved the line and slowly backed downstream, greatly discouraged but not yet defeated.

When I returned an hour later, the silhouette of the alder stand was barely visible against the night sky. It was too dark to cast any distance with accuracy, and I edged upstream hugging the bank opposite the alders to a point 15 feet from where the previous strikes had occurred. When the fly settled on the surface it was less than six feet from the rod tip. I never saw the fly disappear or sensed any tension on the line, only the familiar slurp and I set the hook, raised the rod tip, reared back and held on.

The trout bolted for the alders, and the rod did its work. Held just short of its goal, the fish thrashed briefly on the surface, raced upstream a short distance, turned and headed downstream. Once past the alders, there were few snags to contend with and I began breathing again.

Win or lose, I badly wanted a glimpse of this fish. Too dark to see below the river's surface, I fumbled to reach a flashlight in my fishing vest. With hands occupied controlling the trout, I jammed the base of the light in my mouth and tilted my head to whatever angle was necessary to follow the course of the battle. Tired from fighting the rod, the trout made one long final run while evading the first pass with the net. With the flashlight clenched in my teeth, I used the light beam to help maneuver the fish to a small mud flat where it was netted with comparative ease.

To an avid devotee of night fishing this brown trout was nothing exceptional, however, at 20 inches, it was my personal record for a wild trout of any kind. In retrospect, it was probably unfair to play this fish on so heavy a rod, but fair or unfair, I still use it religiously when night fishing, for in the shadowy blackness with limited visibility and so many unseen obstructions to contend with, a light rod is all but useless against a large trout.

I still question why this fish rose to and was hooked by exactly the same fly pattern on three successive nights. Speculating that more than a single trout inhabited that piece of river, I fished it intently for several nights, yet I had no other rises. Each year I faithfully return to fish close against that isolated alder stand, but I have never again been rewarded for my efforts.

Despite an occasional triumph, failures far exceed my successes. And despite the pleasure of reflecting on the successes, it is the losings which in reality are the most memorable; for I am enticed back each summer to darkness on this lovely river by one unforgettable moment when a brown trout delicately sipped my fly from the surface and snapped a four-pound tippet in one effortless silent motion.

George Hommel

One of the all-time great Florida Keys bone-fish and tarpon guides, he is now proprietor of World Wide Sportsman, a well-known fishing tackle and sportswear emporium in the Keys. Islamorada, Florida.

Tarpon Tale

Back in the late '50s, Dave DeTar, now deceased, was fishing with me as his guide, and we were after tarpon just west of Big Pine Key. Dave belonged to the Miami Beach Rod and Reel Club and wanted to boat his first 100-pound-plus tarpon on a fly. He was using a 12-weight rod and an anti-reverse reel with a pretty heavy drag when he struck a fish that looked to be over a hundred.

After about 30 minutes of aerial acrobatics, the tarpon headed for a small mangrove island that was about 100 feet wide. You could see there was water all the way through it. Well, the fish went straight into the island, and Dave asked, "What do I do now?" I replied, "Throw your rod overboard and maybe he will swim it through," which he did. I then poled rapidly around the island and here came the tarpon miraculously followed by the line and rod.

Dave picked up the rod out of the water and 45 minutes later landed the tarpon. After all that, the fish weighed in at 99 pounds!

Sibley W. Hoobler, M.D.

Has fly fished the same beloved stream in northern Michigan for over 60 years. His streamside cabin remains a gathering place for friends to whom he reads the graceful prose of Henry Van Dyke, and where he listens to fishing stories and dreams of monster trout that have eluded him. Cleveland, Ohio.

Do You Want to Know the Truth?

The stream flowed confidently; there was barely a murmur as it twisted sharply to the right. Only the underlying swirl and the uprising sand betrayed the difficulty of negotiating the curve. The old fisherman and his young friend, who was new to the art of casting the dry fly, stood on a brushy peninsula surveying the darkening scene. A few birds flew about seeking insects on the wing. All was silent except for the faint murmur of the river. The whippoorwills were not yet ready to sing. A small bush leaned out into the head of the pool adding to the dark turbulence.

"He ought to be just below that leaning branch," said the old man, beginning his preparatory, line-lengthening casts. At the proper moment, he released the line, and to his great pleasure the fly landed within a few inches downstream of the bush, its white plume floating gaily on the descending ripples. In a few seconds came that welcome slurp; a big one had taken it and quickly pulled the line with a singing noise for about six feet down to the bottom of the pool. The rod tip trembled as he sulked down there at the end of a 4X tippet. It was the still, silent moment of truth. There followed a heavy, steady tug as he moved down stream toward a brush pile at the river's bend. Fearing he'd lose it, the fisherman applied gentle upward pressure. The fish yielded, and his shining brown specked body could be seen just below the surface. "It's the big one I've heard about," He thought. In a moment the trout dove into the brush; his movement could no longer be felt in the rod. From a pull on the line to extricate him came back only the empty feeling of a lost fly. The pair stumbled back to the car silently, emotionally drained. As if in mockery, the whippoorwills began to sing.

The presence of the big fish had been passed around in almost silent whispers, each informant being sure that his listener had some knowledge of the fact before contributing his latest news. So the rumors of the giant trout had been quietly magnified.

During the next few days, in this prime time of the trout, when the hexagenia hatch was eagerly awaited each nocturne, another young friend, skilled in the casting of a dry fly, came to visit the cabin. As the pine trees were darkening against the summer sky, he pulled on his gear and announced his destination. The host said no word as he declared he'd fish through the river's bend. He thought that the guest deserved first choice on the river.

The whippoorwills had long since ceased to sing in the warm summer evening when the angler returned. "Do you know," he said, "I was casting just below a small protruding bush when I had a fantastic strike. The fish took my line and bottomed. I was thinking what to do when upstream I heard a splashing noise: two men coming down—a long spinning line ahead of them. It tangled with the line to the big trout. Seeing the mischief they were causing, the two interlopers waded down to extricate the line. In the process, they broke my leader." The doleful story, told by the glowing coals of the camp fire, was fittingly accompanied by the baleful whoosh of nighthawks on the wing.

As the morning's shaft of light filtered through the pine needles bringing life to camp, the old fisherman bade his young friends good-bye, with promises to invite them next year. A quiet settled on the cabin. Sitting on the porch that morning alone, he vowed to return that night to match wits with the experienced old trout. He checked rod and reel; he laid out the best flies well treated with mucilin, and he attached a new and tougher leader to the line. Quickly after dinner, he departed to the parking spot so as to be the first. It was not to be. A car blocked the drive-in, and it was evident that some one was already at the hole. The old man drove onto another spot, but he fished without enthusiasm. His mind could not be distracted from the opportunity lost. In fact, it became an obsession leading to a sleepless night.

Early next day he returned to the river bend, determined to seek out the old brown in broad daylight. His trousers were soaked from the glistening dew on the grass as he approached the peninsula and the now-famous spot. As he rounded the last clump of tag alder, a scene of desolation appeared; the long grass lay flat in the morning sun as if crushed by sleeping bags; small bushes had been cut to the ground, and the remains of a campfire blackened the soil for the little peninsula where so many hopeful anglers had stood to cast to the current below the bush. A few lackluster casts brought no rises, nor were there any during the rest of the summer. Some years passed; the scars healed; neighbors no longer spoke in hushed tones of the trout which could so silently and swiftly strike the shimmering fly and as easily break leaders. Often in the evening as whippoorwills would call and night hawks ride the air, the old man would remember those nights and wish he knew the true story of that last one.

Sometimes it is right that we should know the truth. In medicine an appropriate and difficult procedure often dispels doubt and frequently leads to cure or relief of abnormal conditions. Often, however, it is better not to know—where the disease is unlikely to respond to medical or surgical treatment. Sometimes too much knowledge can destroy, as in the plays of Ibsen.

Now when he thinks of those bygone nights, the old man is glad he does not know, for although the unknown persons might have been rude and thoughtless fishermen, he prefers to believe they were two young people camping out in a lovely spot—throwing out with hesitation their first flies— and one of them was rewarded by catching his first big trout. In doing so he joyously joined those whose lives will never be complete without experiences by a stream at twilight in the tantalizing presence of a great trout.

Knowing the truth could destroy that dream.

Reprinted by courtesy of Headwaters Chapter,
Trout Unlimited, Gaylord, Michigan

Joseph P. Hubert

He probably fishes for Atlantic salmon more each year than many anglers do in a lifetime, and as you would expect, he is highly knowledgeable re Salmo salar. Author of Salmon, Salmon, *Joe is also the creator of the Sheep series of salmon flies, which have taken Iceland and other salmon areas by storm. Duluth, Minnesota.*

Richer Than Midas

(an excerpt, with permission, from the privately published volume, Salmon, Salmon, With a Chapter on Iceland*)*

I must tell of a situation involving jungle cock and a close acquaintance of mine. It seemed this fellow had an old habit of scanning the sporting-goods want ads in the papers of any town he might find himself in. His long-suffering goal in such reviews was a Winchester Model 21 with an extra set of barrels for under two hundred dollars. (He's still looking.) One particular morning, in a small Midwestern newspaper, his want-ad search revealed a notice: "Due to illness, fly tier of over 40 years wishes to sell his materials." Now, having only recently become a member of the old school of salmon fishers, he wondered if by chance some jungle might be a part of this inventory. A phone call disclosed that the old dresser did allow that some jungle was for sale. After expressing his intent to purchase it, he received directions to the tier's residence in the nearby town.

A hurried trip found our buyer at the seller's workbench, and after amenities had been exchanged and coffee poured, a request to see the jungle was made. The fly tier said as he was principally a trout-fly dresser, he had little need for jungle cock and really had been unaware of his stock of that feather. He thereupon emptied a box of jungle cock before the stunned eyes of our friend, making a pile consisting of 53 jungle cock necks. A treasure greater than that of Midas! Fists full of diamonds would seem pale beside their value! Here before our fisher-for-salmon was a life guaranteed free from want, a supply of the perfect salmon fly.

Taking a few minutes to recover, he questioned, "Do you realize what you have here?" The old dresser allowed that he did know their value and placed the pelt prices between 40 and 60 dollars each. Upon closer examination it was found that the majority of necks were of exceptional quality and his stated valuation was well within reason.

The question was then asked as to how he came into possession of such a supply. He was not really sure, as he had only recently discovered their existence. It seemed during his recent move from the old farm to town he was cleaning out his barn and came upon a rat's nest half constructed of jungle cock feathers. Upon further search as to the source of their building materials, he found beneath some old cartons this horde of jungle cock necks. Their original source was thought to be a fly-material wholesaler who had gone out of business some 25 years before and had sold his complete inventory of material to the old dresser for a lump sum. He felt this was the only possible source, and the box had remained unopened until the rats had perfomed that task. Well, a price was settled upon for the entire number of pelts, and a call was made to my friend's fly dresser in the East, with some 40 necks being consigned to him.

However, before our want-ad searcher left, he asked the old fly tier what he had done with the rat's nest.

Len Codella

As head honcho of Thomas & Thomas, Len is involved in fly-rod design and manufacture, arranging worldwide fly-fishing safaris, and dealing in antique tackle. Greenfield, Massachusetts.

Episode at Wagon Tracks

Fly fishermen are an interesting lot. They seem to be forever searching for something: a better rod, a more effective fly, a better understanding of their sport, or some shadow in the water's surface. Looking for the first dun of an impending hatch, or the flash of a nymphing trout, a cloud of flitting caddis above the waters of their favorite pool, or rings on the surface to telltale a taking fish.

Most seem to be seeking knowledge of a sort that will put them at least on even terms with the fish they are intent on catching. Many search seemingly forever for that edge, some actually finding it; some are completely content with the search, perhaps down deep hoping never to find it, being completely consumed by the quest.

I believe, at one time or another, nearly all of us have this Quixotic fixation on our sport, being perfectly content to wait it out; somehow convinced that the quest is as important as the quarry; that the catching of fish is not as important as the how, and the successful quest for a single trout with a dry fly is far more significant an accomplishment than catching dozens with an underwater fly. Such is the gist of this story.

It was glorious spring day! Little matter that it was overcast and gray with the promise of a cold rain in the air. The strong cool wind blowing straight downstream gave an ominous suggestion that what might be following this front could be a bit of somewhat less than friendly weather. But what did I care? It was mid-May, the time of the Hendricksons in the Catskills. I was on the banks of the Beaverkill; it was only 10 a.m. and the Hendrickson hatch was due at 2 p.m. I had wangled the day off precisely so that I could take advantage of the superb dry-fly fishing this hatch would offer. I could spend the next few hours trying wets and nymphs for likely takers while awaiting the hatch.

I'd left home a bit over two hours before, driving the 120 miles at a steady pace, planning to arrive late morning and thus giving myself plenty of time for observation and study of the water prior to the anticipated hatch. On the way, I had visions of having the pool below Wagon Tracks all to myself at hatch time, figuring that all the regulars would be dutifully at work this particular midweek day.

Checking the water upon arrival I noted there were at least four fishermen along each bank of the pool I was planning to fish. So much for solitude! But, no matter, it was a glorious day. I even recognized a couple of the fishermen as fellow TGFers and I really didn't mind sharing the water with them and the others already there. As I suited up at roadside, I could feel the life force of the stream. The rushing movement of the water seemed to project a sense of life and of being live that is one of the mysterious rewards of being a fly fisherman. And yet, something just wasn't quite right.

What bothered me was that no one was fishing. These guys were standing around on the banks, in full uniform, rods rigged, ready to go, and yet not a soul was fishing. No one was even carrying on a conversation. It seemed that each had staked out his territory for the hatch, still 3½ hours away, and was contentedly guarding it, being perfectly happy to while away the waiting by staring at the water. Strange scene, this.

I moved down to the water's edge and hailed the first of the stoics I encountered, "Hi there! What's happening?"

"Not much," came the reply. "Waiting for the Hendrickson hatch to start."

"How come nobody's fishing?" I asked in a voice loud enough for all to hear.

"Why bother?" replied another. "These trout won't hit until those insects start to pop later this afternoon."

I saw my chance and took it. "Mind if I try?" I queried. "No, not at all . . . waste of time, though," came the reply from one of the more familiar members of the group.

I proceeded to rig up in order to fish a pair of wets with one eye on the task and one eye on the water. During the process I noticed a flash at the bottom, near the shallower head of the pool . . . then another, and then another, this time a bit off to one side of the main run. Trying to keep my cool for the benefit of my audience, I stepped into the stream, shook out a short length of line, flipped the cast upstream into the tail of the broad, shallow riffle and let the flies tumble down into the head of the only slightly deeper pool. The results of that first cast were electric. Almost at once, I had a solid strike with the fish both hooking himself and catapulting out of the water at the same time. He sure got everyone's attention pretty quickly. After a brief but spirited struggle I was able to release a healthy 13-inch brown.

During the fight, I had kept an eye on the pool, to see if the struggle would put down the other fish. Not a chance. As I looked down the length of the pool, I could see more and more flashes signaling actively feeding trout as far downstream as I could see. My next cast to the same spot produced a double-header! I had actually hooked two trout at the same time, each taking one of the pair of Hendrickson nymphs I was fishing. One of these trout managed to shake himself loose and I landed the other and released him. As I worked my way down the pool, I was into fish after fish, hooking and releasing so many that I lost count, and actually landing three more doubles!

Of course, all of this activity got everyone on the bank thoroughly worked up. I kept inviting those gentlemen to get off the bank and give it a try; announced the flies I was using and offered to share some of mine if they didn't have any with them. To my utter amazement, every one of them deferred, seemingly content to watch the parade, but somehow not wanting to join the marcher.

After more than the required amount of exhorting them to participate, I was convinced that I had done the morally right thing by each of them, and had demonstrated perfect stream etiquette. Comfortable that all question of manners had been addressed, I settled down to nearly two hours of some of the best nymph fishing I've ever had.

I learned a number of things that day on the stream, among them that trout will often feed more heavily on nymphs preparing to hatch, than on the duns themselves. Often this pre-hatch nymphal activity takes place hours before the main event, giving the angler ample opportunity for some terrific wet-fly fishing, if he is so inclined.

I also learned that there are times when an experienced fisherman will "turn off" to the idea of fishing a wet, so strongly may he be intent on "taking them on the dry." I can offer no rationale for this aberrant behavior, but I am convinced that this is what I experienced among my peers on the Beaverkill that memorable spring day. Perhaps none of that group that day wanted to be the first to give up the quest that each had psyched himself for, finding it far more noble to remain steady in the search; the how of the quest being far more significant than the quarry. Having been there too many times myself, I can readily understand. But, that day, I had a ball!

Peter A. B. Widener

Peter released a world-record permit recently because he didn't want people to know where he caught it; he would rather catch the fish than the publicity. There should be more fishermen like him. Palm Beach, Florida.

Catching

For the past 50 years fishing has been important to me. I caught my first sailfish when I was seven with Bert Hitchcock on the old *Goldfish* off Palm Beach. Over time I have owned two or three boats and fished for most every kind of saltwater game fish there is, catching all but a broadbilled swordfish and a mako shark, although I have hooked two of the latter. In addition I've also cast to a substantial number of non-game but very interesting, sometimes exciting, saltwater species.

Several years ago, a superb guide, Bill Curtis, first introduced me to saltwater fly fishing. After an extensive internship, I have since enjoyed a great many hours of rewarding fishing. As a result, I can't emphasize enough how important it is to have a really good guide that you get along well with and whose middle name is "Fish." In addition to Bill I have spent a lot of time fishing with John Emery who, in my opinion, is one of the best of the Keys guides. I give John full credit for finding fish and then making catching them as easy as it is humanly possible to do. Altogether pleasurable experiences have been my lot.

Recently, John, my second son George (who in his own right is probably as good a fly fisherman as anyone I know), and I went to Key West for a week-long fishing excursion. The sky was Keys blue, the water gin clear and glistening. A gentle south-easterly breeze tempered the blaze of the 90° sun. On our second day out I caught an 18½-pound mutton snapper on fly which is an absolutely superb fish on the flats. They only come on for a very short time each year and then only in very few places. They are, I believe, spookier than a bonefish or even a permit and so to catch one is difficult. On our sixth day out I caught a 32-pound cobia on fly. It also very rarely comes on to the flats. This particular cobia was swimming with a nurse shark, the reason being that the nurse shark burrows around on the flats to dislodge food like crabs and mussels. On our last day I managed a 31-pound permit also on fly. It sure would have been some kind of slam if I could have caught them all in one day! The other four days of fishing were anything but uneventful, as I caught four or five tarpon and jumped another fifteen or so as well as two barracuda, one of which went 15 pounds. George also caught a 17½-pound mutton snapper on fly.

The shark problem on the flats can be very touchy at times, but I have lost very few fish to them. Also, interestingly enough, cormorants follow nurse sharks around on the flats. Sometimes you will see two or three cormorants and a mutton snapper all contending for the scraps of food that a nurse shark kicks up. Frequently, I have almost decided to wade until I saw a lemon shark chasing a mutton snapper. The mutton snapper have been in full flight for a channel to get into deeper water while the lemon sharks were gaining at almost twice the speed of the snapper. Having seen numerous lemon lazing around the flats I have been much impressed and, needless to say, take great thought before starting to wade.

During the last three years I have had marvelous luck on fly catching perhaps a hundred bonefish, including one weighing 13 pounds 2 ounces, a number of them that went over 11 pounds, and a lot of 10s and nines. I have also taken ballyhoo, box fish, several varieties of sharks, including a 60-pound spinner shark, a moon fish, blue runners, and many varieties of snapper. I find that a fly rod adds so much more enjoyment to the catching of these fish. It is not all just concentrating on one fish, because in some places there are a lot of different fish that can enliven the sport and really keep you interested. Other good saltwater fly-rod fish are redfish and sea trout. Both regularly hit flys although sometimes red fish only have three-inch wide tunnel vision.

I have found that fish seem to take best with a little chop and a slight breeze. Some times of the year and in some places, the incoming tide will be more productive and, at others, the outgoing is just as productive or more. Very little good fishing on the flats can be found at dead tide. The period 10 minutes before high tide and 10 after the turn of the tide can be very good.

Mainly I have fished Boca Paila in Mexico's Yucatan; Deep Water Cay and other Bahamian hot spots and, most especially, Florida's east coast from northern Biscayne Bay down through Islamorada and Marathon on to Key West.

After all of this I have found that if I can just catch a couple of fish in a day I am very happy and even if I don't, I am still very happy.

Philip M. Winslow, M. D.

An orthopaedic surgeon (ever notice that so many doctors are fly fishers?), who is now retired, Phil has enjoyed a happy life in pursuit of fish that will take a fly as well as upland birds pointed by a staunch and stylish little English setter. He says he is looking forward to, like dessert after a fine meal, a steelheading safari in the Northwest. Henrietta, New York.

A Fly Fisher's Diary

1928

I first fished the fly with any intensity when I was 17 years old just before going to college. I was taught by an old French-Canadian named Joe Forest who ran the LaBarriere Hotel and Fishing Camp between Joliet and St. Michel in the province of Quebec. His two sons, Ernest and Raymond, acted as guides and were caretakers for the then-famous Mattawin Fishing Club. The members of this club, I do not believe, ever knew that we poached their waters. I actually guided for their club one summer and learned a lot about dry fly fishing.

One hot, dry summer day Raymond and I decided to try for some trophy trout. He knew of this lake, but it was a five-mile hike, and we had to take a canoe. Raymond carried the canoe. The French-Canadians were great jokers, and you can imagine how I felt after a five-mile walk, mostly uphill, when I finally took my pack off, opened it and found a rock that weighed 15 pounds!

There was a small cabin on the lake, and we were going to stay overnight to get the evening fishing, as well as the following morning. After a rather fruitless circuit of the small lake with the canoe, we started to get things ready around the camp. I decided to put up a rod to see if we could get something for supper. Since our tour in the canoe had been without results, I immediately accepted the suggestion from Raymond that I enhance the desirability of the fly by adding a large night crawler to it. There was a sharp drop off at the shore near the camp, and it was a favorite place for the lunkers to hang out because we always threw the guts here after cleaning fish. It was also here that my father, the year before, had caught a 7½-pound square-tail. I was able to fling the worm-embellished fly into the deep part of about 40 feet and then propped the rod up on a forked stick like the classical meat fisherman. I then promptly fell asleep. Some time later, I was awakened by the noise of my rod and reel being dragged across some rocks to the water. My frantic grab was successful, and I eventually landed a full grown female Whistler (Golden Eye) duck.

1929

The following year when a freshman in college, in my own eyes, I had become an accomplished and expert fly fisherman although I had not completely given up other methods of taking trout. This time I was with my college roommate Ernest; we were fishing the Mastigouche River several miles from the lake where I had previously taken the Whistler duck. The river at this time was roaring, and our efforts with the fly were not particularly exciting. The depth and speed of the water made it impossible to wade or maneuver a canoe to the area in the river that we knew held some good trout. After many feeble attempts, and with no success, we decided to float some garden hackle down to the quieter water on bobbers to where we knew the fish resided. Meanwhile, my college friend, who was not very interested in fishing (obviously a queer bloke), was back in the woods amusing himself exploring and taking pictures. He had been finding many interesting flowers, shrubs, and butterflies. Anyway, the trout were quite cooperative, and it was not long before we had some dandies of two to 2½ pounds, enough for supper, and we decided to quit.

Several months later the same college roommate came to visit me, and I was entertaining some of my father's friends by telling them of the great trout fishing that we had enjoyed the previous summer. This, of course, included modest descriptions of my prowess with a fly rod. About this time my friend asked if we would like to see some home movies of the trip. Some of the details of the trip were now forgotten, and I expected to see pictures of many large trout. Much to my horror and embarrassment he had beautiful pictures of great clarity and detail of those damn cork bobbers gyrating in all directions.

1934

Several years later, and now in medical school, I made the trip again, this time with my father. Actually, it was a combined hunting and fishing trip in the fall before the start of school and was very successful. The weather was crisp and cool, and we took a moose as well as a deer. The fall fishing was excellent. The males were beginning to clean up the spawning beds, but the season was still open. The fish would take almost any fly with abandon, and the males were very brightly colored. Our guide, Raymond, was a reasonably good cook and made a combined stew of fish and grouse which was delicious.

On one occasion, as we approached the shore and a portage to another lake, I saw a large male trout in shallow water with his back almost above the surface. I had a shotgun at the ready as we knew this particular portage was a favorite haunt of grouse. Without thinking I pulled up and shot the trout. He simply rolled over, and I placed him gently in the bottom of the canoe. My conscience bothered me as I kept staring at the beautiful fish of about three pounds. We left for home the following day, and this fish became mixed in with some of the other fresh-caught fish that we were taking home. The fish arrived with us in good condition, and I forgot all about the shotgun incident. My father gave some of the fish to a very good friend who was an ardent fly fisherman and a real purist. He later thanked my father and reported that the fish were in good condition and most enjoyable.

Several months later my father got a note from this friend with a single #7½ lead shot wrapped in a piece of tissue paper and with a note which read, "Do you always use such large shot for trout?"

Later

After my father's death in 1958, I learned about Atlantic salmon fishing. Why it took me so long I will never know, but perhaps I would be broke if I had done it earlier. My continued efforts finally got me to Helen's Falls on the George River. This is a huge brawling river and is fished by wading the holding spots along its edge. The camp is several miles from the "lies," so a boat trip always precedes the fishing, and lunch is on the river. After a day of fishing and dinner, those fishermen who can stay awake usually gather in the dining tent and swap lies of the day and tie up needed flies. There is always talk about which is currently the most successful pattern and in what size. Several of us take a small vise and material for this ritual.

On one trip, one of the guides was a 16-year old Montreal boy named Doug Koskie. It was his first year on the river. He was a very likeable chap, hard working and anxious to please. He was fascinated by the stories and the fly tying. After watching awhile, he asked Rod Smith, who was at the vise at the moment and spinning some deer hair on the head of a muddler, what the favorite or best material was for salmon flies. Many of us at that time favored the Black Bear with a Green Butt, or any of its other variations. Rod looked at this eager young man and said that absolutely the very best material was pubic hair from a virgin Eskimo girl (an Eskimo girl between six and 16 who can run faster than her brother), but that it was very rare and extremely expensive. At this point, Doug shouted "WHOOPEE!" and exclaimed "I'm rich, my sleeping bag is full of it."

1976

Dougie Koskie was very frank and outgoing and mentally very alert despite his lack of much schooling. He was a delightful companion on the river as he was always cheerful, and he soon learned the holding spots. I will never forget the day when my friend, Carl Jones, loaned him his rod and suggested that he take his first salmon. Doug was reticent at first since it was more or less unwritten policy that this was not done. It was only a matter of minutes, however, before this sharp young man was able to get the fly far enough to be productive. He soon was hooked up and landed a beautiful 12-pound cock salmon. Dougie was estatic, as you can imagine.

We had a new man on that trip, my associate Dr. Carl Harris. Since he had never done any fly fishing and was only familiar with the lakes of Minnesota, we gave him the prize beat for his first day. This was the same beat where Dougie had earlier caught his salmon. Carl was very successful and came home that evening with his limit of five fish. This particular beat was always full of fish after the initial run, and they held right near the bank so that all one really had to do was keep low, get the fly out a short distance, and let the current do the work. Needless to say, Carl was quite puffed up and rightly so. Whoever caught five salmon on his first day?

Later Carl was quite sheepish when he reported his encounter with Dougie. Dougie had asked him how many fish he had killed that day, knowing he was a brand new salmon fisherman. Carl did not brag openly but told him that he was able to bring in five fish and in a tone that did not imply much modesty. Dougie then asked him what beat he had been on, and when told, said "Oh! Anyone can catch them there."

John A. Shields

A supermarket-chain executive who is admittedly, "no fan of spent salmon, the canoe hatch or spawn slingers," John is an unabashed fan of Michigan steelhead on a fly. Cleveland, Ohio.

It's All Timing

April is "Steelhead Month" in Michigan. But not this year!

We all know that steelhead move up the rivers of Michigan the first week of April—some may sneak up the last week of March; they are viewed by the holdover fish as premature adventurers.

My annual calendar always blocks out a few midweek days in April to avoid inappropriate business from interfering with what I believe is the most exciting fishing of the year. After all, where else can you catch trout running six to 16 pounds on a fly from a wadable river?

Mid-March is the time to check in with my friend "The River Watcher" to see how he felt the "run" would be this year—particularly given our warm winter and lack of snow cover. His response: "The run has been on for 10 days already and you'd better come up this week if you don't want to miss it. The river is low and clear, and the fish are very spooky. Besides, this has been the best winter ever—no anchor ice and we've caught fish all winter."

Damn, why didn't I call earlier—and it was already Tuesday! I scrambled to clear my calendar for Friday, called a few folks, and Dr. Phil Sheridan, who had joined me two years prior, agreed to join me again. Thursday morning, Doc, his son Flip, and a friend, Dr. Jerry O'Connor, were on the road up to the Pere Marquette and I followed that afternoon.

A new land-speed record was set between Chicago and the Pere Marquette that afternoon. A business lunch had lasted forever; the guys on the other side of the table didn't appreciate the importance of reaching the river to fish that hour before dark.

I arrived at the PM in time to fish for about 30 minutes—Doc and friends were on the river and had seen no fish. I was surprised by how low the water was—and how clear. "The Riffles," the prime spawning area, had only six to 10 inches of water and although it was covered with redds, there were no fish visible. We left the river disappointed, but hopeful for an improvement the next day.

The evening was spent reviewing with Doc and friends the technique for steelhead. The facts are simple—to catch fish you must put your fly where the fish are—which means you must be able to spot them or know exactly which holes they are in, and you need a weighting system to get your fly to the bottom.

The key to spotting fish is knowing where to look, using polarized glasses, *and* believing that the fish are there. The redds are easy to spot, bright gravel in an oblong shape. The fish lie just above the bright spot in the depression they have dug (the bright gravel is the tailing from the depression). If the water is three or more feet deep or dark, it is difficult to see the fish. Thus one must look for a dark shape which moves—usually the tail has the greatest movement.

Weighting systems are most important—if the fly doesn't get down to the fish, the cast is wasted. I believe this is the biggest problem for most inexperienced steelhead fishermen. I prefer the three-way swivel approach—it casts miserably but is the most effective method I know to deliver the fly to the fish.

The system is simple—a three-way swivel attached to the leader with 18 to 24 inches of tippet (I prefer five or six-pound test) and a dropper of three or four inches including as many lead shot attached as required to get to the bottom, but not so many as to impede easy movement along the bottom. Once you get the feel of it, you easily recognize the *tic-tic-tic* of the lead bouncing along the bottom gravel.

Positioning in the river is also important. The most effective method is to position one's self at a 45° point above the fish—as close as possible yet far enough away not to spook them. Water depth, clarity, and sunlight all influence the distance required. I have frequently seen fish move to within three feet of me in water that was waist deep when the sky was overcast or in the late evening.

The cast should be presented well above the fish, so that the lead is on bottom and the fly, which will be downstream of the lead, is also on bottom. Two frequent problems are casts too close to the fish so that the fly doesn't get to the bottom by the time it passes—or one underestimates the length of his line and tippet thus passing the fly on the far side of the fish.

Back to fishing! I find sleeping, when I know I want to get up before daybreak and am excited about fishing, almost impossible. So it happened this trip—I woke about 2:30 a.m. and heard a soft rain on the roof of the lodge—good news! A soft rain means overcast, and even a little color in the water. I rousted the guys at 5:30 a.m. Dawn was breaking and there was still a drizzle. I am always impatient to get to the river as it was this day. Damn—why does it take so long to get everyone into waders and rain gear?

When we reached the river—the first look, "We are alone. Thank God!" Then a look into the river—"Hot damn," at the first redd were two nice fish, a few hundred feet up. Another nice fish was working under a branch; on to the Riffles. Well it was tough to say *but* those shapes out there had to be fish!

Young Flip Sheridan entered the river to fish under the branch—I sent Drs. O'Connor and Sheridan to those shapes which were in the prime redds in the Riffles. I moved to the head of the Riffles—but no fish.

Moving upstream with a hope and a prayer, I found two fish working a redd where there has never been one before—slipping into the water I positioned myself slightly below it and began to cast. The fly was of my newest tie—the Gubbins famous strip nymph on a #6 salmon hook: rabbit body fur, tied matuka-style with mono eyes, a turn of grizzly dyed brown for legs, and a wing case of turkey quill.

Well I cast, and cast, and cast: the fish were spooky and I was totally unsuccessful, even with a change of fly to a Spring's wiggler and a skunk. Finally I moved up above the fish—tried to keep my silhouette low, put the strip nymph back on and began to cast. (How much easier it is to deliver the fly from above!) About the 10th to 15th cast the fly stopped. I struck hard and was on to a good fish.

Then up he came—not five feet from me upstream with a great jump—a nice male of about seven pounds with some color—bright red cheeks and a slash of red down his side.

Then up again, though not so high, a quick turn and down the pool, with me struggling to get him on the reel. Two good runs and damn, he's under a stream improvement. How can I get him out? Finally I try slack; rats, he went downstream and he's around a piling. I give him slack like crazy to release the tension and stumble across the river to the piling, doing a nice job of taking cold water in my waders.

Well, what to do? I climbed up on top of the stream improvement, try to pass my rod under it—to no avail. I'm freezing; then I note the piling is not attached. So it's easy to pull the line around it; stupid me! I reel in the slack line and as I take in even more slack—a tug back! That fish had come upstream and was holding behind a midstream rock not 10 feet from me. We are back at it; he runs downstream when I holler to my friends for help. Great! They are busy landing a fish for Flip—they hold it up—a beautiful bright hen.

Now it's my turn. I work the fish to shore, and disappointment—I've foul-hooked him just under the jaw—all the fun's gone! It just doesn't seem fair—even if I hooked him when he struck. It's not kosher to foul hook any fish. We beach and release him. It takes a few minutes for him to gain his composure as he fins in the shallow riffle. Then away he goes: good luck!

Flip's fish is a beauty—a six-pound hen, bright silver and fairly caught. A great grin on his face says it all. By the way, those shapes I sent the doctors to fish, were just that, "shapes." It's time for breakfast!

After hot coffee and eggs, dry clothes, and so on, it's back to the river. Doc O'Connor worked the remaining fish on the redd where I had caught my fish, and I moved up several bends to a stretch of gravel on which I've found fish but never landed one because of the two brush piles above and below the riffle.

Bonanza! Maybe six to eight fish are working the area. I ease into the water and start on the lower fish. Because of the shallow water, I kneel and am able to get within 20 feet of several fish. *Bang*, the strip nymph strikes again! A fast run and, damn, he's off. Another strike! But no fish. I've frightened the lower fish off the redds into deep water.

I move to the top of the riffle and position myself below several fish—still using the Gubbins Special. A take. Something's funny. It's a 15-inch rainbow. Rats. A normal bragging-size fish is a disappointment when steelheading, but he'll make a nice meal, again proving the success of the strip nymph.

A few more casts and again a nice take. This time I have him, several good runs, and I'm keeping this one in the middle of the river. I'm still on my knees when he heads upstream with the reel singing. Help! He's in the damn woodpile. I feel the leader rubbing against the limbs and the line goes limp. Has he turned around? No way. A five-pound tippet doesn't take pressure well, but it does hook fish!

Well, the story is getting too long, but the fishing got better. I found two fish laying next to a large log at the end of the high-bank pool. After watching them porpoise a few times, the male hammered my big stone fly nymph and, after a short struggle, I beached a nice nine-pound male which I had photographed to record the fact and returned him home to make another female happy.

Late that afternoon, I returned to "The Cedars" and saw several large fish working a redd. Repeated casts produced no results. Again I tried the strip nymph, shortened my cast, and three or four times the male shot off the redd obviously chasing my fly, but no take. Then *bang*! What a fish! During several good runs, Doc, Sheridan and company walked up and I hollered to get them on the river as there were still fish working the area. But I couldn't move this one. I was downstream of the fish and putting all the pressure the five-pound tippet would take. Thirty minutes and a hundred yards downstream I beached a beautiful male which later measured 33 inches and weighed 13 pounds. What a great way to end the day and the trip.

A few hours later I was back in the car heading for Chicago with less than 24 hours on the river. It was all in the timing. The rain came pouring down that night and the fishing was over and as I write this 10 days later, not a fish has been seen since.

Good timing is better than skill.

Walter F. Lineberger, Jr.

Walt is currently boss of Windy Water Ranch and, formerly, a prominent banker who retired to the Western good life. He is an expert fly fisherman who lives in a fly-fishing mecca. Ennis, Montana.

Just Another Lousy Day in Paradise

I have had the good fortune to own a ranch located in the Madison River Valley of southwestern Montana for the past 15 years. One has a choice of almost any type of trout water he could desire within a radius of 75 miles from my home in Ennis. The Madison itself offers a wide variety of fly fishing for good-sized rainbows and browns. At different seasons and, for that matter, at different times of day, you may use dry flies, wets, nymphs, or streamers with success. Some areas are good for wading, while others are best approached by floating in a McKenzie River boat.

Other relatively large nearby rivers are the Gallatin, the Jefferson and its principal tributaries, the Big Hole, the Beaverhead, and the Ruby. The Gallatin, Madison, and Jefferson rivers converge to form the headwaters of the Missouri, which is one of the finest large trout rivers in the U.S.

Add to this array of blue ribbon trout waters, the Henry's Fork of the Snake River and the Firehole and the Gibbon, which combine in Yellowstone Park to form the Madison, and one begins to have some conception of the opportunities that exist. And I haven't even mentioned the availability of the famous Yellowstone River, with its tributaries, which lies within the magic 75-mile circle.

A lesser known source of good fishing, are the spring creeks and tumbling mountain streams which usually flow through private ranches. The spring creeks are predominately inhabited by browns and the mountain streams contain mostly rainbow.

For further variety we have mountain lakes, which usually require packing in by horseback to catch some of the three to five-pound native cutthroat trout. Henry's Lake, which lies just beyond the Montana border in Idaho, produces large cutts, rainbows, and crosses of these two plus big brook trout.

You may ask how does one decide, among all this enticing smorgasbord of fly fishing, where, when, and how to fish? For my part I try to partake of some of everything. The season and weather will dictate some of the choices, and preference and inclination will make the final decision. Since I do live here, I can afford the luxury of being opportunistic in choosing the best times and places.

I should here confess that my favorite form of fly fishing is dry; I like to wade; I release all my fish unless injured, and I use the lightest rods and leaders that conditions will permit. However, I do fish nymphs and other wets when fish will not take a dry, and I readily admit that this type of fishing often requires more skill and frequently produces larger fish than fishing dry flies. I hope this disclaimer keeps me clear with my friends who prefer to fish wet. I have found that trout can often be persuaded to take a dry fly even when there is no visible hatch or any evidence of rising fish. by the same token, there are times that the best placed and floated dries will not induce a strike and yet a small nymph in the surface film will generate a riot. A sunken and slowly retrieved wet can also produce extravagantly in this mountain area.

I find that at my age—I have been retired for eight years—I can no longer wade the heavy water of the big, swift flowing rivers except in the more sheltered and shallow areas. The ideal combination for me and many of my contemporaries, is to float the big rivers and cast into much of the prime water as we float. We then pick the good areas to wade and have the guide either beach or hold the boat while we wade and fish these spots.

I cannot emphasize enough to those of you who may not be familiar with fishing Western waters, the importance of obtaining the services of a good guide. The fish move about in the larger rivers from the banks to holding areas in the middle. Many of the most productive holes are not visible to the uninitiated. I have observed over and over that good guides will consistently catch (and release) many, many more fish while floating through the same stretch of river than the less experienced.

My enthusiasm for this Western fly fishing is so great that I should at least mention a few of the drawbacks. There is an ever present threat of wind. Winds of 25 to 30 mph can raise hell with your casting. A good graphite rod designed for a six or seven-weight line will usually take care of most situations. Other big river situations will call for longer casts than some of you may be accustomed to in Eastern waters. Always bring a down jacket, a rain jacket, and polarized glasses (the sun is brighter out here). Weather is good, but uncertain.

Like anyplace else, western-Montana fly fishing can be poor on a given day; however, I like knowing that the fish are there and that it is just a question of attracting them.

All of our stream fish are wild trout and this provides a much more sporting form of fishing than the put-and-take trouting of many areas. These fish have to be rugged to survive in this environment, and they demonstrate this when they are hooked. Even the brown trout, which are supposed to be underwater fighters, frequently jump like rainbows. A 1½ to 2½-pound rainbow will make you think he weighs four or five pounds.

At this point I would like to share with you a day of fishing on a wonderful little Montana spring creek which I had with our eldest son a couple of years ago. Walt III is an excellent fly fisherman who lives in Chattanooga, Tennessee. He visits us about one week a year. You can understand why I took him to one of my favorite streams. This creek rises from a number of springs in a large meadow and meanders for several miles through an area devoid of trees until it finally joins a large river. It is gin clear, 30 to 40 feet across at its widest, with numerous pools and runs, but few real riffles because the drop is very gradual. The banks are grass covered and somewhat spongey. The stream carries a fairly large volume of water and the banks are undercut. It is necessary to approach the stream carefully to avoid spooking the big brown trout which tend to lie under the overhanging banks and feel the slightest vibration of the turf. If wading is practical at a particular spot this masks your approach. In the slower parts there are patches of moss and these are loaded with freshwater shrimp. Most of the brown trout are from 12 to 17 inches long. A few real monsters are present. These larger fish tend to migrate here from the big river in spawning season.

We started fishing about 10:30 on a beautiful morning in mid-August with each of us taking a stretch of about one-fourth of a mile. We first tried #14 to #16 drys of various patterns and were getting a few rises along the banks— usually within two to four inches of the bank. I took my first brown at the end of about half an hour on a #16 ginger quill. He was about 16 inches long and gave me a good fight accompanied by several beautiful leaps. As I slid him out on a grassy indentation in the bank, I marveled at his lovely coloring and then took my time admiring the snow-capped mountains on either side of the valley. A long look showed son Walt fighting what appeared to be a good fish in the distance.

In another hour I had released another three or four fish of about the same size as the first, but only a few were feeding. We two met for a consultation and, in doing so, noted that the warm sun's ray had brought out a number of grasshoppers in the meadows. A search of my flies produced a box of varied sizes of Elk Hair Hoppers which looked like they should really produce results.

We each tied on a hopper and started fishing upstream. The result was immediate and dramatic. We were taking trout almost every cast. They took at the banks, in the middle of the stream, and over the moss beds. I don't think we caught anything under 14 inches and the largest was 19. The larger fish would dive for the moss beds or try to rub the hooks out on the undercut banks. It was a wild circus of leaping, straining trout. After we had each caught and released about 30 browns we were worn out and, for once, surfeited with the intense pleasure of playing these magnificent fish. I have repeated this peformance on other days, but never have I enjoyed it more than on this beautiful day and in the company of our son.

I like the solitude and detachment that come while wading the smaller streams, but I also truly enjoy the companionship of fishing with a good friend on a float trip. One fisherman sits or stands in the bow of the boat and the other sits in the stern with the guide at the oars in the middle facing downstream. The guide takes advantage of the current, but uses the oars not only to guide the boat, but also to slow its forward progress to give a good float for your fly. Distance from the bank is sufficient to avoid spooking the fish, if one is casting to the bank, but close enough to permit you to cast to the bank. If the fish are lying close to the bank, as they do early in the season when the hatches are coming off the willows and grassy cover, you must put your fly within a few inches of the bank. Later on when the fishing pressure becomes more intense and the hatches spread across the river, the trout will move toward the center. This is when a guide's knowledge of the good holding areas and ability to read the water really are most important.

In all my years of floating the Madison I have made many friends among a number of outstanding guides. However, I have formed a particularly close friendship and developed a deep respect for the ability of "Mac" McPhetres (now retired from active guiding). Mac and I have fished together for about 20 years. He is a hard taskmaster on your method of presentation, but he leavens this with a great sense of humor. Mac still despairs of my tendency to use too much line and failure to always mend my line. If I miss a strike it never escapes his eagle eye, and I am frequently rebuked by some appropriate quotation from Shakespeare or a more earthy source.

I like to be in the boat with a good fisherman. In the frequent windy conditions of the Madison and other big rivers, a certain number of tangles are inevitable. This is particularly true when we use two flies and the patterns tend to be of the larger Western variety. The repartee and laughs that one has with a fellow fisherman and guide in the confines of a McKenzie boat gives a spice of friendship that cannot be duplicated. Some of the friends that I have particularly enjoyed fishing with over the years are Dave Vhay, Al Whitehouse, Frank Silver, Lee Bassett, Jeff Dorsey, Bill Bricker, Ray Jeter, and our sons Pete and Walt.

Mac is a firm believer in the two-fly practice for this type of fishing, and I confess that he has made a believer of me. The end fly on dry fly presentation matches the hatch and the dropper is usually some form of Trude which can float dry or sink just below the surface. Each fly seems to act as an attractor for the other and doubles are a sometime thing. Ask my friend Al Whitehouse about his double on 16-inch browns.

The guide will jump overboard and hold the boat to permit a more thorough fishing of the particularly hot areas if the water permits. Better yet are the places where I can wade without being swept downstream. Some of these spots hold an unbelievably large number of big fish. Frequently you will want to switch to smaller flies in quiet waters where you can see the fish feeding.

The waters of the Madison below the town of Ennis break up into several courses known as the "Channels." this division of waters has shallow and slow flowing spots that are ideal for wading. In the afternoons the caddis fly hatches are out in force. My decision to try to acquire a ranch in this area was confirmed in 1963 when I caught and released over 50 trout in a few hours in the Channels. This area can only be reached by floating since it flows entirely through private property.

Actually I got my first real taste of Western fly fishing in the High Sierras of California over 60 years ago. The fishing was so good in those tumbling, rushing, rainbow filled waters that the trout didn't mind my unskilled casts. I caught hundreds of rainbows, brookies, and some golden trout on our two-week pack trip and was immediately admonished to release all but what we wanted to eat. I am still a firm believer that the best way to introduce a novice to trout fishing is to put them in a place where they are sure to catch lots of trout, preferably wild. These Western mountain streams are ideal.

One of my favorites is the upper Ruby River of Montana, which in turn flows into the Beaverhead and, this in turn, joins the Jefferson. The stream flows through private property, but may be fished for a reasonable rod fee. Here, and in similar streams, one may catch trout without the selectivity and finesse that are called for on most streams. It is still exhilarating to fish this type of stream and just enjoy the way these trout attack a fly. Many of my friends who are accustomed to fishing stocked waters cannot believe that these wild trout possess so much vigor.

The fact is that no matter what type of water you are fishing, you are surrounded by beautiful scenery. The "Big Sky" is an unbelievable blue, and the waters are clean and clear. It is a paradise for fishermen.

Romi Perkins

Being married to Leigh, "Mr. Orvis," Perkins makes her Mrs. Orvis, which suits her just fine. The two of them are probably fly fishing's most traveled couple. It's all business, of course. What a way to go! Manchester, Vermont.

A Sad Day at the Orvis Pond

Back in 1965, when Leigh had just purchased the Orvis Company in Manchester, Vermont, one of his nieces was a supplier to the company. She had a small manufacturing operation which produced exquisite decoupage switchplates. She would arrive in Manchester every six months for meetings on new products and production schedules, and bring her children along. This particular June, little Kent, who was around 10 or 11 years old, wanted to go along to the office building and fish outside in the trout ponds. It was a Monday and there were no fishing schools that day, so permission was granted. Uncle Leigh outfitted the lad with a tonkin cane rod and retired to his office where he was interrupted every 15 minutes by little Kent, who would proudly walk in unannounced, dragging a fish behind him.

The first two times, Leigh congratulated the boy and showed him where a refrigerator was, to keep the fish for dinner. The third time, Uncle Leigh suggested sharply that Kent should release the trout he caught from then on. After a short lecture on conservation which the boy seemed to absorb, the

44

avid novice fly fisherman returned to the pond and Leigh settled back to the desk.

Fifteen minutes later, he heard quite a hubbub out in the store. It seems that Kent had made a cast and hooked into a five-pound brown, which had lived there in the pond for seven or eight years. He was a great pet of everyone who worked there. Old Gus was his name, and no one had ever caught him in all that time.

It happened that the previous owner of Orvis was in the store that morning. Ducky Corkran, a dignified and handsome man of 70, was there to get some salmon flies for an upcoming trip. He looked up to see Kent coming in the door dragging Old Gus behind him. It was obvious that Gus was beyond reviving. His tail was bedraggled from being hauled through the gravel parking lot. His eyes were unseeing. He was a goner. Of course, Ducky recognized the fish at once, and stepped over to Kent and demanded to know what he thought he was doing, catching the pet of everyone in the Orvis family right out of their pond. All the store employees were goggle-eyed, frozen where they stood. Tears were streaming down some faces. Kent looked up at Ducky through his tousled hair and said, "Cool it, Pops, my Uncle owns the joint."

W. Michael Fitzgerald

Mike admits that even after obtaining two degrees from Ohio State, he still thought a nymph was a woods maiden, and a blood knot a surgical procedure. However, after seeing the light 18 years ago, Mike has made up for lost time by founding Fish and Game Frontiers and fly fishing on five continents and many adjacent islands. Wexford, Pennsylvania.

Education of a Bonefisherman

It all began years ago when friends in Pittsburgh talked my wife Susie and me into joining them on Andros Island in the Bahamas for a few days of bonefishing. "Be sure to bring your fly rod—you've never experienced anything like the first run of a big bonefish," they declared.

My roots were firmly established in fresh water, moving fresh water, holding trout, salmon, and smallmouth bass. Those rolling streams which course through wild and remote places where eagles soar, loons call, and a fire feels good at night. That was my idea of fly fishing.

Being committed now to a subtropical island in the month of May, I decided I'd better read, what I could, fast. Out of the files came those great narratives by Joe Brooks, Lefty Kreh, and other storied anglers who had begun to preach the gospel about fly rodding in saltwater. I was skeptical, but great tales they were, and I thought just maybe this bonefish was a pretty exciting fellow.

As our little plane circled Andros before the final approach, I was enchanted by the spectacle of that brilliant array of water colors throughout the shallow areas—cobalt-blue deep water, green channels, multi-hued coral reefs, and the expanse of white flats. Besides being beautiful, they looked very, very fishy.

The first afternoon, I found it was even hotter than I expected, one of those sultry-humid Bahamas days, made tolerable only by the fresh breeze coming off the Atlantic. We got settled in, and through the hotel made arrangements for fishing the next morning. It was no surprise when the guy who took care of these things informed me that my guide was called "Bonefish Jack." Secure with that knowledge, I discovered something else that afternoon: the Harvey Wallbanger, which had never passed over this palate before. They tasted so good at beachside that I had two more and almost missed dinner. But we were ready the next morning.

Bonefish Jack looked the part, all right, with his sweat-stained straw hat framing an ebony face that seemed to have a permanent scowl in place. Faded denim shirt, cutoff Levi shorts, and bare feet completed what I assumed bonefish guides should look like. Susie and I immediately felt overdressed in snow-white tennis shoes, khaki cottons, and Orvis fishing hats.

As a quick opener, Bonefish Jack looked at my fly rod and said, "Mon, what dat rod for? You gonna ketch fish or jes' act like you trying?" I allowed as how I was going to do exactly what he told me, and that never having done it before, would welcome any help and advice he could give. His scowl deepened noticeably.

Out we went at high speed in a 16-foot skiff across a broad bay, which became shallower by the minute, and then Bonefish Jack stopped the motor, stood up on the rear transom and began to pole quietly and with purpose. For an hour-and-a-half, we skimmed quietly along and saw not one fish on the flat. We sat like stones in the boat, not knowing what to do, what fly if any to put on, and were not sure we could see a fish even if one was there.

The water was like glass, and with the hazy sun rising, we felt like ancient mariners. Saltwater and sky shimmered into one as the temperature headed toward 90°. My khaki shirt slowly turned two shades darker. We kept thinking about those cool mountain streams.

At this point, B. Jack stopped the boat, got out and looked at my fly rod and "Bonefish Special" fly. I thought at least he'd like that fly because he shared its name. With a snort, he clipped it off and tied on a long shank #2 hook. "Dem fish want a meal, Mon. Dis is what dey want." He produced a small plastic bucket from which a strange scratching noise emanated. Lifting the lid revealed a dozen plump crabs with bodies the size of a silver dollar. He crushed one suddenly and threaded the fragile looking pieces onto that #2 hook and handed me the outfit.

"I'm not sure I can cast this." I said lamely, at which his scowl deepened again.

"We see, Mon. You should have brought spinning rod." With that, Jack began to walk, pulling the boat and making Susie and me feel even more uncomfortable. At one point, I got out to lighten the load, trying to remember about "watermanship," something I had read about. After about eight steps, which I thought were stealthy and well-taken, Bonefish Jack ordered me back in the boat. "You sound like water buffalo, Mon."

Suddenly, Bonefish Jack stopped and cocked an ear to the east. By now, I had stripped a little line off the reel with coils in the bottom of the boat and still wondered how I was going to lob this mass of crab to any bonefish. We heard the sound—something like rustling leaves—just out of sight on the steamy surface of that windless flat. Then we could see the disturbance on the water pushing our way as the noise became more distinct.

"Bonefish, Mon. Dey come, get ready!" Meanwhile, I had not read anything about hearing bonefish before seeing them, but I could sure hear them now and still not see any fish well. I stood up and tried to lengthen some line, with a couple of very careful lob-casts, looking each time at that hook to see if any crab was left. Miraculously, most was still intact.

Certainly, the fish were there, a school of 100, maybe 200, dark shadows moving with purpose, changing direction constantly, tails flashing in the hazy morning sun.

"Cast, Mon, two o'clock—25 feet and not too far!" commanded Bonefish Jack. Man, was I eager! I had the presence of mind to stay very slow on the backcast, seemed that mass of crab weighed a ton. It took forever to course through the air. Then I drove it forward with much strength of purpose. Instantly, I knew the result of the cast, but had no idea of the effect on that school of bonefish.

Three pieces of crab the size of a quarter flew off the hook in spite of my best efforts at a parachute cast and sped like arrows 40 feet right into the middle of the school, and my bare hook splashed down 10 feet short of target.

That school of fish exploded like a small charge had been detonated in the sand. I'll never forget the sound of their surge and the lightning speed of their close-formation disappearance.

It was then very silent for a few seconds. I gazed at the swirling sand and mud over a 150-foot stretch of water where the fish had been. It wasn't silent long: Susie managed to snicker, punctuated by a stream of profanity from Bonefish Jack. The first thing I really comprehended that he said was, "Goddammit, Mon! Dat de worst cast dis man ever has seen. Here I poles de boat and poles de boat for two hours, shows you biggest school of fish I'se seen this year and you does dat. Why you do dat to Bonefish Jack?"

I was humiliated, intimidated, and our relationship went downhill from there. I was hot, tired, thirsty, fishless, and from somewhere deep in my embarrassed gut emerged the faint taste of yesterday's Harvey Wallbangers.

A cold beer made things better, but I decided I wasn't having fun—and after the first bonefishing result, absolutely dreaded the next opportunity. It came an hour later. The next time, Bonefish Jack had me cast that blob of broken crab 20 feet at 11 o'clock to what appeared to me to be a barren flat. Then he backed the boat up 15 feet, moving like a panther through the water, instructing me to pay out a comparable amount of running line. Then we waited. Ten seconds later, two fish appeared like ghosts in the general vicinity of where that crab was resting on the bottom.

"Move it one foot, Mon." commanded Bonefish Jack. That I managed to do without screwing up. Both fish put on the brakes, lunged to their left, and two silver sickle tails broke the surface, and I couldn't feel a thing.

"He eat it, Mon—set dat hook!" I raised the rod and met an unyielding tightening that felt mighty good. There was a stand-off for one second, then one head-shake, and the next few moments weakened my knees. Never had I heard a single-action fly reel make a sound like mine did as that fish took off at incredible speed. Thank God, there were no loops of line to worry about, because in what seemed like an instant, the fly line was gone and the backing was melting like butter in the sun. A great vee of water spread behind the fish, and a little rooster-tail of water shot up as if behind a miniature racing hydroplane where the fly line met the surface.

I held the rod high, but everything felt out of control. The fish showed no sign of stopping or losing strength or speed. Bonefish Jack was now in the skiff, pole in hand, ready to follow when it happened. Deep on the spool furrows appeared in the backing, beyond where it had ever been used before, and in one of those furrows was a gnarl, which stopped that run like a brick wall.

In an instant, the rod lurched down to that sickening horizontal position, something snapped, and it jumped right back to vertical. The silver torpedo was gone.

Again, a short period of silence. Susie and I looked at each other with our mouths still half open in amazement at the performance that fish had given, from the take through that incredible run.

Only the forlorn sound of empty reeling filled the void until Bonefish Jack laid it on me again with inimitable Bahamian profanity. He said something about the tide being wrong and we'd better head back, and that was fine with me. We no longer belonged out there on that particular day with this particular guide. Susie and I exchanged knowing smiles—she knew it and I knew it—that in spite of our frustrations, one run by a six-pound fish, the screaming reel, and the previously unknown dimension of power/speed/weight we had never experienced before in our fishing, had us hooked for good. We never wanted to see Bonefish Jack again, but we were looking forward to the next time on bonefish flats.

After the verbal beating we took that day, it was nearly two years later that I worked up the courage to expand our bonefishing horizons. I had long since sworn off crab and continued to read everything I could get my hands on, while practicing my casting like a man driven. We found it at Boca Paila and Ascension Bay in Yucatan, Mexico with the late Tony Gonzalez, and a delightful little Mexican guide named Arturo who, with a knowing and engaging, gold-toothed smile, would only mutter, "Mucho malo" in response to a misguided cast. He would then pole resolutely on, fishing the flats with eyes like an eagle. I also learned that in waters like those, you might expect your next shot in 10 minutes rather then two hours, like our first time around.

Now, years later, with miles and miles of sparkling saltwater flats behind us, the bonefish are still very much a part of our fly-fishing lives. We "discovered" Christmas Island in December, 1982, with endless pristine flats that are literally teeming with these mint dime-bright silver bullets, which you must hunt like turkeys, stalk on foot, and cast to carefully. Still, if you make a mistake, they're gone, but if you get it right, they're eager to take—and what a take it is! Then you know a fish five pounds and over will give you that searing run, which can still make you weak in the knees. The really big ones are at Christmas also—12 pounds and up. I know, because I've lost two fly lines there the past two trips.

What a wonderful getaway it is to leave western Pennsylvania in January or February and head to where the palm trees sway and the trade winds blow, and where you can work on one of the most noble fish that swims, the fabled gray ghost. Sure, we still cherish those trout-filled streams, and the bonefish have made us pay our dues, starting at Andros and over the next 15 years. But if that great question is put to me "If you had only one day of fly fishing left, what would you choose?", I'd agree with Lefty and go bonefishing—without crabs and Bonefish Jack!

Richard T. Baker

Dick grew up in Indiana when "one fish or one quail was a big deal;" went to Ohio State where he "learned to make money without working;" retired early to spend more time fishing, hunting, and playing golf, which he says is similar to herpes—there is no way to get better. Cleveland, Ohio.

Bear Facts

For several years, Claude Blair and I, along with other buddies, have fished Alaska in the vicinity of Lake Iliamna. During the salmon spawning season, the large rainbow trout come out of the lake and follow the salmon up the many streams to feast on salmon roe. The trout do not stay too close to the salmon because of their sharp teeth but, instead, usually about three or four feet behind, and when the salmon expells the eggs, the trout dart forward and gather them in. Fishing for these big trout is one of the most exciting fly-fishing experiences you can imagine. The best method is to very quietly wade the river and watch for trout. The salmon are very easy to see because of their reddish color, but it takes a little practice to be able to spot the trout. When you see a trout, you cast a wet fly, which resembles spawn, just behind the salmon. When the trout takes and, you set the hook, it immediately comes out of the water and gives you an extraordinary battle.

The fishermen are not the only ones interested in the salmon run. The big Kodiak bears congregate along the rivers to feast on the salmon and, during the height of the run, it is not uncommon to see many bears fishing the stream. Our guide had always cautioned us about them; the standard practice was to yell at a bear in the stream, or along the bank, and presumably said bear would take off through the bush. On one of our trips, we were fishing a fairly small stream which was full of both salmon and trout. I had waded ahead of our group by maybe 50 yards and was standing in the river up to my hips when a very large bear came down to the water's edge. Bears do not see exceptionally well, but they do smell terrifically (both ways). Evidently this spot was the bear's special fishing hole, and when he spotted me in the water in my brown float jacket, he apparently thought I was another bear poaching on his territory. He immediately let out a growl and came into the water after me.

Our guide had warned us that the worst thing you can do under those circumstances is to try to run from the bear. You don't have a chance since the bear is so much faster. The only thing you can do is to wave your arms and yell at the top of your lungs at the bear. Instinctively I wanted to run, but somehow I managed to gather up whatever courage a certified public accountant might have and shouted and waved at the bear as loudly and vigorously as I could. The bear came to within 30 feet of me and stood up on his hind legs, snarling and growling, evidently trying to decide whether to attack or not. Finally he turned, went back to shore and started downstream, but when he got wind of me, he immediately turned and came charging back toward me at speed. I thought this was the end. He advanced to about 30 feet again and repeated his prior performance. After several very long minutes, he finally turned and vanished into the bush to my great relief.

When the rest of our party came up, and while I was still shaking, they said that when the bear stood up in the water, it looked like he was standing right over me. Needless to say, after this experience, we changed our modus operandi: when we saw a bear near the stream, or in it, we surrendered the territory and gave him a wide berth!

Author's postscript: As a final note to what was actually a very good and very productive Alaskan trip, the fact was that I didn't find out who my friends were until a month later. I had played golf with Claude Blair, and after beating him on the course, he bought my dinner at the club and we played gin rummy in the evening. I again upped my winnings and, as we were getting ready to leave, he said, "You know, Dick, if I had known a day like this was coming, when you were faced with that bear, I would have rooted for the bear!"

Ernest S. Alson

Ernie began fly fishing in 1960 when he was befriended by Joe Brooks in the Florida Keys. Joe gave him a list of places to fish with the suggestion to visit at least one of them a year for the rest of his life. Ensuing years have been spent following Joe's leads to trout in Montana and Argentina, marlin in Venezuela, sailfish in Florida, bonefish and tarpon in the Keys and Bahamas, Atlantic salmon in Iceland, steelhead in the Northwest, and saltwater fly fishing all over. Harrison, New York.

I Wonder

That last morning we parked where the man from Orvis suggested, below Muddy Lane along River Road, downstream from Manchester. We bushwacked our way in through a jungle of second-growth trees and a tangle of thicket, winding up just where we wanted to be: at the Battenkill, not far from the New York border. It must have been 20 or 25 years ago; the three of us were up from Harrison for the Green Drake hatch on the first weekend in June.

It was beastly hot, not at all trout weather. The water temperature was in the 80s. Nothing stirred for three days. The only action was a flurry just after sunset for 30 minutes or so when the midges were out and the rings of rises showed all over and nothing would take, not even with 7X and #22's.

On that last day, I waded downstream about half a mile and found a surprisingly wild flume. On the far side, where the bank was steep and rocky, tall trees, swamp maples and locusts, shaded the river. Above was a rustic cabin that looked empty. Below, the dark water boiled white through a narrow opening, creating a swirl of bubbles and a current downstream, 50 feet or more.

The near bank was all gravel where a deep back-eddy washed foam toward the flume. I still had on the 7X tippet and one of those #22 black gnats that Tommy likes to tie. Slowly I made my way to the head of the pool debating whether to try a wet or a streamer. The first flash in the back-eddy registered. Probably the glint from a soda can, I mused with a cynicism heated by the sun. But, as I took a few more steps toward the head, *whoops*, there was that flash again.

This time I knew it was no man-made object, but a rolling fish at my feet, no more than a yard away and too close to cast to. So I did the natural thing and shoved my left boot under whatever it was, and lifted up. A huge spotted tail emerged, attached to a monster body. Imagine my surprise! Heaving my rod onto the bank I splashed farther into the stream and threw my arms around a fish, a giant fish, and tossed it up on the bank.

I hustled out of the pool and found the trout; a brown slab-sided monster with an undershot jaw staring at me out of a single dead eye. It had already surrendered, something it had never done in life, to the lack of oxygen in the warm water and had played out its final moments in the back-eddy when I arrived. The plastic tape markers on my rod showed the big brown to be exactly 30 inches long.

I slashed a sapling with my knife, shoved a forked branch through the giant's gills and, grabbing my rod, waded upstream to locate my friends. When I spotted them, I gave a blast on my whistle and held up old Jasper for them to view. You have never seen any faster, wader-clad, 200-yard dashes in your life. "Where did you?" "How did you?" "What did you?" The questions tumbled faster than the flume.

My only comment: "There I was, in this slide pool, with a #22 black gnat and a 7X tippet on my line when I landed this 30-inch trout." Their gaze was so awestruck that my guilt surfaced and I then confessed that I had truly landed it, but not on my line. Mark weighed the big brown; his scale waggled and stopped at 10 pounds even.

Rather than carry the monster back to our car where my camera lay baking in the trunk, I propped it up on its belly under a shade tree, placed a few large rocks around to hold it in place, stuck my #22 black gnat in its jaw—and left.

The following March, *Field and Stream* carried an article on New England area streams which reported ". . . the good old Battenkill, now mostly a put-and-take river, still gives up a beauty now and then. Last June, a local angler weighed in a 30-inch 10-pound brown which he had caught on a small black fly that morning in a remote pool of the river."

I wonder . . .

Peg Keller

Defined by her children as a professional volunteer and domestic engineer, she loves traveling, raising sheep and Labs, gardening and fishing. She also considers herself very lucky when asked to share a rod with husband Robert. Wittman, Maryland.

Sharing The Rod

The Cast:
Peg: her turn on the beat.
Bob: Peg's dutiful husband.
Harold: the other rod on the beat.
The Place. Vidadalsa, Iceland

The water was deep, the wind moderately strong, the day overcast, and the fishermen were eager.

There was a hole across the river that Peg had been told was the place to fish this beat. Being only a two-year Atlantic salmon fisherwoman, Peg always approached her time on the river with sheer determination to catch a fish, no matter what the size, just to catch a fish. Idleness was not one of her pastimes, whatever the occasion.

The approach to this hole was from the middle of the river, which meant the water would be about two inches below the top of Peg's waders. Dutiful

Bob would always be at her side acting as lifeguard holding onto the belt around her waist. With this moderately strong wind blowing, the casting was somewhat difficult, especially in this depth of water. Peg made a couple of casts, working her line out for the most part, sloppy at best. On the third cast a mouth rose to the surface and gulped the fly. *Zzzing*—they were off— all three of them—Peg and Bob toward shore and the fish all over the place.

Other rod, Harold, at this point, decided to rest and perhaps because Peg had borrowed his Hardy reel with an intermediate line on it, thought he'd observe the goings on and perhaps offer a little advice on the situation.

A half hour went by, Peg was in the water, out of the water. She was trying not to let this powerful and active salmon go downstream. There would be a lot of ground to cover down there. *ZZing, zzing*, jump, bow, jump, bow!

"I'd say it's a 15-pounder," commented Harold. "Tighten the drag," shouted Bob. "Move up, move back." "Keep your rod tip up." "Stay with the fish." "Run . . . ."

Harold came up to stand near Peg when activity subsided for a brief moment. "You'll probably get 500 words of advice," he comfortingly said.

Peg was having trouble with the drag. No matter how many times Bob yelled "Tighten the drag," it would only go just so far.

Downstream this thrashing beauty drove, ripping the line into the backing. There was no choice but to cross the stream. So with her lifeguard at her side across they went. Once, twice, three times. Word 250-plus was "Don't try to cross there, it'll be over your head." So back to the shore.

"I'll get the tailer ready," Bob cried. "Don't lose my fish by horsing with that," pleaded Peg, "He isn't ready."

"Hang in there, you're doing fine," said Harold. Words of praise were welcome to Peg's fatiguing arms and determined spirit. An hour had gone by. Finally, after about a hundred more words of wisdom and the blessing of a tiring fish, it was happily beached on the sandy shore.

The fish scale was found in a vest pocket and the beautiful Atlantic weighed in at 21½ pounds.

Is this what is known as "sharing the rod?"

Fritz Neubauer

An extremely knowledgeable, professional outdoorsman, he is proprietor of a Fishing and Hunting Club, a Labrador retriever aficionado, and trapper. Also a good man to have as friend. Hunting Valley, Ohio.

Skill and the Lord

"Fritzel machs schnell! Der Baron ruft dich geh mit ihm Forrellen Fischen." That was my grandma telling me that the Baron wanted me to go with him to carry his German brown trout. That was my introduciton to a fly rod, 60 years ago in Austria. The real reason he wanted me along with him was to catch grasshoppers and crickets when the fly didn't produce. I learned about purists when I was six years old. The cheater! There was hope for him, though, because he positively would not use "garden hackle." One day when the fishing was poor, I went to my grandpa's manure pile to get some worms, but the Baron said, *"Nein, Fritz."* I was just trying to earn the *Groschen* (penny) he would pay me.

Next to duck hunting with my uncles, the sport I found most fascinating was fly fishing. My grandma would fill the creel with watercress, and I'd tuck the trout away as the Baron handed them to me. I was usually so excited to be part of the sport that I'd frequently get in the way of his back cast. It never took long to get all the trout he wanted because the sport was reserved exclusively for nobility. But this distinction didn't mean that we never got to eat trout. My enterprising Uncle Ernst would walk along the boardwalk at the lumber mill with one of his hands casually plunged in his pocket. Actually, his hand was controlling a short line which ran down inside the length of one leg of his trousers, and he was trolling as he walked. He was an expert at this and always got us our meal.

He taught me well and, years later, during the big depression in America, my Uncle's trick came in handy as I walked along the Cleveland Electric Illuminating Company's fence at Gordon Park. It fed many hungry people in my neighborhood. Carp, shad, sheepshead, white bass—anything went. Our family would get the fillets, the Vishnowsky's would get the heads for soup and the Troy's would fry up the rib cages. It was a tough time to come to America.

Like all immigrants, we quickly learned that the Land of Milk and Honey with dollar bills growing on trees was a fantasy nurtured in the minds of those who yearned for a better way. The day before we departed, my grandpa, the mayor, fire chief and owner of the lumber mill in town, shut off the mill stream and turned me and my buddies loose on the drawn down mill run. Everyone stood on the bank and cheered as we threw browns up to 10 pounds up on the bank. My grandma fried them up like wiener schnitzel, and I'll never forget it.

With the memory of an Austrian trout stream still in my mind, the only place I could find to fish when we first arrived was a sewer outlet on what was then the Bratenahl Country Club. Although I was keeping our family and the neighbors supplied with fish, it ended very quickly one day in July when I took my mother to my fishing "hole." *"Gotten Himmel, Fritz!"* When she saw what the carp were eating, I wound up floundering in the water with the fish. And that was the end of that.

For most of us during the Depression, fly fishing was something you read and dreamed about. I'd show my mother the pictures in *Field & Stream*—a fisherman wearing waders and a hat full of flies, standing in a beautiful trout stream. She would remark, "Be happy with your throw lines. How can you use a fly rod at the Illuminating Company?" She was right. I'd get laughed off the breakwall, and Doan Brook had no trout, only carp.

My mother knew she had to find something to occupy me and my boundless energy and one wonderful day, she found the Rocky River. It was a two-hour ride by streetcar. She would sit with her knitting while I dreamed my fly-fishing dreams. When we finally got to the Metropolitan Park and I saw the river, I thought I was in paradise! I'll never forget the day. It was June 15, 1932, the Opening Day of bass season. (Ohio had closed bass fishing from May to June 15 in those days.) I almost wet my pants with excitement. Looking upstream from the Hilliard Bridge, I could see fly fishermen whipping the water to a froth. And there I stood with my throw lines, worms and doughballs. *"Mutter, bitte! Ich muss eine Fliegen wand haben!"* (Mother, please! I've got to have a fly rod!) I forgot the throw lines and just sat there with my mouth watering. Mother answered, *"Fritz, Liebchen, es kost zu viehl, wir haben nicht das geld."* (Fritz, Liebchen, it's too expensive and we haven't the money.) My hopes were shattered and my heart sank.

I probably made a complete nuisance of myself that day trying to help the fly fishermen, but they all put up with the little Kraut kid. I was the bass measurer. There was an 11-inch size limit in those days (and there still should be). Finally, after a heartbreaking number of eight and 10-inchers, I saw a rod bend that looked good. When the smallmouth jumped, everybody yelled, "Hey, Dutch, get the landing net. It's a keeper." I didn't have to stretch that bass to make 11 inches. It was a beautiful two pounder. My homesickness was over. That smallmouth on a fly rod in America meant more to me than the Baron with his five-pound brown in Austria. It meant that I didn't have to be a Baron to use a fly rod in America.

From then on, it was fishing every Sunday. I made a deal with my mother—I would go to church if she would take me to Rocky River. The streetcar ride seemed endless. At each stop, I would hope there would be no one waiting so we could get there faster. We transferred streetcars at Public Square, and the wait could be an hour, an eternity. I made friends with many of the fly fishermen by catching hellgrammites and soft-shelled crabs for them. My mother always packed extra sandwiches and kuchen and, while they were eating, they would let me use their outfits. It had to be still-fishing because they wouldn't trust me whipping a line. The Pat's Pixie (a lure designed by Pat Patterson, a well-known local outdoorsman and fisherman) with pork rind was the best smallmouth lure then along with the Trix Oreno, a metal lure shaped like a Dardevle. They were tough on fly rod tips if you didn't know how to handle them. How well I know. Mine were always taped up.

I made a brush pile in the river which was a hangout for rock bass and an occasional smallmouth. I'll never forget my first fish on a fly rod. It was only a six-inch rock bass, but it gave me more of a thrill than a six-pound carp or sheepshead on a throw line. My first bluebill at the 140th Street breakwall and my first fish on a fly rod are two of the high points in my life as an outdoorsman.

I must have been a real pain in the neck to Merle Marx at the Five Points Sporting Goods store. I'd beg him to just let me feel a fly rod. The $6.98 for the rod, $4.98 for the reel, $2.00 for enameled line, and a couple of bucks worth of lures and leader was far beyond what my mother could afford. She had a helluva time getting a nickel for a hamburger and another for milk, and many a day I would walk the five miles to school because I didn't have the penny for student fare on the streetcar. With today's economy, these things seem hard to believe. I had a paper route with 20 customers at five cents a week. By saving every penny I could, I finally put a dollar down on a fly-fishing outfit. I would practice during lunch hour at school. 1-2-3-4, forward from 1 o'clock, elbows in and snap your wrist. Merle would keep yelling at me from the store, "Too far back, dammit!" My buddies thought I was a complete nut. Level-wind casting reels were just coming out at that time, but I stuck to my fly rod.

Life suddenly became wonderful! I discovered the Shaker Lake area with Horseshoe, Green and other lakes. The Lee Road bus from St. Clair took me right to this outdoor paradise. I learned to trap muskrats and raccoons there and, one day, while checking a muskrat trap at the water's edge, I thought a trap snapped on my fingers. Actually, I'd stuck my hand into the mouth of a snapping turtle. I managed to pull it out from under the bank but, unfortunately, it refused to turn me loose. For once, the Lee Road bus driver didn't have to yell, '"Please step to the rear," when this 12-year old Kraut kid got on the bus, tears streaming down my cheeks carrying a 15-pound snapper under my arm, still firmly attached to my fingers. Lee and Cedar Road was as far as they would put up with me, but that was good enough. The gas station owner on the corner was an old-time hunter who used to let me warm myself on cold winter nights after I finished my trap line. He knew exactly how to handle the situation. He heated a poker red hot and poked it up the turtle's rear and the turtle let go.

In those days, Friday fish fries with turtle soup were the thing. From the Hermit Tavern at Five Points to Noble's and Donavan's Loop at 140th Street, the taverns offered me 12 cents a pound live weight for turtles. I was in business. The fly-fishing outfit was as good as mine. Shaker Lakes, Euclid Creek, Bluestone Quarry—I got a couple hundred pounds of turtles the summer of '33 and finally got my first fly fishing rod. I was the Mr. Orvis of the neighborhood.

What a beating that outfit took! White bass at the Illuminating Company, perch off the Gordon Park breakwall, catfish at Mentor Lagoon. Thank God for the extra tip that came with the outfit. Split bamboo wasn't meant for the use I gave it. Friction tape in the fly bag was a must.

As I am writing this, I'm sitting alongside one of my bass ponds. I have a State of Ohio Hatchery License and I'm raising smallmouth bass, trout, and pan fish for stocking ponds. When we fish at any of our ponds, there is a "no kill" policy. Hanging on a rod rack are two Orvis graphite flyrods, Battenkill reels, also a number of Orvis spinning outfits—a far cry from my first Depression days outfit. It's for a good cause, though, and it makes me feel good to think that, in some small way, I'm helping to keep Leigh and Romi Perkins going on those little fishing excursions to New Zealand, Iceland, Scotland, and Christmas Island. That is a good cause, isn't it?

The Orvis outfits have come a helluva lot easier than that first fly-fishing outfit. The newest was a gift from my wife, Dee. When I told her the story of my first rod and how much it cost, she said something like, "Don't worry about it, you're worth whatever this one costs." Now you all know when your wife says something like that to you, you've got to say something nice back. I came up with, "Ok honey, I'll teach you to fly fish." What a mistake. When it comes to hunting and fishing, my wife had an uncanny knack of coming up with the impossible. After a lot of coaching, she finally laid a dry trout fly out on one of my trout ponds. No sooner did it hit when it was sucked under. After a half hour of deep runs, Dee was begging for me to take the rod. I told her, "It's your fish, baby, and you're onto something good." I was hoping it would break water so we could get a look at it. I had visions of a record brown, left over from years and years ago. After almost an hour of this tug-of-war, she finally got it into the shallows. What did we see? Whiskers! A damn five-pound channel cat. Where he came from is still a mystery. But there is one thing for certain, I have never heard of anything like that on a dry trout fly before. Incidentally, he ate better than a trout.

Most fly-fishing nightmares are of a back cast hung up in a tree. I've got a back cast story that came out a little better. After WWII, I was convalescing at Percy Jones Hospital in Michigan. I had a gunshot wound in my right elbow and managed to convince the doctors that fly fishing would be very effective physical therapy. Next, I finagled a fishing permit for Gull Lake at Kellog's Rest Camp. One afternoon while I was out in a boat catching one-pound bluegills, I was trying to get a lot of line out to a weed bed when suddenly, on my back cast, my line started going out. What a catch! I had hooked a sailboat with six coeds from the University of Michigan. By the time I got that hook out of the sail, we'd become the best of friends. Maybe that's why bluegills on a fly rod are my favorites.

About 30 years ago on a beautiful, warm Sunday afternoon in May, I was bumming around my game farm with my friend Leigh Perkins who is president of the Orvis Company and who I've ribbed a little in this story. I noticed schools of fish coming up out of Bridge Creek up the overflows into my ponds. I said, "Suckers." Leigh said, "Like hell they are! Look again. They're bass!" He was right. No sucker mouth on these fish. I couldn't believe it and had never seen anything like it, or, that many fish. I had an old casting outfit in my Jeep and one lure, an orange Flatfish. Every cast connected with a largemouth from one to five pounds. Leigh was already late for a dinner engagement so we released all the fish and left. The next day, I came back with all my bass fishing buddies, equipped with a fish carrying tank and an aerator. It was the chance of a lifetime. With the bass I saw the day before, I would be able to stock all my new lakes and ponds. Hours went by. We didn't get a hit. Sadly, the big run had gone through. Several days later, I found the bass, three beaver dams upstream on beds at Widgeon Pond and immediately called my very good friend Hughie O'Neill.

If anyone ever lived up to the title of this book it would be "Uncle Hughie." We met when I stripped off his old enameled fly line and put on a line that had just been put on the market, the Cortland 333. The look on his face was something to behold when his line slipped smoothly through the ferrules. Uncle Hughie was the President of Leaseway Transportation, a millionaire over and over, and he became my friend for life over a $3.98 spool of fly line. He always wanted to take me bonefishing or salmon fishing. I'd laugh and tell him I was happy with my fly rod fishing for the trout of Ohio—bluegills. I took him to Widgeon Pond, one of the many ponds and lakes on my game farm. The females had laid their eggs and the males were protecting the nest. They hit anything that came near the nest. Small bass poppers were made to order. Uncle Hughie declared it a perfect day, better than bonefishing, and that, of course, made my day. It must have been a special day for him because as we were enjoying our shore lunch, Uncle Hughie—a life long teetotaller—had his first beer.

Although Uncle Hughie's conversation could be salty at times, his cardinal rule was to never take the Lord's name in vain. This put quite a strain on this inarticulate immigrant's vocabulary, because most of my favorite expletives were unacceptable. Fishing a beaver pond with a fly rod and not being able to express myself in those rich phrases that rolled off my tongue so easily was difficult. One day when we were fishing together, there was a big bass feeding in a side lagoon with a log across the mouth, a real challenge. I urged Uncle Hughie to try his luck. He handed me his rod and said, "This one's for you, Fritz." Carefully, I slipped out of the canoe and flipped a bass bug over the log toward the bass. He hit it immediately, and as I was trying to figure out what to do, he gave a tremendous leap over the log and I landed him. A beautiful five-pounder. "The Lord was with you on that one, Fritz," Uncle Hughie declared. Under my breath I murmured, "It was just plain skill. I must have learned something after all these years of fly fishing." But do you know, after all the different things that happen in a lifetime of fishing, some wonderful, some disappointing, some strange and unbelievable, I just wonder if perhaps Uncle Hughie was right.

BEAT TWO
Keith C. Russell

The Top-Secret Secrets of Fly Fishing—Part One

What species would fly rodders fish for if they could fish for only *one*? Which *one* location? Which *one* fly would they use? What *one* type of presentation? *And* what are the reasons for these answers? It's all revealed here for the first time by the world's best professional and "professional amateur" fly fishers.

This may be the really big fly-fishing news of the '80s! Think of it! Over 100 of the leading professional and "professional amateur" fly fishers from all over the world have been polled by this writer for their answers to the above penetrating questions.

What 24-carat nuggets of information! The results of millions of dollars and hundreds of thousands of hours expended; the careful consideration of the species sought, from bluegills to blue marlin; the studies of their habits and habitat; the tens of thousands of hours of fly selection; the final determination of the most productive presentation; the tremendous amount of accumulated experience from around the globe.

This unique poll was conducted in 1985 among specially selected participants, of whom 54 are fly-fishing professionals (those who make their living from fly fishing). Of the remaining, 45 are "professional amateurs" who have sought the Holy Grail of fly fishing throughout most of the world, and nine are half-and-half, or perhaps more accurately, semi-pro (that is, they are closely connected with fly fishing but do not make their living directly by it or from it or whatever. I hope you understand. If so, please do let me know. So I'll know.)

First, the species above all others named by this very special group of fly fishers as their favorites in all the world, fresh water or salt, if they could fish for only *one* were, in alphabetical order: Atlantic bonito, Atlantic salmon, bluefish, bluegill, bonefish, brook trout, brown trout, cutthroat trout, Pacific sailfish, rainbow trout, smallmouth bass, steelhead, tarpon, trout (all species).

With a grand total of 108 voters, 13 fish received anywhere from one to 40 votes, while 11 ballots were cast for trout in general: the cream of the crop, folks, a most interesting list.

Atlantic salmon led this most preferred group as *the* species, with 40 ballots equal to 37 percent of the total votes cast. However, 15 votes or 13.9 percent were in favor of brown trout; 10 (9 percent) named rainbow trout, two (1.9 percent) went for steelhead; another two gave the nod to brook trout; one fisher selected cutthroat trout; and 11 experts (10.2 percent) came down in favor of trout generally. Thus a grand total of 41 votes (38 percent) went to trout of one kind or another.

The "net result," therefore, fly-angling brethren, is essentially a dead heat, a tie between Atlantic salmon and trout for the purple ribbon. But it should be said that this was not a personality contest, as you will see in detail a little further on. A great many factors were given thoughtful consideration in determining the way the ballots were cast. Here is how the voting went, and by whom.

First, one nod was given the Atlantic bonito by pro Tom Rosenbauer of Orvis News. Tom recommends Martha's Vineyard for this saltwater fighter and a #1/0 Chartreuse Deceiver cast to breaking fish and retrieved with very fast strips. He stated, "Atlantic bonito are seldom caught from shore on the Atlantic coast, but do come in during the fall. The strike is very quick, and the first run will often take 100 yards in a very few seconds."

Next we have the bluefish, another saltwater battler, which was given a single vote by George Reiger, pro and conservation editor of *Field & Stream* magazine. George prefers a Cape Charles, Virginia, location using private creations featuring mylar and bucktail. Thanks to this species' teeth, none of his flies last very long, thus giving him ample opportunity for further experiments at the bench. He advises a "stake out" anchored in shallow water similar to that for tarpon and waiting for tailing fish to come by on the tide. "Further, they arrive in numbers, fight remarkably like the Atlantic salmon, and most Chesapeake blues are of comparable size: six to nine pounds, with a few in the 12- to 16-pound range."

Moving on, we find Bob Stearns, another *Field & Stream* professional, who labors there as saltwater fishing/boating editor and who cast the one ballot for Pacific sailfish. He's not fussy about where to find these sails but does go for a foam-head popper, 8 inches long and white with blue back. Bob elects the usual billfish presentation of teasing the sail to within casting range via a hookless teaser. The boat is then taken out of gear and the fly cast. "It's extremely exciting," he says, "and besides, what other fish can you catch that's as long as the fly rod?"

Now we come to the smallmouth bass, one of those species of pound-for-pound fame. This brawler got four votes from a pro-am and a trio of play-for-pay'ers. The former, Dick Baker, urges Michigan with a popper and concludes with the sage (?) remark that "fly-rod smallmouth on a popper are better than sex." Presumably he knows. All the while Gerald Almy from *Sports Afield* magazine won't say where, but does choose a Black Sculpin/Marabou Muddler hybrid with a twitching or stripping retrieve as the fly and method of his choice. Ed Gray of *Gray's Sporting Journal* also declined to divulge location but likes a Mickey Finn and five-weight equipment. Dave Whitlock, who did L. L. Bean's fly-fishing book, reveals a preference for either an Ozark or Ontario stream using "a hairbug fly retrieved in a slow, erratic, floating and diving manner because it simulates something that is truly alive and vulnerable as a food source."

Next we arrive at the irascible bluegill, which was named by five citizens: two "professional" do-it-for-fun'ers and three "non-hobbyists." First to the pro-ams. Bob Buckmaster recommends Wisconsin lakes, #12 (#12?) Black Wooly Worms and a slow retrieve on three-weight equipment. He reasons that bluegills "are beautifully colored, strike aggressively, and if they weighed five pounds you couldn't land them." Bob Elman, author, editor, and publishing consultant, who is sort of half pro and half amateur (self-proclaimed) likes his own back yard: Merrill Creek Pond, above the dam, Stewartsville, N.J. Bob also goes for "a small, nameless, dingy green popping bug with a splashy (sloppy) cast and increasingly jerky retrieves as level in thermos subsides." He vows the bug works best when first immersed in Rector's scotch (well-known floatant). On bad days he may add a teeny pinch of attractant (New Jersey night crawler). On worse days he dispenses with the bug entirely and uses a #8 snelled hook encased in attractant. Tsk, tsk!

The pro's are another matter. "Uncle Homer" Circle, angling editor of *Sports Afield*, flatly states he likes "bluegills in all fifty states on a green sponge spider with white rubber legs." He says to "hold the fly under water, squeeze out the air, and let it soak up water slowly. Between top and bottom a whopper bluegill may inhale it and put a goshwonderful bend in your light fly rod. They're delightful to hassle with, and the afterglow of fine eating caps off a memorable day." Dick Kotis of Fred Arbogast agrees with Uncle Homer, the only difference being his fly preference: water crickets, either wet or dry. Tom Paugh, editor of *Sports Afield*, goes for a Virginia farm pond with poppers, "mostly still, with only an occasional 'pop'." His reasoning is perhaps best of all: "for solitude!"

Next on our star-studded menu is the silver king, the magnificent tarpon, with six ballots to its credit from 1½ professionals and 4½ pro-amateurs.

Leading off is Stu Apte, former airline pilot and for many years now a pro fly flinger of the first water, who declares that given the constraints of this poll, he "would without question choose sight fishing for tarpon on the shallow flats of the Florida Keys (all tarpon addicts named the Keys) using an Apt Too fly (furnace saddle and gray squirrel tail neck on a #4/0 hook)." Next at bat is Gene Hill, (the half-er), *Field & Stream* columnist, book author, sage of the outdoors, fishing and hunting, and of matters pertaining thereto. Gene's a Keys man, too, thinks fly selection is not really that critical, and depends on a favoring wind and a little luck to guide his "usually sloppy" casts. He bases his pick on "the stalking of the fish, the locale, and the singular power of the tarpon."

Tarpon aficionado Joe Hudson thinks a black fly with hackle and wings of vulturine guinea fowl at the end of a double hauled line is the most effective, while George Kirkham admits he "just gets more thrills going after big fish!" Avid and active Rip McIntosh prefers a black fly with red or blue and declares that "nothing matches the acrobatics of a big tarpon on fly!" Our tarpon report ends with perhaps the best known tarpon specialist of them all, record holder Billy Pate. Billy, not unexpectedly, adds Homosassa to his location preferences along with the Keys and selects a saddle-hackle fly presented with a slow strip. He says going after tarpon is hunting as well as fishing, and that "the tarpon is a natural fly-rod target, taking flies sometimes when they won't take a bait fish. If you do it right with a fly, he will usually eat!"

Moving across thin water only a short distance, we sight the "gray ghost of the flats," the elegant and very rapid bonefish, which garnered nine votes for the top spot from six pros, two pro-ams, and one half-er. First up is pro Leon Chandler from a leading fly-line company, Cortland, who gives his vote to old Mr. Bone in the Bahamas, preferably the Exumas, and uses a brown, white, or yellow fly depending on conditions (color and type of bottom, light, etc.) and who likes to fish to 'em while wading. He also likes the kind of places they live—warm, clear water flowing in over the flats—and the stalking, watching for cruising or tailing fish, and that first run of a hooked bonefish which he says "has to be one of life's greatest thrills."

Half-er Mike Fitzgerald, of Fish and Game Frontiers, selects the bones of Christmas Island in the Central Pacific Ocean. He prefers a barbless #4, gold or silver Crazy Charlie fly cast while stalking, and his reasoning is multiple: (1) on C. I. you do it on your own without a guide marking the fish; (2) it requires "hunting" the fish with mind-cleansing concentration; (3) there is a premium on careful and accurate presentation, often in windy conditions; (4) the powerful, visible take; (5) the exhilarating, sometimes incredible first, long, high-speed run ("I swear they're faster and stronger here than their Atlantic/Caribbean cousins"); (6) "There are greater numbers of bonefish on C. I. flats than anywhere else I've seen or even heard about"; (7) very large bones (over ten pounds) are present in good numbers—record-quality fish; (8) the marvelous warm, sunny, stable climate provides a true year-round season ideal for flats fishing; (9) all catch and release at Christmas; (10) "The most expansive bonefish flats I've seen are here, giving the angler virtually unlimited hunting range," and finally (11) "There's the bonus of trevally fishing on the flats and at drop-off edges—and they're something else." That sure says it all, Mike.

Next voter, well-known, now retired Florida Keys guide, Captain George Hommel of the World Wide Sportsman in Islamorada, goes for Keys bones with a custom, green body, white hair-wing fly and a very slow retrieve. He states, "Nothing can compare with their slyness and speed," with which Bill Hunter of Hunter's Angling Supplies echoes agreement except for changing the fly to a tan/white upside-down tie. Thanks, Bill, for the tip. Pro-am Bob Keller of Maryland's Eastern Shore says ditto, but prefers a pink fly and out-of-the-way locations like the Turks and Caicos Islands.

Now to Lefty Kreh, fly-fishing professional of repute and some kind of thrower, who is not too particular location-wise: he just likes the Keys, the Bahamas, *and* Christmas Island (who doesn't?) using the Bonefish Special fly. Lefty reasons: "Bonefishing is regarded as the wild-turkey hunting of angling. The fish have sharp eyes; they flee at the slightest sign of anything wrong; and you can use relatively light tackle." Fling-for-fun-er Dick Pope, Jr., of water skiing and Cypress Gardens, Florida, renown, agrees with Lefty, selects a brown and/or white fly, and adds, "Bonefish are also extremely unpredictable." Amen, Dick. Mark Sosin, fishing editor of *Sports Afield*, also agrees with the foregoing but prefers a snapping shrimp fly. He comments, "It is a demanding sport in which presentation is critical."

Bringing up the bonefish caboose is Dix White, who owns the Wayland, Massachusetts, Orvis store. Dix opines for Deep Water Cay, just east of Grand Bahama Island, and a Pinder brown shrimp (Crazy Charlie pattern) fly plus "a reel buzzing like an angry hornet."

So there you have the ballot counts—some of the votes expected, but mixed with a few refreshing surprises—plus some secrets of fishing for the various runner-up species. But what of the two main contenders, trout and Atlantic salmon? As patience is an acknowledged angling virtue, I have no compunction about telling you that, to find out, you'll have to delve further into this book. You'll find Part Two of my "Top-Secret Secrets" poll—on trout—at the beginning of Beat Four; and the final part, on *Salmo salar*, leads off my final Beat.

Why I Fly Fish

The reason, or reasons, why I fly fish is something that I don't think about very often. Perhaps not as often as I should because, you see, such a subject involves introspection, a searching within one's self, which probably a substantial majority of today's adult population past the half-century mark is somewhat reluctant to attempt, things being the way they are. And I am one of the majority.

Nevertheless, the effort is, I think, a worthy one. Certainly a very considerable number of men and women throughout history, and possessed of vaster talent than mine, have thought it desirable to reduce their feelings on the subject to words. I am moved to do no less.

Now to say that fly fishing is a religious experience might be stretching things a bit, but it's close enough as to be almost borderline. To be specific, fly fishing, like church attendance, is therapeutic. Each one of us needs some outside help from time to time. And we each must find it in our own way. If you're like me, pure fresh air and tall green trees stretching into the distance are your cathedral and moving water is your constant, continuing baptismal; its sound is your litany. Surely beauty of sight and sound, and awe, awe in the presence of nature's wonders, which can only be the result of the hand of God, are related to a religious experience. Who is not moved under these circumstances?

In sum, fly fishing for me is more than a sport or recreation. It is truly a perfectly delightful, soul-mending experience. How is it with you?

The Candy Fly of Boca Paila

There are many names of many places around the globe, the sight of which on a printed page or the sound of which on someone's lips, to the fly fisherman at once conjures up a mental image of wondrous, storied, fish and fishing; Shangri-Las, if you will; meccas that are only to be discussed in whispers and with reverence. Such pearls as the Miramichi, Restigouche, and Grand Cascapedia in Canada; the Grimsa and Laxa i Adaldal in Iceland; the Beaverkill in New York; the Battenkill in Vermont; the Au Sable in Michigan where Trout Unlimited was born; the Brule in Wisconsin; the Snake in Wyoming; the Yellowstone, Madison, the Big Hole, Brodhead, and the well-known "unnamed tributary of the Missouri" in Montana; the Deschutes in Oregon; the Alta in Norway; Tierra del Fuego in Argentina; Chile; Islamorada in Florida; and Deep Water Cay and Great Exuma in the Bahamas; and Christmas Island for bonefish; Homosassa Springs in Florida for world-record tarpon; and then there is Boca Paila on Mexico's Yucatan peninsula where the Gray Fox of the flats abounds, if not for size, then in mind-boggling quantity. Which, as it is said, ain't too shabby.

Let's go there in May, in prime time, and see what the fishing gods decree. There were the four of us: the Senor and wife Barb, Margie, and El Viejo, that's me. It was a trip long planned, once delayed for two years by the Senor's bout with the Big C and finally back on track, thanks to expert medical attention, radiation, a stout will, and God's will. The flights: Cleveland to Miami to Cozumel to dirt strip at Boca Paila to dirt strip at Ascension Bay to houseboat, our home for the next several days. Accommodations on the latter were a might tight, but we were all good friends, so what the hell. The groceries were definitely better, centering around fresh fish and lobster, which we enjoyed broiled, baked, boiled, fried, hot, cold, and have you ever tried a lobster omelet? Yowsa, lip smackin' great!

Oh yes, about the fishing, and therein lies the tale and the tails. In February of the same year, Margie and I had spent a week over on Deep Water Cay with John and Anne Dickinson, who ran the joint, and very, very well, too, and with Joan and Lee Wulff, Pringle and Ed Boyd, and Evelyn and Carl Navarre, who owned the famous Cheeca Lodge at Islamorada, all of whom know a bit about bonefish, tarpon, permit, and related matters. The week had been a gas in all respects, and, it was determined, was deserving of encores, plural, in the future. Soon after returning home, I received a package from Lee W. containing a handful of Wulff-tied and Wulff-favorite, yellow surface stone flies, which his accompanying note proclaimed, "those Boca Paila bonefish will take like candy." With a mental blessing upon the Chairman of the Board, I stowed his flies with all the rest of our gurry where they remained until, I think, it was the second or maybe the third morning of our houseboat stay. The bonefishing to that point had been good by Boca Paila's standards, which meant it had been super great outstanding by the standards of most of the rest of the world.

So OK. That morning, as I searched my bonefish fly box for a winner first crack out, quite literally, my eyes and fingers, and then bringing up the rear, my mind or what's left of it, stumbled over Brother Wulff's yellow surface stone flies, the "miracle," candy flies, which no respecting Ascension Bay bonefish could possibly resist. Of course, nothing else would do, and at the end of my leader, it went with great expectations. Our leader would never lie to his disciples.

At the first opportunity (bonefish) which presented itself, out went my dream and a prayer. It hit the water good, looked good, and I felt good about it, particularly when Old Mr. Bone charged that fly like there was no tomorrow and lit out for parts unknown but distant. Naturally I was pleased, but little did I know at the time that those bones that morning were going to act like kids loose in a free-for-the-taking candy store. I mean, what they did was go wild, berserk. It was a real genuine, honest-to-God, Hey Rube. They were all in love with that Candy Fly and just couldn't get enough of that wonderful stuff.

When it was time to stop for lunch and head back for home base, the count stood at 30, plus my guide had taken three, all released, and averaging maybe four pounds. I had been in bonefish heaven.

Back at the houseboat, Senor Davis thought I was lying. Well, of course, naturally he was jealous and said he wasn't goin' on any more safaris with a liar. But I knew he didn't really mean it, so I didn't care what he said, I had been *there*. I had seen the Holy Grail. I had been taken by the hand and shown the way. Thanks, Mr. Chairman.

Now for the postscript with a punch for those of you who are still with us. It seems that while those terrific Boca Paila bonefish guides may never have heard of Lee Wulff, perish the thought, they are now sold, sold, sold on what they call the Candy Fly, the bonefish fly to end all, the best thing to hit the Yucatan since sliced tortilla. Es verdad!!!

> Please don't cry, Boca Pai-la bonefish,
> Permit and tarpon too,
> Just wait until proximo ano
> And we'll be coming back to you!

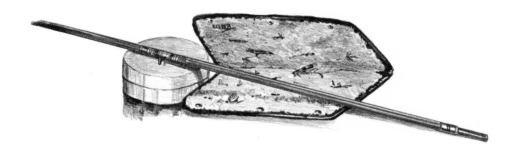

Grimsa Saga

We had Leifur's heppni on the River Grimsa: good fortune on Grimsa, Iceland's world-reknowned Atlantic salmon river, about 2½ hours by car north and a little east of Reykjavik, the capital of this beautiful land of fire and ice and Atlantic salmon, the king of fish and the fish of kings.

Gardner Grant, former prexy of the Fly Fisher's Federation and current head honcho of the American Museum of Fly fishing, fishing his umteenth year in Iceland, put together a group of irregulars, eight rods strong, for the second week in July for a go at *Salmo salar*. Those paid up and present included G.G; his double buddy, Mike Owen, formerly National President of Trout Unlimited; Ed and Pringle Boyd; Tom and Yvette Cole; Charles Leavell; father and son Everett and John Kircher; and my Margie and me. For some of us it was our long awaited first time at bat in Iceland. Others were veterans of several trips to Iceland's piscatorial plate. All had been actively calendar watching for our salmon safari to begin.

New York's Kennedy Airport to Iceland's Keflavik Airport is an "interesting" trip. Check the quotes! Icelandic Air's "cattle cars" are mostly filled with college students on summer break, on their way to Europe the cheapest way possible, plus salmon and brown trout anglers making their annual pilgrimage, in addition to returning Icelanders from holiday or relative visiting. In summer, every seat on every flight is filled with bottoms, and a happy air prevails, sometimes described as a 4½ hour cocktail party. G.G. had looked after our welfare with "choice seats," meaning they were all together, and we were all old friends by touch down.

To say that Iceland is a fascinating country is a gross understatement. Start with approximately 225,000 people, all of whom are either handsome or pretty, depending on their plumbing. Add a 100 percent-plus inflation rate, a 40 percent prime interest rate, no unemployment, and everyone smiling and friendly. Believe it! All true. And you might also include the cleanest air and water anywhere. There is *no* pollution. All is not quite perfect, however, witness the six-month long days and six-month long nights, with attendant side effects. However, I like it just the way it is, and, I hope, stays.

Salmon fishing in Iceland is not exactly roughing it. In this case, on the lovely Grimsa, overlooking the home pool called Guilfoss, the almost new, angled architecture from Ernie Schwiebert's drawing board, red-roofed fishing lodge, nestles right into the countryside like a member of the club. We would be happy there. So, too, our stomachs, if not our bathroom scales. Icelandic table fare is irresistably good. Properly centered around the pale pink flesh for which we sought and had traveled many miles in the seeking, it is prepared in all imaginable ways, both cold and hot, to wit: smoked, gravlox (my very favorite), salad, soup, cold poached, hot poached, grilled, broiled, baked, boiled, and no doubt several other ways, which escape my failing memory. And it is all so very, very good, as is everything else before, with, and after. (Please hand me my napkin for I'm drooling.)

The fishing schedule: 7 a.m. to 1 p.m., and 4 p.m. to 10 p.m., for a total of an honest half a day, and all in daylight, calls for good beds, in addition to good food. We had them. The lodge mothered us well. Most important of all, the Grimsa looked after our souls and fed our psyches too.

The salmon fishing? Well, it is not for scores or scoring, for only each individual knows what it means for him or her. If measure one must, then I can report a bottle of white wine consumed for every fish killed, and our week was the season's high. So count the wine bottles for your answer.

For Gardner Grant, it was old hat that is forever new: always experimenting, trying something new in fly or tackle or technique; always enjoying just being there, doing one's favorite thing in the world, in one's favorite place in the world. What more could anyone possibly ask?

For pretty Pringle Boyd, it was her maiden trip for salmon. A good fly fisherwoman, she shared a rod with Ed, caught several fish and just generally had a ball.

For raconteur Ed Boyd, experienced on Atlantic salmon, bonefish and tarpon, the first half of our week was frustrating, very much so, for it seemed everyone else was into fish, and he simply couldn't even buy a hit. Midweek everything changed, and he netted every fish struck and caught up in a hurry. Damn good, I'd say.

For Mike Owen, it was the exact, 180° opposite. Although certainly experienced on salmon, for some reason never determined, he had difficulty keeping them on and netted about half those struck. Those netted, however, amounted to a very satisfactory result.

For Tom and Yvette Cole, who'd done it all before, more than a little, it was another return to mecca, which they hope to repeat ad infinitum. Count me in with them.

For Charles Leavell and me, it was also our initiation to the fraternity, and we lost our virginity with gusto. In fact, *con muchissimo gusto*. Like most, I'll never forget my first visit. Following the strike was the terrible fear that I would do something wrong and lose him. No one happened to be around at the time, including my guide, Diddi, who was off somewhere tending the Boyds, so I knew I would have to beach the fish.

When eventually I did, and *numero uno* was safely grassed, the wonder of it was almost overcoming. All I could do was say thank you to the fishing gods and sit, and look, and admire that wonderful salmon. Right then I knew that I was the one that was really caught, and I couldn't have been happier.

For Margie, it was another in a long line of fishing and hunting safaris to dozens of new and strange places all over the globe. To me, she's the best of all because even though not a fisherwoman or a hunter, nevertheless, she goes! What's more, she's the first to say what a smashing time she's having, and I know she means it. Thanks, Margie.

For all of us, the beauteous, bountiful, storied, Grimsa is now permanently enshrined in our minds and hearts. Make that hearts and minds because the heart is more important. All rivers call with one siren song or another, but the Grimsa's call is something different. I think perhaps because it is such a very close and personal call, that it becomes so special. Special it will always be.

The Nursery

It happened a few years back at the classy Castalia Trout Club in northwestern Ohio, perhaps the Buckeye State's most prestigious private trout water. It was fun and frustrating, unintentional and embarrassing. It took place during an Ohio Ducks Unlimited Council meeting thanks to Castalia Club members and long time D.U. supporters, Rusty Heymann and Jim Secor, whose guests we were so fortunate to be.

We arrived at the Club about noon one beautiful September day. Following refreshments and lunch, a Council business meeting was convened and, after a productive session, was adjourned in the late afternoon, whereupon we all took to the stream for some R & R before dinner.

Since I figured that most of the guys would be trying their luck pretty close in, perhaps in their hurry to wet a line, I determined upon the opposite tack and headed for the back forty. Arriving at the point on the Castalia water where it departed club property, I began slowly working my way back upstream, taking a nice rainbow now and then and generally just having a ball. It was late afternoon on a most beneficent day when time seemed unimportant and I was quite content to continue the scenario. Belatedly the thought seeped into my tranquillized brain that it was rapidly getting on toward dusk and I was soon due back at the club house for dinner, that is, if I wanted any.

Reluctantly I quickened my pace while still taking time to cast into likely looking water along the way. The Castalia stream snakes along in horseshoe bends, S curves, and double backs with foot bridges strategically placed to shortcut one's journey out, back or in between, and I had a map if it came to that. So why rush? The next I knew, so help me, it was dark and so was the moon and I was without flashlight or matches. What the heck, I figured. All I have to do is keep going upstream and eventually I'll get back to the Club. Without taking the short-cut bridges it might take a little longer but no big deal. It was too black to read the map.

A few minutes later in the still of the night I heard someone approaching. It turned out to be Jim Glass, at that time Executive Director of the Ohio Wildlife Legislative Fund, which has been so successful and has since gone national with Jim still at the helm. Jim had overstayed like me and so we joined forces to find our way. The first thing we accomplished was to try a shortcut and ended up completing the proverbial circle right back where we started from. Discarding that approach we finally agreed we were lost and would make our way back eventually even though we might as well forget about dinner.

Soon after, as we were slowly winding our way in what we hoped was the right direction, we came upon the damnedest rise of trout I have ever witnessed. The huge pool in which this heart stopping action was taking place appeared like a heavy rain shower was in progress. Hundreds of trout, or so it seemed, in the pitch dark, were participating, taking advantage of some kind of super hatch which, of course, we couldn't see.

There was only one thing to do and we did it. Our rods were still set up. We both cast, were struck, played and netted rainbows of about two pounds each. We cast again, were hit, and Jim landed his. Worse luck, I was too anxious, struck too hard, and broke off my fly. I was out of business as it was too dark to tie on another. I almost cried. All the while Glass is whooping it up, casting, hooking, playing fish. Those rainbows couldn't get to his fly fast enough. I was reduced to netting his fish for him without so much as an offer to use his rod for one cast or two or even a thank you. Some pal.

Well, he did eventually get his fill. Even gluttony has its limits. I've conveniently forgotten how many fish we finally lugged back to the Club, the majority his. The lost were welcomed home. No one had even worried about us. We had a drink, maybe two, and a cold supper. But I had the last laugh. While Jim was catching fish like he died and went to heaven, except for my netting activities, I didn't have a helluva lot to do. I watched him for a while, but a person can get tired of that in a hurry. As it happened, during the process of being bored by it all, while looking around the area, I noticed for the first time a dam-like structure at both ends of our pool. I wondered and suspicioned but said not a bloody word.

After dinner, in the middle of a nightcap and a review of the evening's fabulous fishing, the question was where, oh, where did this wizard event take place? When pressed for an answer, I casually mentioned the concrete dams, upon which a horrified hush fell over the group assembled.

We had partaken of forbidden fruit. We had fished the Club's *nursery* where their hatchery breeders were kept. With all due modesty I stated that I had taken only one.

My Moby Dick, Jr.

Bill Humphrey beat me to it! As a matter of fact so did Herman Melville when he wrote *Moby Dick*. However, who would have dreamed that a well-known modern author, whose works have been primarily in the fiction area, would come up with something called *My Moby Dick* in which he writes about a giant, one-eyed, brown trout. A prodigy of the species. A fish to make all other trout seem mere minnows. Humphrey spotted such a fish in a small Berkshire Mountains creek, in Melville country, and determined he must catch it. "I had not lost a leg to him," he says, "but he had certainly taken a big bite of my brain." He recognizes that he has been "singled out" of "millions of fishermen" to receive this revelation, "to pursue this monster."

But for fickle fishermen's fortune it would have been me that was singled out first, for I too had an encounter with a one-eyed, brown trout of reasonably substantial proportions. My own experience with my "Moby Dick, Jr." actually happened coincidently soon after my having read Humphrey's classic little tale. It took place at the incomparable Rolling Rock Club in Ligonier, Pennsylvania, which sports one of the loveliest little trout streams anywhere. True, most of the fish are stocked, as they are so universally throughout the United States today, but at the Rolling Rock hatchery with fisheries biologist, Horace Stiff, in charge, they really know how to rear those browns, brookies, and rainbows so that when they are released in the stream they are at their fighting best. Horace and his staff, under the supervision of the R.R. Fishing Committee, are also much concerned about living quarters for the trout. Thus they provide excellent cover, keep the banks of the stream in good repair, and generally maintain the stream itself in the best possible condition.

Unfortunately, I don't get there as often as I'd like, but then I guess you can say that about a good many things one particularly enjoys. Margie and I do, however, manage to spend perhaps three to four weekends a year in that beautiful valley and on this particular occasion, as they have been so many times, Barbara and Bill Davis, the Senor, who has been my long-time best friend and hunting and fishing partner, were with us. The Senor and I had agreed that on this trip we would devote our time almost exclusively to fly fishing. I must admit, however, this was not without its negative aspects. Specifically, I fell in the first morning. Now it isn't that I haven't fallen before. Maybe fallen in isn't quite the proper term. In over the waders (sometime referred to as wet fly fishing) may be more accurate. In this particular situation there wasn't any question about it. I just plain stumbled and fell over a bowling ball-size rock which sneaked up on me without warning and placed itself where I couldn't miss it. So over and in I went and the first day I fished most of the day wet. Not wet fly, wet drawers.

The following morning we were both out early, this time on different stretches from the day before. After fishing upstream through one pool un-successfully, I sneaked up on the next higher one and there at the foot of the pool, in rather shallow, clear water, I spotted a brown trout of definitely larger than average R.R. dimensions slowly finning away on its feeding station, awaiting the arrival of goodies from upstream. Casting a #14 Light Cahill about six feet in front of his nose, it floated nicely as you please right past him without so much as a welcoming nod. Twice more I laid it out for him picture pretty and twice more my offering was disdained.

At that point a second trout, one which I couldn't see, rose a few feet beyond my big brown. Thinking this newcomer might also be of a size, and apparently it was hungry where the other was not, I decided to make my next cast to him. Unfortunately, I was a mite short and so got no acceptance while the Cahill floated downstream, this time on the other side of the biggie on which I had been working previously. And this time, *wham*! Brownie took and then took off, and proceeded up, down, crosswise and diagonally to cover about every square foot of that pool plus several encores. Having done his thing, he then quit cold and came quietly to net. Of course I was delighted to have successfully negotiated his capture but somewhat surprised at the suddenness of his capitulation. An examination quickly told the story. That brown was not only long but unusually skinny for his length. The clincher was that it was blind in the left eye. Thus came the dawn: my fly which had thrice been ignored had floated down his left side. Hungry or not, he simply couldn't see it. No wonder he was a bit thin and somewhat undernourished—he was unaware of half of his available food supply.

Nevertheless he did win the Club's dry fly brown trout contest (length times weight), did my Moby Dick, Jr. Which is more than Bill Humphrey can say, who, on the other hand, does say, what he says, better.

The following year I got lucky and again won Rolling Rock's dry fly brown trout contest but with two differences from my experience with my Moby Dick, Jr. This time the big brown took a #14 Dark Cahill and when landed was found to possess two good eyes and was fat. Thus gaining a measure of credence from my obviously jealous fishing partner of the year before, the Senor, who for the past 12 months had referred to my one-eyed monster as "the Snake."

BEAT THREE

Lionel Leach

A Britisher to the core, "Bulgie" is a fly fisher for all seasons. An artillery officer in Kenya at the outbreak of World War II, he experienced tremendous fishing and shooting all the way up Africa; then to Baluchistan and Burma chasing and being chased by Japanese and survived both! A fan of Glen Morangie, a single malt Scotch, over which he and KCR became good friends. Stevenage, Herts, England.

The Best of Times

A fisherman hopes to win against all odds, and sometimes he does, but often he fails, as the following two simple tales will show. An angler in Scotland, many years ago, hooked a large salmon and found that he had neither net nor gaff. The fish was tiring and, as he brought it to the bank, he could see that the hook was attached to the slenderest piece of membrane in the side of the jaw. He shouted to his wife for help and when she arrived he asked her to take off her bloomers (for it was in the days when ladies wore such things) and to wade into the water behind the fish which he gently eased back into its final resting place. With one great heave the gallant girl heaved fish, bloomers, and all onto the bank and fell on them in watery triumph. So much for the success story—now for the failure.

Our son, Stephen, when he was studying law, came to Scotland to fish with us on the River Shin in Sutherland. He had never caught a salmon and was very keen to do so. Each evening he fished late, and, on this occasion, I sat waiting for him in my car on the road high above the pool where I could just see him casting. I heard a shout, seized my gaff, and ran down the steep path to the river. There I saw a 14-pound salmon capering about and realized that the fish was foul hooked. It had gone beserk as foul-hooked fish frequently do. Stephen told me, amid the mad rushes which the fish made, that he had lifted his line from the water to make another cast, the salmon had jumped and he had a struck it in mid-air, the hook was lodged tight just below the vent.

It took the best part of an hour before the fish was within gaffing distance; by this time it was dark and as I peered into the river, to my surprise I saw *two* fish keeping station side by side—the hooked fish and a satellite; I am told that this sometimes happens.

I have always secretly prided myself on my skill with my long-handled Scottish gaff, which is one of my most cherished possessions. At least I have now seen sense and use a salmon net whenever I can, but pride must have its fall and had I used a net that night Stephen would have had his fish. I struck at the wrong fish, there was no leader to steady it and it rolled from under the gaff. The hooked fish took fright at the commotion going on beside it and went out into mid-stream where it wound itself around a rock. Stephen muttered something like "Silly old bugger," just loud enough for me to hear. I jumped into the river fully clothed and stumbled across the current, floundering like a land-locked whale. When I reached the rock I just had time to see the leader snap—our fish (if I may call it this) gave a tired flip, its belly showed white in the moonlight, and it was away.

My real story of failure and success begins on the west coast of Ireland in Connemara in the early 30s, which is a long time ago! My parents, who were home on leave from India, had taken me there on holiday to learn to fish. We were fishing the Kylmore Fishery out of Lenane, mainly for sea trout, so the tackle was light and it was "fly only"; the sea trout ran from two to four pounds and sport was good. What I really wanted though was a grilse or a salmon. I knew that a few had come up so each night I dreamed of such a fish. One sunny afternoon toward the end of our stay, I was fishing from a staging just below the castle when suddenly, from the green depth of the pool, came the fish of my dreams. I can see it now, it swam quietly after my fly, opened its mouth and turned away—the line began to strip off the reel and we were away. Sadly the fish was stronger than my leader, it could have been 12 pounds or more, but I shall never know for after 10 minutes the leader broke and so did my heart.

Bad times are generally followed by good. Twenty-four years later I was sitting on a high, green bank above the River Eo on the borders of Galicia in northwestern Spain watching my wife, Joan, fishing below me. Standing on the rock beside her was Chamber, her ganchero, the splendid ghillie who had lost one eye in the Spanish Civil War in the bitter fighting around Oviedo. He was shading his good eye with his hand the better to see the fly in the water.

The river below me ran a light blue over white stones, totally different in color to my Connemara river of years ago, but again from the bottom came a fish, a large one; I saw it open its mouth and turn away. I did not dare shout in case Joan struck too soon, but then I saw the line go taut and the rod bend. The strike was perfect and so was the fish when it lay on the green grass among the wild flowers. It weighed 16 pounds and Chamber called it "guapo' and so it was.

Why Chamber? (Pronounced in Spanish with a soft "a" and the accent on the last syllable). The reason for his nickname was that he always carried an umbrella hooked to the collar of his jacket and hanging down his back. "Chamber" was short for Chamberlain, the British Prime Minister at the time of the Munich crisis who, invariably, carried an umbrella.

Those far off days of the 1950s in northwest Spain were happy times for us. We were both young so the long journey down France, across the Spanish frontier at Hendaye and then a farther 500 miles west over poor roads meant little. We made many friends of all nationalities, but particularly Spanish— they are our friends still and our families keep up the friendship in the next generation. I went back five years ago—it had not changed very much except that the Spanish Tourist Office had increased the rod capacity of the rivers and there were fewer Atlantic salmon—as is the case everywhere. An old man in the bar of the Hotel Fuente at Cornellana recognized me even after all those years and said "'Senor, your friend Don Eduardo is dead, Don Jose Maria is dead, your ganchero Turnisco is dead, I think it is about time you followed them, for they will be waiting for you on the river up there" pointing to heaven. I might have had my doubts if he had said "waiting on the banks of the Styx!"

As our family grew up we fished nearer to home, mostly in Scotland on the River Deveron near Banff and the River Shin in Sutherland. Happy family holidays with Joan, our two boys and myself, sharing a three-rod beat for our six days of fishing. Every year Hughie Mackintosh, our ghillie on the Shin, would greet us as a family and tell us tales of what had happened before we 'came up' or after we had 'gone down' the year before. This was in the early 1970s when salmon were more plentiful than they are now. We usually managed to catch up to 18 fish in the week, but we worked hard for it. Sadly stocks have now diminished not only on this side of the Atlantic, but wherever Atlantic salmon swim. The rodsmen blame the estuary netsmen, who blame the drift netsmen, who blame the deep sea fishermen. But whatever the cause Scottish rivers are at an all-time low and the runs of what fish come in are getting later and later. We had only five salmon in our week's fishing last year; this year we shall not go north, but this is partly due to old age, for in a fisherman hope springs eternal. Our memories remain with us, so do the 12 rods in a rack on the kitchen wall and the many photographs of friends and fish from all over the world.

Sometimes, in those days when we were in funds, we went fishing farther afield. On one occasion to Kashmir, where the fishing was a fiasco due to the late spring, but the holiday was a success due to the beauty and peace of the Nagin Lake and Ghulam Badyari's houseboat. The next year we chanced our luck and went to Ethiopia to the Bale National Park 200 miles south west of Addis. I had chased the Italian Army all the way from Somaliland to Addis in 1941 and then westward from there along the road which runs through the lakes to Sciascamana. We followed this road 25 years on, even found my old howitzer gun pits, but turned south at Sciascamana and up into the high ground around Bale.

The rest house, just a stone shell, was at about 10,000 feet. It was cold at night, even a frost one morning. We camped in a bare room and were joined by many others who had come there to fish. The bird life and scenery was attractive, the fishing excellent, except that the river ran through the plain below us in a gorge which was about 35 feet deep. It was not easy fishing for now and again you had to climb out of the gorge to bypass a deep pool and a cliff face. Friendly, small boys threw pebbles at you and even tried to urinate on you. It was an experience, a fishing trip we shall never forget.

Sadly two of my friends who were with us on this trip have been drowned in recent years, one while duck shooting on the Kinankop in Kenya and the other in a fast flowing trout river in Chile. Both were tremendous sportsmen, both good friends whom I had known from the days when we drove the 2,000 miles from Kenya to Eritrea in 1940/42.

The rivers in Chile can be dangerous. Seven years ago we nearly lost two of our party on our first fishing trip to that part of South America. This experience, and two further ones in storms on Lake Rudolf or Turkana as it is now called, had made me deeply suspicious of small boats and boatmen. But since that first trip in Chile in March 1979, Joan and I have returned on two further occasions for to us it is the most exciting trout fishing in the world. I cannot say that either of the first two trips yielded many fish but on the third trip, with our friend and guide, Mike Konak, who took us to Lake Yelcho south of Puerto Montt, we had some of the finest fishing in the world. Not only was the fishing good but the hotel at Puerto Cadenas was excellent and the scenery beautiful.

On our way south that last occasion, we found ourselves once again on the night sleeper from Santiago to Puerto Montt. It is not a fast train but they call it El Rapido and it is comfortable. The staff bring pisco sours to the sleeping compartment before the evening meal and there are fresh strawberries for breakfast. From Puerto Montt we flew with the Garcia Air Charter Service in a twin engined plane. We were due out at 5 p.m. but it was 7:40 p.m. before the plane was airborne. We had a head wind over Chiloe and by the time the pilot turned inland at Chaiten (the ugliest town in the world) it was already getting dark.

He flew along the valley, well below the peaks rising either side of us, until ahead I could see the grey glint of Lake Yelcho. At the seaward end was a very small dirt strip, it looked like a postage stamp from above, hard to make out in the fast-gathering dusk. Mike cheered us up by saying the pilot was a good man and so he was. He put his airplane down with precision, threw out our rods and baggage, and with a confident *"adios"* disappeared into the night. I have flown with many bush pilots in my life but he was as good as any.

Ramon and Juliana Ojeda, who own the small hotel at Puerto Cardenas, could not have been kinder to us. The hotel is simple, spotlessly clean and the food excellent.

I woke up early next morning, dressed and went outside to the most startling view I had seen for years. The sun was just showing over the glacier opposite the Sillon del Diablo. The ice on the lower slopes where the rays had not reached was purple, up the glacier the color changed to pink, and then a blush onto bright white. The air was clear, the lake still, except for the circle of a large fish feeding on the surface. It was a perfect setting and I blessed Mike for bringing us back to Chile and to this lovely spot.

After breakfast we went fishing, Joan with Mike in a boat with an outboard, and I with a great barrel-chested boatman called Ala Din, and so we fished for six perfect days. Fishing statistics are generally stretched but by common consent we had caught 63 trout—browns and rainbows—weighing a total of 208 pounds. All but a few were released. Five of these were around the six-pound mark, four of five pounds and 17 of four pounds, but we were agreed that it was not the number and size of the fish which pleased us most, it was the beautiful lake, the way in which the Patagonian trout took the dry fly, and the warm reception and kindness we received from everyone we met. The high mountains, the glaciers, the changing colors of the lake, make Yelcho a fisherman's paradise, the one to which Joan and I would return if we could.

Richard J. Kotis

Owner of internationally known fishing lure manufacturer, Fred Arbogast Company. When asked once if he would be interested in selling his company, Dick's answer was, "Listen, I fished 180 days last year. And I'm going to do the same this year and next. And the next. Now, come on!" Akron, Ohio.

Notes from Dick Kotis' Diary

We were making a movie on Johnny Cass' houseboat, the *Casamar*, at Big Pine Key. An outdoor writer; Erwin (Joe) Bauer, was the script writer for the pic and the photographer was Karl Maslowski. At the time Erwin was probably the most prolific outdoor writer in America, and Karl was one of the best outdoor photographers. Our quarry was the Big Four of the Florida Keys: tarpon, bonefish, permit, and barracuda. We were fortunate to have some wonderful weather and were able to accomplish our objective except for the permit.

The *Casamar* on which we were living was a very large houseboat that had two twin-bedded rooms and a living lounge that was convertible to a third bedroom. Visualize if you will that the houseboat would swing on its bow anchor and, therefore, the two front bedrooms were constantly experiencing a cooling breeze making it very comfortable for the guests to sleep. Joe and I were sleeping in the living lounge on hide-a-beds. This room is directly behind the bedrooms and, therefore, doesn't get the benefit of the breeze. As anyone having been in the Keys knows the mosquitos there can be about as large and vicious as they are anywhere in the world. At about one in the morning, Joe Bauer, after constantly slapping, hiding under the sheet, and going through every other maneuver known to fishermen, finally decided to get up and take matters into his own hands. Not wanting to wake our roommates, he fumbled around in the dark until he found a pressurized can of insect repellent. If I remember correctly, his exact words were, "Don't worry, Dick, I'll kill these little — ." and immediately started to spray the entire room. At the time, I simply buried my head under the sheet and decided that I would spend the next five hours dreaming of catching that big bonefish or tarpon on a fly the next day.

Can you imagine our great surprise in the morning when we awoke to the most beautifully newly decorated lampshades, walls, pictures, and what have you, for it was not insect repellent that Bauer had employed so generously, no indeedy, but a can of silver spray paint that was being used for maintenance purposes on the houseboat.

A fascinating exhibition of athletic prowess also took place on that trip while we were fly fishing for bonefish. One of the easiest ways to move the camera boat behind the poling boat is to have a nice, strong young man (in this case Peter Maslowski, Karl's son) pole the boat and, while waiting, to keep it steady and in the exact position the photographer wants it. At that time, Pete's experience had been primarily in fresh water. He was a student in college and, as I said, his dad was one of the outstanding outdoor photographers in America. Pete was doing an absolutely tremendous job of wading in anywhere from knee to chest-high water and keeping the boat exactly where his dad wanted it in relationship to the sun and anglers. For any of us who have fished the Keys, it is a fascinating water wonderland where, in fact, you are "hunting" for fish while at the some time watching constantly for rays, turtles, sharks, and what have you. As we crossed a particular bar and picked up a nice bonefish, we noticed a five-foot nurse shark cruising our flat. Having had the opportunity to coach youngsters for many years in both high school and college, I know the physical effort and skill it takes to high jump five feet from a standing position. And I've never seen anyone standing in waist-deep water vault himself into a boat that was approximately chest high so magnificently. Obviously, a nurse shark was as frightening to Pete as it was to me when wading the flats. How appropriate it would have been had the camera been on the crew rather than the angler.

There is nothing, of course, like being at the right place at the right time. A number of years ago, I took a trip to Great Bear Lake and a side trip to the Tree River. As you may know, the Tree is well-known for its world record Arctic char. There isn't any river in the world, in my estimation, where there are more big Arctic char than there are in the Tree River, and, if you are there at the right time during their spawning run, which usually occurs in late July or August depending upon weather conditions, the chances of your catching a big char are very good.

Normal procedure in fishing the Tree is to fly in late afternoon (there are 24 hours of daylight), fish late into the evening and the next day until the next group comes in to fish the river in the late afternoon. Bill Murphy was our guide and took some of us by boat to some small islands located in the river and others across the river to the far shoreline. The small island I was on, for some reason or another, was extremely productive. My fishing buddies could not reach it by casting and I was having an absolute ball catching these huge Arctic char. Each time I would hook one I would have to go as far down the island as I possibly could and, hopefully, have enough backing to keep the fish on after it ran down through the rapids. After losing many because of their size and/or the water, I finally hooked into a magnificent fish that I knew I wanted desperately. He ran through the first set of rapids downstream to a pool and I thought I had it made. At the second set of rapids I was down to the position on the reel where I could see the arbor. Fortunately, Bill Murphy who was returning from dropping off one of my fishing companions, picked me up and we drifted down through two more major sets of rapids gaining line all the time. My char then decided to stay in a large, calm pool area and we eventually got downstream from him simply by drifting through and keeping tension on the line. We landed that char because we were downstream of him and so he was fighting the water and the fisherman, and it is presently one of my most treasured trophies.

John D. Wheeler

A practicing attorney and trouter, he recently took up Atlantic salmon fishing—a sport from which he may never recover. Hunting Valley, Ohio.

Ernie's "Wong"

This story requires a little background. Several years ago, while fishing with some children at a pay trout pond, I observed that the only other party fishing was a Chinese family with five children. My kids managed to tie into a couple of trout—soon after which the fishless Chinese family started closing in on our territory and ended up in our back pockets. It turned out to be a lot of fun as we all had a good time; but meantime, I coined the phrase that we had been "wonged." Since that day, if I intended to join my fishing partner and fish at close proximity or vice-versa, I announce I am "wonging" him or I am being "wonged."

I was on the last leg of a three-week fishing extravaganza back in 1981. After eight days of trout fishing in Montana, I had continued west to Seattle where I hooked up with Ernie Schweibert's Alaska party. That year, Ernie had decided to spend two weeks in Alaska during prime time for large rainbows which is the last week of September and the first week of October.

The first week was spent at Kulik Lodge where each day we were able to fly out to fabulous fishing and big bears. You've all read about this fishing so I won't bore you with it here. Suffice it to say that: first, it was every bit as good as the best you've read; second, it was damn cold—with snow and high winds; and third, Ernie caught the largest rainbow and otherwise displayed his mastery of the art of angling with the same degree of precision and detail expressed in his books and sketches. He truly is an expert of the highest order. But even the experts have their days.

The second week, four of us (out of an original party of 10) accompanied Ernie to a lodge owned by Cliff Pulis located on Slop Bucket Lake in Illiamna, which is located at the northeast corner of Lake Illiamna. Cliff and his girl, Sue, were marvelous hosts. Ernie had been invited there to come and join Andy Puyans who spent a great deal of time fishing with Cliff. Andy is also nationally known for his fly tying and fishing expertise. The moment I saw him in the stream, I knew I was with a true predator. I had seldom seen such intensity and he does catch fish!

One day near the end of the week we flew to the Upper Tularik River. It was a frightfully cold and windy day with the wind-chill factor somewhere in the neighborhood of 0°. That's cold for most any purpose but especially fishing! On the way to the river, we passed over several smaller lakes that had completely frozen over due to the bitter cold. One of our party asked the pilot if he could land our plane on those frozen lakes—to which question the pilot promptly responded, "Yep, . . . once!" The Upper Tularik flows into Lake Illiamna like its sister river, the Lower Tularik. It is not as well known or as heavily fished but it also holds large rainbows.

There were six fishermen and as we first hit the ice cold water near the mouth, Ernie announced with his usual degree of authority that we should all spread out so as not to interfere with each other's fishing as "there is plenty of water in the stream." Obligingly, I moved upstream.

Two or more hours later, all I had to my credit were a few grayling and a couple of two-pound rainbows (small by Alaskan standards). I was so cold that my entire body hurt and it was impossible for me to remain in the cold water any longer. I worked my way back downstream toward the mouth. As I approached, there wading up to his waist was Andy Puyans with about a 10-pound rainbow leaping in the air on the end of his line! The others were standing on the bank near a fire prepared by the guide. As I approached, they advised me that this was about the sixth fish of this size hooked and landed by Andy—while the rest, including Ernie, had yet to hook collectively one large fish!

Most of us had been fishing an imitation salmon egg. Unbeknownst to me, Andy had been using a strike indicator! This is a small, hand-tied, fluorescent, red-dyed hair "float" attached to the leader about 10 feet above the fly. I assumed Ernie, as a purist, had refused to resort to such tactics. But, now that it was late in the day, the facts finally sank home. These huge fish were simply mouthing the imitation egg and then spitting it out. The effect on the line was imperceptible. We all probably had hits that day, but without the indicator it was absolutely impossible to detect.

Ernie was cold but not as cold as he was determined to protect his reputation. Such resolve is indeed admirable. He forced himself back into that cold stream up to his waist. He started downstream from Andy but cautiously worked his way up against the current. Suddenly, it dawned on me—Andy was being wonged by Ernie. He ended up right at his shoulder and the two discussed technique as only experts can do (if you know what I mean).

Andy finally came ashore to warm up by the fire before the flight back to camp. Ernie hung in there and then came the moment of redemption as he tied into a whopper and in the purest form—without the "bobber." Ten minutes later we saw Ernie gently remove the hook from the mouth of a beautiful rainbow, which weighed about 12 pounds, and then released it back into the stream. It was a gorgeous fish and the biggest I had seen during the entire trip.

Ernie had finally redeemed himself but by this time it was too cold and too late for the rest of us. We headed home, having learned a hard lesson from an expert: When the fishing gets tough and you won't use a "bobber," try a "wong."

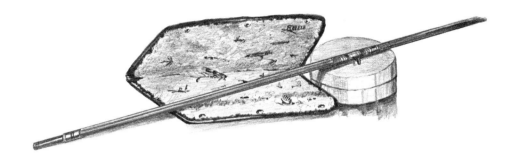

Howard Steere

Head man in charge of, and responsible for, the design and manufacture of all Orvis fly rods. Howard does a super job at it, too. Manchester, Vermont.

Doubtless

It was in a small town in Maine during an earlier time when bamboo fishing rods were in their heyday, fiberglass was just coming on the market, and any fisherman worth this salt would not be without a few Parmachene Belles or Professors in his vest. Nobody had heard of emergers or thorax patterns.

Sonny, a boy who had another year and a half to go before he would reach the magic of being a teenager, waited his turn in the old one-chair barber shop. This Saturday morning in mid-May was no different from any other as the shop was always busy on Saturdays.

Bill, a man in his early thirties, sat in the corner reading a week-old issue of *Life* when Francis came in saying his "Hi's" as a few of us moved down so he could sit next to Bill. "We going out this afternoon?" inquired Francis.

"Ya, pick you up about 2?"

"OK, pumping station, though. I tied up a bunch of Leadwings Thursday night."

"Sounds good, but we've got to get back to that fast section below Alfred

Morrow's with streamers before the water gets low. Frannie, did you see the big brown Sonny caught a couple weeks ago?"

"Guess I was the only one who didn't see it. He must have carted that fish all over town showing it off."

"What did you catch him on, Sonny, a night crawler?"

"No, worms."

"Down to the river?"

"Yes, the sluice pool right at the mill."

As Sonny climbed into the waiting chair, he caught a glimpse of the funny look Francis gave Bill and wondered what they might be thinking of him killing a 24-inch fish caught on worms. Just the other day, the mechanic at Bracy's Garage had told him these two always use just flies and always let the fish go. A half-hour later found him in the fishing section of his uncle's hardware store smelling of witch hazel and looking for some leadwings.

"Need some more hooks?" Uncle asked as he came over.

"No, sir, not this time, I want to learn to fly fish and I need some leadwings."

"What size would you like?"

"I really don't know what they are."

"Well, the wet version is a type fished under water and works real well in most places around here during this part of the year. This is a Leadwing Coachman," he said as he picked a small fuzzy-bodied fly out of what must have been hundreds in little boxes on the shelves.

"You should have two #10's and two #12's anyway, and I'm going to give you a couple of these Hare's Ears. You've got to fish these pretty much the same as you do a worm. Going up to Perkin's Brook?"

"I was going to, but I overheard two other fellers talking about going."

"Probably Francis and Bill. If it is, you should get there early and watch them, you can learn a lot from those two. What other rods to you have besides your Father's baitcasting rod?"

"Just that telescoping Bristol I got for Christmas."

"You leave both at home and go down and tell your Aunt to let you take the three-piece South Bend that's strung up on the porch."

"That's a bamboo rod isn't it?"

"Yes, but you'll be all right if you feel the rod, and don't worry about it."

"How much do I owe you for the flies?"

"Have you got 50¢?"

"Yap, they cost more though, don't they?"

"No, just 50¢.

"I'll be up to fill the standpipe around five tonight."

"If you want, we could do some dry-fly fishing."

"I'll see if I can stay through supper, maybe you could give me some pointers on casting. I hear it's real tough."

Thanking his Uncle for the help, Sonny headed home as fast as he could make the old bicycle go. With permission from his mother and a supper she put up for the two of them, he was off to get the rod.

Waiting on the bank in back of the pumping station up from the brook,

Sonny watched as the new '47 Chevy pulled in. A thin layer of dust from the two-mile ride in from the main road already covered the shiny black finish of the car as Bill and Francis hurriedly put on vests and assembled their rods.

Bill, noticing Sonny, asked in a disappointed manner, "You been through?"

"No, I'll wait until you two get well along."

"You've fished here before, haven't you?"

"Yes, on and off last summer."

"Well, we're going to start at the Dam Pool and fish upstream and it wouldn't bother us if you fished downstream below the dam while you were waiting."

"I'd like to watch you for awhile if you don't mind."

"Fine, you fly fishing?" Francis asked, walking over.

"I'm going to try."

"Good for you!"

They watched as Bill crouched down and sneaked closer to the faster water coming in at the head of the pool. Casting a few times, he put the fly in upstream from him, following it along with the tip of the rod while taking in slack. Another cast, this time out a little farther.

"I've got one."

The line ran first across the pool, then down toward the dam, and now slowly back toward Bill. He reached into the water with a twitch of the wrist, and the fish was gone. Francis allowed it was a fair trout, and that he would have taken him on the first cast if Bill hadn't rushed up to be there first.

Sonny could wait no longer as it seemed like hours, surely a half-hour had past. But he could still hear the teasing between Francis and Bill upstream. Putting the rod together, he noticed the fly on the gut. Very much like the Hare's Ears but with real stubby wings. *If this is good enough for Uncle Buster, it's good enough for me to try. I wish I could have asked Bill what he was using. At least I can try casting in the big pool, Bill made it look easy.*

All attempts were hang-ups; in the grass, either on the bank or behind him. After taking the knots out of the gut, he tried working the line out and swinging the fly. Letting it sink a little and working out more line as the small amount of current pulled the fly down and away, Sonny found he could at least get it out to where a fish might be.

He worked his way around to fish the small pool below the dam where he would not be seen. Having fished this pool a few times before, he knew where the fish would be if the heavy spring run-off hadn't changed the pool much. It hadn't, the deep run was along the whole back side, mostly shaded by the half-grown leaves from the low overhanging alders, inches from the surface. The old sunken tree was still there.

Flopping the fly up into the faster white water and following the line with the rod tip, he could just see the gray of the fly against the partly sunlit bottom as it was being carried along by the current, past the large rocks on to the undercut beneath the sunken tree. An instant flash and tightening of the line against the reel made it buzz as a little more of the line was being pulled off. The fish ran up and across the pool, now back to try to get under the sunken tree. It seemed quite large as the rod trembled in his hand, a feeling he never had with the steel bait casting rod.

With a little more pressure, he brought the tiring brookie within reach and knelt to release him, pausing a few seconds to admire him before doing so.

As he sat on the edge by the dam thinking of the brook trout he had just let go, and how much he had enjoyed doing so and, in fact, enjoyed the whole afternoon, he was certain that no matter what it took, he would learn to be a fly fisherman that summer, maybe even a good one. That 11-inch brook trout was his very first on a fly—doubtless it would not be his last.

Linda Morgens

Linda is perhaps best known for her creative development of the "pounce" method of reducing Atlantic salmon to hand. She is a former director of the American League of Anglers and is currently a National Director of Trout Unlimited. South Norwalk, Connecticut.

"Lefty"

Once I won an all-expense-paid, absolutely free, Atlantic salmon fishing trip to Iceland because I sent $10 to a club "for the conservation of trout." Conserving trout sounded like a good idea even though I never expected to win anything. As a matter of fact, winning was so unexpected that I never bothered to tell my husband Ned about the $10 raffle ticket, or the trout, or anything. I just forgot about it.

After a confused Ned received the congratulatory call and I explained things, we began preparing for our "free" trip. Since both of us wanted to go, we purchased all the necessary extras for a second person, as well as the proper equipment for our new quarry. Upon arrival in camp, as we struggled with donning our gear in the minute bedroom, I heard a mumble, then a low groan, and then some very colorful language coming from Ned's edge of the room. It seemed as though our faithful purveyor of fishing goods had sent him two left wading shoes for his stocking-foot waders and, being neophytes, we did not check our gear before leaving. The real problem was that Ned's foot is a size 13 and in a country of only two hundred-and-some-thousand folks, the chances of borrowing someone's wading shoes in a size 13 are slim or none. None reigned.

Sworn to secrecy, I followed Ned to the river, which was accessed by various steep-sided paths, very fitting for mountain goats. All week Ned struggled in his ill-fitting shoes under the watchful eye of our guide, Jonas. This was OK until one day during a slow session, Jonas began to tell me some funny stories about his past clients. "Well," I said, "if you promise not to tell, I can tell you a funny story that is happening right now." After I related Ned's troubles, Jonas started to laugh. However, he couldn't stop laughing and he continued until tears were in his eyes. I felt uncomfortable at this exaggerated display so I said "I know it's funny, but it really isn't *that* funny, is it?"

"Oh, yes it is, Mam," he replied, "because all this time, this entire week, I thought your husband was a cripple!"

Thomas R. Pero

Long ago and far away, Tommy Pero was castigated by his father for not sitting still on the designated tree stump, waiting for a mud-loving brown bullhead, known locally as "hornpout," to chomp on the worm-baited hook. "That kid is no damn good," his father said with disgust to Tommy's mother, who was seated on her lawn chair and generously sharing her paperback with the mosquitoes. "He'll never be a fisherman." Pero has now somehow made it to age 32 and, in the intervening years, has chased spotted fins from Scotland to Tasmania. He has even become editor of Trout *Magazine. All this has disproved his dear departed father's prediction about his lack of enthusiasm for angling. Bend, Oregon.*

A Roll of the Dice

It was the last week of August, the final week of fishing, at the close of the most depressing season on record for many Atlantic salmon streams in Canada. My wife, Debra, and I had secured permits the previous January to fish the St. Jean river in Quebec, a salmon fishing roll of the dice. Arriving in the village of Gaspé, after a 20-hour drive, it did not look like a lucky roll.

"I'm afraid you're a month too late," the pretty, dark-haired young woman at the office of the *Ministere du Loisir de la Chasse et de la Peche* said and frowned. "The river's very low and the last salmon was registered in July."

But late summer is a pleasant time to be on the Gaspé Peninsula. The green foliage has reached maturity, here and there stands of poplars are beginning to show touches of yellow; immense flocks of gannets are still gathered on the cliffs of Bonaventure Island; the nights are cool, the mornings crisp and clear; and we decided to stay.

An evening thunderstorm rose the river several inches before our fishing was to begin. Rain can be a godsend on a salmon river that's low. Even so, prospects didn't improve measurably. A mid-day walk from pool to pool, all clearly marked with signs, turned up no one fishing. A pair of dark, stale fish was spotted off a high bank in a still, clear pool.

The next morning I set out down the path, through the ferns in the early light. I was enjoying casting, feeling the smooth rhythm of the thick line in the air, the warmth of the sun on my face, watching the little black-hooked, upturned-eye fly swimming through the crystal water. I spent all morning fishing one pool after the next, as much exploring as seriously hoping for a salmon to grab my fly. The river seemed empty. Only in one pool, at its head where the water gathered speed and was constricted through a deeper slot, did I detect even the slightest response: tiny taps on my slimly dressed Silver Rat.

"Parr," I thought to myself. "Maybe sea trout."

The next morning we spent some time photographing the river.

"I think we should go over to the Matane," I said to Deb. "Just forfeit our permits. There's nothing here."

"Where did you get those taps yesterday?" she inquired. "I'd like to take a few casts there before we leave."

We wandered downstream and she worked methodically through the pool several times, changing from a wet to a dry then back to a wet.

"I'm getting taps, too, but they're real light."

"Sea trout. Let's go," I prodded, sitting on the rocky bank, twirling the handle on my reel. "Let's go have a look at the Matane."

"Try your Bomber," she suggested. "Throw it up into the fast water. I had some taps there."

I tied on the big, bushy fly for a couple of perfunctory casts. The heavy run was only a rod length or two out from the bank; I was virtually dapping. On the third or fourth float through the little waves my fly disappeared. I struck hard and felt something solid.

"Sea trout," I announced over my shoulder.

Just then seven pounds of salmon catapulted into the air, my Brown Bomber firmly imbedded in its jaw.

"Some sea trout!" Deb yelled.

For the remainder of the week we had the run to ourselves. It was full of fish. We landed six, hooking twice as many, and prompting many other short takes, heart-stopping swirls, and looks at the fly. We took our time, resting the water frequently, watching for patterns. Typically, a pass through first thing in the morning with a sparse wet fly or small nymph would produce movement. The water temperature was about 55° as we began fishing. It started rising as the sun grew stronger. By late morning, as my stream thermometer passed the 60° mark, another flurry of activity would ensue—this time on the surface. At this time of day, the salmon seemed most interested in floating flies. The afternoon was a lull. Things would pick up again toward evening, the last hour of light being most worthwhile. All the time our only company was the distant buzzing of a chain saw cutting winter firewood.

Our largest salmon came on the final day of our trip.

We had brought our dinner down to the river and started a fire. After we ate I waded across the river and began casting a White Wulff at the head of the run, floating it over and over the little patch of slick water where a good number of fish had shown themselves. Meanwhile, Deb was working the tail of the pool, where the day before I had found a pair of fresh grilse. While working over a fish (which I eventually took) I had spied another darker fish in relatively shallow water across the current. It looked like a small salmon, maybe seven or eight pounds. I floated a Royal Wulff, then a Bomber, then a MacIntosh over its nose with no apparent reaction. Deb tried with identical results. She was now back there, I guessed, giving it one more try.

The sky crackled upriver and it began to rain. For 10 minutes the rain poured down, beads of water forming around my nearly sunk dry fly. Suddenly I heard a great splash, looked up to see Deb's rod arching, heard her reel whine. She had hooked the fish! I danced across the riffle and ran down the bank. For the past few nights, as darkness gathered, we had heard something splash loudly at the tail of the pool. It sounded like a boulder being thrown in. I wondered if it was the fish as I waded into the shallows to tail my wife's salmon.

"Don't you dare lose it!" she commanded shrilly. "It's a big one!"

"'Is it the same fish we worked on yesterday, the one that was holding right out here next to the rock?"

"Yes, but he's a lot bigger than we thought."

"What did he take?"

"Butterfly. Right in the middle of the rain. He just slammed it."

Deb worked the big salmon into the shallows. It still had life in it as I attempted to wrap my hands around its body in front of the tail. The fish raced away, reel protesting. Again its impressive length was finning weakly in the shallows, leader drawn taut, rod bowed. I grabbed and held on for dear life. In one sweeping motion of water and fish the 14-pound prize was on the bank.

It was dark and the rain had stopped as we started home. Everything was wet. Spruce needles stuck to the silver sides of a heavy, happy burden swinging on the path in front of me. I looked back and saw the faint embers of our fire. I listened to the rapids and filled my nostrils with the deep, sweet night air.

Frank R. Richardson

*A high-ranking U. S. Fish and Wildlife Serv-
ice man, his career assignments have placed
him in many great places to fish. Six years in
the Smokies found him in the center of the
best wild trout fishing in the East. He didn't
waste the opportunity. He has had similar
good fortune in the Great Lakes, Alaska,
Colorado, Florida, Wyoming, Idaho, Washington, and Yellowstone country. Atlanta,
Georgia.*

Ah, The Art of Fly Fishing

The act of fly fishing has little to do with science. Actually, anyone can
become a fly fisher, at least within one's own personal definition, as the
result of circumstance or the expenditure of a few sheckles at your friendly
neighborhood tackle shop or through a mail-order catalog. However, to be
recognized by the loosely knit brotherhood of fly anglers as an art form, it
takes considerably more . . . like membership in the Fly Fishing Federation
and Trout Unlimited and the ownership of enough rods, reels, lines, flies,
boots, nets, and other assorted paraphernalia to start your own fly shop, plus
a library of unread books on fishing and an accumulation of fishing cronies
who will desert their spouses for various periods of time using rationales
that only the tooth fairy would believe. I admit to membership in this group.
However, my prose for this tome will not be of great fish but of two memorable incidents which took place years ago as I learned and polished the art of
fly fishing. A crony from North Carolina, a giant in this piscatorial craft, my

close friend and angling confidante of three decades, shared these episodes that I am about to relate.

It was back in the late '50s, a time when felt wading shoes and Polaroids first began to appear as a necessity to the fly angler. Come with me now to the Cane River Valley on the north slope of Mt. Mitchell, which has the highest elevation in the East. North Carolinians who seek trout know well the Cane's reputation as a magnificent trout river resource. In this valley, at the end of a dead-end road (a piece of real estate that only an angler could or would call a road), just above the juncture of the Sugar Fork with the Cane, sets one of the architectural wonders of western North Carolina. Creatively called the Cane River Camp, this is a frequent address for some fishing and hunting folk who refer to themselves as the Cane River Club. This tabernacle for trouters, constructed sometime during the first 20 years of this century, rises three stories in height, has walls of 40-inch diameter logs of hemlock and poplar, which are clerestoried at the roof, and two mammoth fireplaces, one at each end of the structure, made of large river rocks. The centerpiece of this edifice is the large living, dining and fly-tying area. Rooms for sleeping are kept to a minimum.

Please have patience because there is more. It is possible to sit in the great room and see the moon and stars. On one occasion I witnessed the entire constellation of Orion the Hunter from a strategic spot near one of the fireplaces. The two fireplaces do a great job burning wood, but do little as heating units while the air conditioning system has always worked and is especially efficient in winter and on the opening of trout season, always a cold day in April.

The constant challenge always was staying warm. Each opening day saw new theories tested. Enter then a new thermal pajama and the first electric blanket for the Cane River Club. My double buddy from North Carolina, Hugh C. Chatham, III, lint peddler for Chatham Blankets of America, had secured electric blankets for each of the dozen beds. At dinner that evening, which always took place some two to four hours later than the civilized are used to, and following much elbow bending, a lively debate ensued between Hugh and J. Fuller Brown, a Virginian who was addicted to the exclusive use of the Hare's Ear fly. Our Virginian was an advocate of his new thermal pajamas, while Hugh championed the electric blanket. The two continued to argue the issue all evening and finally left together for a bedroom which they shared. Ever the good samaritan, Hugh had gone to each room, turned on each electric blanket, and set the temperature dial at the mid level. It was a time for chicanery. Enter Hugh's brother, Dick, who stealthily switched the control dials on the small bedside table between Hugh's and Fuller's beds. He then set the dial that controlled Hugh's blanket to low and Fuller's to high. As they settled in bed, the "discussion" went on unabated. This devious switch had an obvious conclusion. Hugh slept cold. Fuller slept extremely warm. At breakfast one of Hugh's first comments was, "Fuller, where did you get those thermal pajamas? You had that electric blanket on low all night and sleep like a baby and I nearly froze with mine on high." I can report that in the end, Chatham's electric blankets ruled the day, er, night.

Another of the many pleasurable and pleasant memories of Cane River was the day Hugh and I decided to fish some of the headwater brook-trout streams. These streams are characterized by king-size boulders (many the size of a small house), deep quiet pools, waterfalls, cascades, impenetrable laurel and rhododendron thickets, timber rattlers, no trails, and a super abundance of brilliantly colored brook trout. Fishing these waters is a worthy challenge for a young man and idiotic for one of my present years. On this day, Hugh and I and our mountaineer guide were somewhere between that time frame. The day was clear and warm, the fish were active and cooperative, and our mountaineer guide filled us with the delight of what great pools lay ahead. As the terrain increased its resistance to our entry, we were reduced to breaking down our rods and crawling on hands and knees through the thicket to reach the next pool. As we rested, Hugh rhetorically asked, "Have you ever seen a rougher place to fish?" Our guide, in typical mountaineer fashion replied, "Yep—right up ahead." Ah, the art of flyfishing!

The Cane has produced other memories: a magnificently mantled male brown in September; the mid-summer removal of a cannibal brown who would allow no other trout in his pool; a startling eyeball-to-eyeball encounter with a rattler; and always that wonderful telling and retelling of the day's catch, the best flies, the gentle gig of your cronies, faux pas, and more. Ah, the art of fly fishing!

Ferdinand J. Hruby, M.D.

A classic inveterate sportsman. Chagrin Falls, Ohio.

The "Granny" and the Salmon

Back in the days when catching an Atlantic salmon to a Middle Westerner was the equivalent of shooting an elephant to an Eskimo, the big fishing and hunting magazines would occasionally publish the exploits of salmon anglers on far northern ocean-run rivers. These stories often appeared in spring issues of the magazines and, after the inactivity of winter, were read with avidity and considerable awe. As a young boy I yearned for similar experiences and confess that the desire to engage in these pursuits proved a very strong motivation in my young life. In the great depression, pilgrimages to Norway, Iceland, and Scotland had not as yet come into vogue, and a trip to Nipissing or Temagami was the thrill of a lifetime.

At any rate, with the passage of time and after a few years of active medical practice, I found myself packing my old Ford station wagon and heading east for a crack at an "honest to God" sea-run salmon. Although a dedicated angler, my experience with a fly rod was almost totally confined to bluegill fishing in lakes and ponds around my home in Chagrin Falls, Ohio.

On rare occasions I would have the opportunity to fish at Castalia, Ohio at one of the private trout clubs. My status as a fly fisherman was reflected by my equipment which consisted of a L. L. Bean "all purpose" fly-rod outfit purchased with funds earned one summer picking apples. Though inexpensive, this outfit was far from shabby—after all, the rod was made of genuine bamboo! Glass rods had not as yet made their appearance and no one dreamed of graphite. To the best of my recollection I believe I spent less than 25 dollars for the whole outfit—rod, reel, and line. Of course, there was no minimum wage in those days either and gasoline was 22¢ a gallon.

The drive from Chagrin Falls to Fredericton, New Brunswick was magnificent what with crystal clear days and nights, the foliage of early September, and the pastoral landscape. Naturally on the way up I paused in Freeport, Maine to pay homage to Mr. Bean and his store—the premier haberdasher of my youth and the purveyors of traps, hunting knives, boots, and all the other items so essential to young sportsmen of that era. As I arrived I noticed a pay phone under a tree in front of the store and decided to check in with my Cleveland office one last time before crossing the Canadian border. This was a mistake because if I had considered the news from home an omen I would have turned around and headed straight back. To my consternation I learned that our dear friend, Eunice, long-time desk clerk of the famous Island House Hotel, Port Clinton, Ohio, in the Sandusky Bay duck country, had passed away in her sleep. This was devastating news and I immediately placed a call to her husband who for years had been my walleye fishing buddy and with whom I had shared many memorable experiences around the islands of the western Lake Erie basin. A neighbor answered the phone and told me that, "Jim was at the funeral home." When I asked for the mortuary number so that I could talk to him there, a long silence ensued. Finally, in strangled tones, the neighbor informed me that Jim had dropped dead as he left the house to make funeral arrangements for Eunice! Learning of these occurrences was a truly inauspicious start of a salmon trip for which I had no reservations, knew nothing of the territory, had scanty equipment, and little real knowledge of what I was about.

Hours later my spirits had risen only slightly as I approached the beautiful Miramachi Valley and stopped for gas and information. The proprietor of the gas pump directed me to see "Mr. Doak of Doaktown" who ran "Doak's Tackle Shoppe" and who knew "all there was to know" about salmon fishing. On arriving at his shop I saw it was devoted exclusively to fly fishing and a sign admonished all who entered to refrain from profanity on threat of immediate expulsion. A few religious admonitions were also tacked up on the walls between the gear. Automatically I took off my hat.

Meeting the straight-laced Mr. Doak was an experience in itself, but I soon discovered that his reputation as the guru of salmon fishing was well deserved. He promptly advised appropriate flies and leaders and spoke with reverence of this pool and that pool quoting sizes, weights, and catches with abandon. Nothing happened on the Miramachi that Mr. Doak did not know about. As sales progressed he was gracious with his advice. The camaraderie vanished, however, and he gaped at me in amazement when I informed him I had no place to fish, much less to stay. He was truly incredulous! Such ignorance was never seen on the sophisticated banks of the renowned Miramachi where plans were laid and reservations made years in advance!

Finally his disdain yielded to pity, probably partly because of the posters on his wall, and a charitable impulse took over. He allowed as how he would make a call in my behalf. We both thanked God that his effort was successful and I was instructed to hurry since his friend "Mr. Bamford" was anxious to "get in the water." Arriving at the camp an hour later I immediately jumped into my hip boots and, with Mr. Bamford, rushed to the river.

When Bamford saw me assembling my old outfit and looked at my untapered Ohio-style, fly line, he shook his head but refrained from any comment. He did take the liberty of personally selecting one of Mr. Doak's guaranteed flies and quickly attached it to the hairlike end of one of Mr. Doak's guaranteed, ultra-tapered leaders. With a prayer I walked into the hallowed waters.

As I fanned that heavy fly it looked as big as a sparrow to me compared to my black gnats and bluegill spiders. About 20 feet from shore I whipped out a trial cast. The line rolled on the water and the fly finally hit the surface with a *plop*. I didn't have a chance to be embarrassed because there was a splash, the rod jerked and all hell broke loose. I was terrified! I did the only thing I could do; I ran through the water and hung on for dear life. According to the profanity interspersing the instructions from shore, I apparently was doing everything wrong. Thank God, Mr. Doak wasn't around because he would have been scandalized by his old friend and his new-found disciple and customer. I was soaking wet but at last I was able to horse that fish into the shallows closer to shore. Now the profanity and cursing quadrupled in volume; I couldn't bring my leader through the tip guide for I had tied the only knot I knew, the old standard "granny." The leader was as taut as piano wire and a mighty fish thrashed wildly at the end of it! With a mighty oath Bamford jumped in the water and somehow we managed to unceremoniously pull, shove and lift that fish to the shore. The salmon weighed 14 pounds! I was jubilant! "Man," I thought, "this salmon fishing is the greatest. Now for a few more!" In my naiveté I did not realize how fortunate I was, and as it turned out Mr. Doak later informed me that it was the largest fish caught on the river that week! It was delicious and we devoured it with gusto!

Mr. Bamford would now have nothing further to do with me if I didn't go back to Mr. Doak's store and get a decent reel and a proper weight, tapered fly line to match my old bamboo rod. Naturally I bought this equipment and thereafter I fished for three straight days from day break until dusk and caught the sum total of three grilse. So goes salmon fishing.

Of course, I hung on to my old fly line because what good is a heavy, tapered line if you're fishing for bluegills? Come to think of it this equipment must still be in the basement. After all bamboo does not rust and it's a Bean outfit! It sure would be good to eat a baloney sandwich, drink a beer and catch a mess of bluegills after all these years! I don't think that those pretty girls on water skis at Sea World have scared the bluegill population at Geauga Lake too badly. It's spring now and those little buggers should start rising. "Hey, Honey—where did you say you think that old Bean rod is?" Maybe there is a reward for writing this story for my old duck hunting buddy, Keith Russell, after all!

Robert L. Herbst

The Executive Director of Trout Unlimited; and formerly the Assistant Secretary of the Interior for Fish and Wildlife and Parks, the Commissioner of the Minnesota Department of Natural Resources, and the Executive Director of the Isaak Walton League. He is the best thing that has ever happened to T.U. Annandale, Virginia.

If They Should Never Swim Again

If they should never swim again,
against current, through pool, or watery chain,
Those wary trout that roam
the vast, aquatic, uncharted, unknown,
If in the spring's awakening,
the surge of life should fail to bring
The missing fish to the surface
in the quiet of our fishing place,
If from the depths of placid pools,
the waters were not so cool,
And catches only a memory,
how dull and drear the spring would be.
If I should lift my eyes on high,
and see not a hatch of green drake mayfly;
If midway resting on a riverside trail

held only vision of a lifeless stream so pale,
If in the sunset afterglow,
there were no streams to bubble and flow,
If that domain through which they swim
were lost through ruthless plundering
Then truly, they would cease to be,
and my life poorer and less free.

Joseph Gladysz

A beggar for a local philanthropic institution, he is a fine fly fisherman and fly-tier who also services local "greats" for Atlantic salmon fishing in addition to his own requirements. Brecksville, Ohio.

The Cure

I almost missed my first chance to go steelhead fishing because of a case of viral pneumonia contracted shortly before the trip, and I was most apprehensive while waiting for the doctor's decision about being able to go. Luckily, I had a doctor who believed in fresh air, cold water, and fly fishing as a cure for all my ills.

Plans were begun some months before when John Wheeler and I had been invited by John Shields to fish his club water on the Pere Marquette in the northwest corner of Michigan's lower peninsula. We spent the time in avid preparation reading about steelhead fishing and tying steelhead patterns. Finally, we met on a Tuesday evening after work to make the seven-hour drive from Cleveland to Baldwin, Michigan. The trip flew by as we traded fishing stories.

Wednesday morning dawn found us in the river. The Pere Marquette is a beautiful stream. Its banks are covered with sweepers and log jams and it has a crystal-clear, heavy flow of water covering the gravel bottom. John S. put John W. and me on an undercut bank that was known as a good holding spot for steelhead. We began casting our heavily weighted flies along the cut. Shields told us to try and feel the split shot, tick-tick-ticking, along the bottom.

Wheeler connected first. The big male came out of the water and tried to tail walk across the stream. The fish was as thick as a football and could only get half of his 30-inch-long body out of the water. After a few more runs, I helped John net his fish and then set off upstream still looking for my first fish. On a high bank overlooking a log-infested pool, I saw a dark shape on the bottom. I moved into position across from the fish and made my first cast 10 feet above it. The fly never reached bottom. I lengthened the cast and tried again. My fly line was floating toward me when it stopped and, reaching back, I was into my first steelhead! By applying heavy pressure I was able to keep the fish out of the log jam and it finally ended up below me. I reached for the reel to try to pump the tiring fish upstream and realized the spool wouldn't turn! It had somehow become discombobulated by the heavy pressure and line could not be retrieved or let out. I stood there frozen like the reel. If I moved toward the fish or applied more pressure, it might try to make another run and I'd lose my first steelhead for sure. Wheeler had happened by during the fight and saw the predicament I was in. He ran to get a net, but before John could reach the fish the hook pulled out. As I looked around for a 10-pound rock to "adjust" my reel with, Wheeler continued to pursue the tired fish in shallows and managed to put it in the net.

This, of course, is the absolute worst thing that could have happened. Wheeler insisted that any subsequent telling of this story should begin with a disclaimer giving him complete credit for the fish.

The second day was better than the first. Fish continued to pour into the stream and there were new redds everywhere. The fish were eager and seemed to take any pattern: Spring's nymphs, big black stones, strip nymphs and even a damsel-fly nymph imitation—all were in demand!

Toward the end of the day we all were fishing the same riffle near the club house. John Shields was hooking a fish on what seemed like every cast. Unfortunately, each fish would run downstream and break off in the heavy current or along the brush-infested banks. Shields was determined. His next fish ran through a log jam downstream, then held in a deep pool. John could not free his fly line so he cut it in half, untangled it, and tied the two ends back together. No luck. The fish got off but Shields still wouldn't quit. On his next cast, another fish grabbed his fly. Instead of running for the heavy downstream current, this fish bolted upstream. Shields braced himself in the current and pressed his nine-foot rod into a semicircle. The fight was headed John's way when his rod tip shot straight up into the air. The knot on his spliced fly line had come loose. John stood there dumbfounded as 30 feet of his fly line, attached to a big steelhead, headed upstream to some unknown destination.

This was our signal to stop fishing. As we packed up the van to go home,

Wheeler commented that our total of over 50 fish, between eight and 12 pounds, was as good a two days' fishing as he had ever seen, and that included Alaska.

Now I'm not recommending steelhead fishing as a cure for pneumonia, but in my case, it sure worked. It's one cure I'll take every time.

Salvatore Palatucci

A school teacher who became a professional conservationist. Sal was hired by Trout Unlimited to develop a national Special Project fund-raising program which has succeeded admirably. Vienna, Virginia.

A Little Knowledge Can Be Dangerous

Have you ever added a little too much garlic to a sauce that only needed a tad more? Or thought that the bicycle you were going to throw together for your kid would only take 15 minutes with the instructions they sent you? Well a similar thing happened to me when I got started in fly fishing. Having learned to hunt for trout with the venerable worm, once I decided to try what looked like a fascinating art form—fly fishing—none of the people I fished with knew anything about the mechanics or tackle involved, so I had to learn it from a book—and therein lies the root of the title of this tale.

To digress for a moment, I was the type of kid who after hearing half of a great idea, read one fourth of an instructional guide, or heard any adult begin something with "Now this is how you. . . ," I would immediately dash off to complete the obvious. This led, historically speaking, to a lot of broken docks, incomplete projects, and an occasional discovery, but that's not what happened with this new "art form."

Somewhere between the introduction and glossary of Ray Ovington's *Tactics on Trout*, I left out whole bunches of mundane details about putting the right tackle together to become a masterful fly fisherman. And while this shortage of details led to a host of fishing problems, none vexed me as much as leader crafting, for it almost ended what has since become a semi-pleasant sport (fly fishing). Looking back I'm embarrassed by my stupidity but one old timer had a great time at my expense so maybe it was worth it.

I had gone fly fishing about six times in the Catskills of New York State and had yet to catch a single fish, even a chub. In fact that statement is inaccurate because I had yet to complete a single cast where the fly didn't end up on top of a twisted clump of monofiliment, also known as my leader. In dealing with this frustration, my two primary reactions were to (1) cast harder, in an effort to unfold my leader and (2) go finer and longer with my leader although the reasoning for that gem escapes me at the moment.

Subsequently, on two separate occasions, I drove back to Long Island where I lived with a sprained arm or shoulder and on all six return trips I cursed everyone from Theodore Gordon to Henry Thoreau thinking they were obviously insane and let whoever fill in the damn rivers. By the same token, I also tend to be a stubborn son of a bitch, so I wasn't going to stop trying. If Ovington obviously didn't know what he was talking about maybe someone else did. But before I could get another book I met the old timer referred to earlier.

I saw him coming down the Willowemoc and couldn't help but notice how effortlessly he cast and how sweetly his fly lit upon the water. And there I was beating the river to a froth and occasionally launching a rod tip across the current. Of course like all good trout fishermen when he asked me how I was doing I lied, but I was also intrigued because what he was doing looked like so much fun. So I thought I'd steer the conversation around to "The Fly" thinking that must be the problem for me.

It was only then that the incompleteness of my education became obvious because as the old gentleman followed my fly up my leader to my fly line, he burst out laughing and I mean really hard. "'Son,' he asked, "where did you get this leader?" "I made it myself," answered I with somewhat shaken pride. The Gent: "How are you able to cast this, son?" Me: "Well, eh, to be honest I have been having a little difficulty getting all my casts to lay out now that you mention it." The Gent: "I can understand that, son. I'd have trouble too casting 15 feet of 6X tippet material!" And then he started laughing again.

Near as I can figure out somewhere between "long and fine" and "the lighter the tippet the better," I added too much garlic.

It was a tough experience to live through but now I can catch chubs regularly!

Harry L. Tennison

"My appreciation of the out-of-doors started when I was living on my grandfather's farm. We ate dove, quail, deer, duck, squirrel, rabbit, possum, and raccoon plus armadillo, which is not bad. And, of course, we ate catfish, which is still one of my favorites. I know now how lucky I was to be raised that way and feel that if more kids were raised the same way now we would have fewer of them in some sort of trouble. So go fishing, and take a kid with you. Both of you will never forget the experience and be all the richer for it."

Harry is a consummate conservationist, the founder of the respected Game Conservation International formed "to prevent the end of the game" and to help in the saving of some of those fish, animals, and birds that were once taken for granted. Fort Worth, Texas.

The Ol' Gray Fox Takes on Fly-Fishing Royalty

Spending the first two weeks of your married life trout fishing out of West Yellowstone, Montana is the perfect way to find out if the girl you married is going to be happy in the out-of-doors. Of course, I already knew that she loved to shoot dove, for we did that on our first date.

My wife Gloria and I have fished all over the world since that day long ago when we received two fine Hardy rods and reels as a wedding present and it has been pure enjoyment for both of us to have shared so many experiences. We got hooked on tarpon and bonefishing a few years back and that cost a bundle, as we now own a condominium in Islamorada, Florida and have enough fly rods and reels to start a small store, not to mention the dozen or so pairs of waders, of which only two sets don't leak at the present time.

The first week of June we will be off to Norway to fish the Gaula River. Last year was my first on the Gaula, having done all my salmon fishing—Atlantic salmon, that is—in Iceland and Canada. My first two hours on the Gaula produced three fish larger than I had ever seen in Iceland. The first one I caught weighed 24 pounds and I thought I had died and gone to heaven when, only half an hour later, after resting to try and realize that I had actually caught an Atlantic salmon of over 20 pounds, I went back to the river and in five minutes time had on another fish that was a mate to the first. Following two beers, much back slapping, jumping up and down, and then sitting down for another 10 minutes, it was back to the boat and back on the river. Thirty minutes later, I had landed another fish that was larger than either of the first two. By then I was so tired from fighting those fish, I just said, "That is enough for one old man, I don't want to have a heart attack on the first day." Besides I wanted to get back to a telephone and ruin a beautiful party that would start in about five hours where five of my Iceland fishing partners would be in Texas.

I also called Gloria and told her what it was like to be sitting in that boat on the Gaula River that was big and wide and deep and beautiful. Our guides were from Sweden, and were headed by Ted Dalenson and Johann, his partner, along with five others who were all members of a fly-fishing club in Sweden. They guide more for the love of fishing than anything else, as they all do other things to make a living. Ted and Johann had put together this package, making a deal with each individual farmer along the river. All of them spoke excellent English and could even understand my language, which is Texan. And could they ever cast! All of them could hang 100 feet of the prettiest line out over that river I had ever seen. They made their own flies using a new material called Flashabou, which looks like decoration off a Christmas tree and works like no tomorrow.

Those fish on the Gaula hit with authority, and I, being dumb and stupid, almost gave my fishing partner, Bill Heller from England, a heart attack by hitting back the same as I do with tarpon. Only one big healthy strike, the minute I felt each fish take, then you just hold on, and as Ted and Johann told me, "'Lead them to the bank, and they will follow, just like a little dog."

Some of them would lead, but then four of them that week decided they didn't want to be led and off we went down the rapids, stumbling over rocks, falling against trees, and all the time trying to keep the line tight and put pressure on the fish. Bill was yelling at me, I was yelling at him, while Ted and the rest of the guides were all giving me instructions. All I was trying to do was not fall in that roaring stretch of water for the rapids were at least half a mile long and the river about 300 yards wide. Thank goodness only four of those big fish decided to go downstream. I ended up not losing a one of them, why I don't know, the way I was fighting them, but as I told Bill and the rest; "If a hundred-pound tarpon never broke off the way I was fishing, then I thought these Atlantic salmon wouldn't either."

We would go down river, into those rapids, for at least 300 yards and many times I was down to the last few feet on my reel, the same Billy Pate reel that I use on tarpon. My rod was a 14-foot piece of graphite that really took a beating, as did the 15-footer I also had along. One day I even took my tarpon rod out, which is only nine feet long, but it did the job, too. I guess a really good Atlantic salmon fisherman would laugh and make fun of how I was fishing, but it produced fish. Some purists will also say that the way I was fishing was not very sporty, but I was putting fish on the bank, and that is the name of the game, and I was using a fly, not hardware or salmon eggs, or what I consider the worst of all—*worms*!

What I did do was to let out a lot of line, into the backing, with a quick sinking tip, for the water is very fast and deep and the salmon are at the top of the rapids, resting after the 40 or 50 miles they have come from the sea. I was teasing the fish, the same as I did as a kid, fishing in still water in a small lake on the ranch. We called it "jigging" and also other names, but it started out working for me, and kept working for Bill, too, although he is such a fine fisherman, he really didn't need any help. We had along with us another very fine fly line caster who couldn't figure out what I was doing and just about hit the panic switch by the fourth day, for by then I had landed 14 of the biggest fish I had ever seen, the largest being 30½ pounds. I averaged 25½ for the six days and probably could have caught more fish but, by then, after the first day, when I had caught two fish, I simply sat on the bank, swapped stories with the guides, drank cold beer, ate charcoal-broiled salmon or steak, and enjoyed just being alive. I also was having a grand time watching this Yankee who was with us trying to hook a fish. He fell in once and darned near drowned, but he was a great sportsman and just kept on fishing. Finally I showed him what I was doing, but he never seemed to get the hang of it the way Bill Heller did. Bill also wanted to catch a fish from the bank casting and did manage to catch two small ones—they weighed about 18 pounds each!

Fishing from a boat on the Gaula is most interesting, as the boatman, in effect, does the casting for you by moving the boat across the river laterally, which swings the fly for you as if you were about on a 30 to 40° angle from the fly, the same as if you had made the cast yourself. The "jigging" is done by using your free hand to constantly strip the line about five to six inches toward you. This makes the Flashabou spread out as you release the line after each pull that you make and, evidently, it does attract the salmon. I do hope it keeps working for me, as I will be back on that same spot this year.

Now I'm not going to tell you what else is on that fly, or what sort of a fly it is, but if you want to call me, I'm in the Fort Worth telephone book. You Atlantic salmon fishermen are most welcome to call, but remember, most fishermen lie a little every now and then.

For years, when nothing else would help, my friend Earl Wilson and I would go to using the "hitch" in Iceland, which Earl showed me how to use. It is simple to tie a couple of half hitches at the back of the eye of the fly you are using, the tight part of the half hitch to be facing you so that when the fly appears on the water, which is about the time your line comes tight, tip held high, about 45° away from where you are standing, the fly will ride on top of the water, leaving a vee behind it. If all goes well you can really have some fun, for the salmon sometimes will come all the way out of the water to eat that fly. Evidently they follow the fly, or else come right up from where they are holding, to take. It is exciting, for a 15-pound Atlantic salmon makes quite a roll when he takes a fly in this manner. Many times I have pulled the fly out of the mouth of a salmon, so you must be cautious when you make your strike. Most of the time the salmon is hooked before you can move, because they take it so fast, and, at other times, they just sort of suck that ol' fly in and then settle right back down.

I used this method on the George River in September, 1984, while fishing with Jim Rikhoff. On two pools in particular, I usually have caught my limit—four fish in two hours. The smallest I have caught on the George was seven pounds but most of them were in the 12 to 15-pound class and they really put up a scrap, for the George is also a big, heavy river and you cast from the bank, except at two of the beats, where it is very dangerous—one slip and you are in trouble. That is why I use the Bruce and Walker 14 and 15-foot rods. They are not hard to cast and, having learned the Spey from my English friend Bill Heller, it is easy to just stand still, with no backcast at all and roll out 60 or 70 feet of line. With the length of the rods you can easily lift that fly up in a hurry and get it skimming across the water.

During our last day on the George we needed three more fish to make it an even hundred for the week for a party of eight. I had skipped the day before and naturally got on everybody for not catching any fish. "OK, Texan, go catch us three fish," they told me. "That will not be a problem, because I have number eight beat today." With that, one of the fellows, another Yankee by birth (so he couldn't help himself when the panic hit him, as number eight had been the most productive of any of the beats except number three), suddenly said, "To hell with that, you've fished eight more than anybody and I haven't fished it but twice, so you can just go somewhere else." He seemed to be pretty serious, so I just looked at him for a minute until one of the other fellows, a non-Yankee, said, "Harry, you come with me and show me how to use that big rod and that hitch you have been talking about." "Fine with me," I said and off we went to the boats which would take us up the river.

When we unloaded my friend hung back and asked me, "Did you know which beat he had?" When I told him I didn't, he smiled and said, 'Number three!' It took 15 minutes to walk to number three, over the rocks, and when we got there he said, "You go ahead and show me how to use that big rod." I gave him the rod but he repeated,"Oh, no, I want you to fish and I'll watch." I made some short casts and showed him how to lift the rod to make the fly skid across the water and he finally said he would try it. After wrapping the line around his head twice and trying to cast with just one hand he finally gave the rod back to me and said, "To hell with it, Harry, you fish."

Lady Luck was smiling, for on the second cast I was into a very nice salmon which came out of the water and really put on a show for us. This one weighed about 13 pounds. Thirty minutes later I had two more in the holding pond, which was made by damming up a small stream that ran into the river, and then I just sat on a rock and watched him fish with his nine-foot rod. He could cast very well, but somehow he just never got the hang of where to put that fly, which was right in front of a big rock about 30 feet out in the river, so when we went in to pack up and leave he still hadn't hooked a fish. Funny thing, neither had anyone else on the river, except one man, and that was just his fourth fish for the week. The man who had taken my beat caught nothing. The lesson to all of this is that if you are going to be smart-assed, then you had better be lucky, too. I'll take luck every time, with, of course, the experience that comes from fishing with some people through the years who really knew what they were doing such as my friends Perry Bass, Bill Heller, Earl Wilson, and Paul Leonard and, of course, the wonderful guides I have come to know in Iceland and Norway. One man, Diddi Bragason taught us all how to use the hitch when all else failed. Ted and Johann taught me about the Flashabou so when I fish I have all these men to thank, and yet Gloria still beats us with the biggest fish and wins all the money. We bet pretty heavy—$10 each and my friend Bill Heller, who usually catches the most, still keeps on losing out on the biggest fish each year. We will be together again this year, Bill, Perry, Earl, and Paul, and I still believe that, when Gloria shows up, she will win again. We are trying to figure some way to bar her from the Gaula.

Now let's fish for tarpon for awhile. I have had the good fortune to fish with most of the good guides in Islamorada but I won't name them for fear of hurting someone's feelings that I might leave out. They know what they are doing and I have never seen so many men who will work so hard to put you close to a big tarpon. I've lost more fish than I have caught and I haven't caught enough to claim to be any sort of an expert on tarpon fishing, but just that first one was enough to tell me that here was a worthwhile way to spend your time.

Tarpon fishing is hard work, plus a little skill in casting a fly line with a heavy rod, or at least it seemed to be heavy the first time I picked one up. I felt like I was waving a broom handle and I imagine I looked like it, too. Billy Pate and Stu Apte showed me how though, along with Forrest Haynes, Hal Chittum, and a dozen other of the great guides at Islamorada, along with my friend Joe Hudson. I will never be in their class and I know it, but they have put me into some great moments hooked up with a tarpon on a rod that weighs about five to seven ounces with a 14 or 15-pound test leader.

As I wasn't doing too well with the big rod, I told Stu that I was going to use my Atlantic salmon rod. He just grinned and said, "Well, Harry, OK, but we might be out here for quite a long spell if you hook into something big."

Fortunately we didn't hook into something big, only one that weighed perhaps 35 or 40 pounds. I thought it weighed a ton when it hit and felt like I was going to lose fish, rod, and all, but fortunately I had been listening to all the guides talking, and also to Stu, as the tarpon started his act, which was just beautiful.

The tarpon had come from behind the boat and I threw the line right past Stu's head and it landed about 50 feet back of the boat. "He's going to take it!," was all I heard before I felt that tremendous surge of power as the tarpon shot out of the water.

Having fished for Atlantic salmon my knowledge came in handy, because you do the same thing with a tarpon that you do with a salmon, you bow to him when he comes out of the water and I had to bow seven times in the 15 minutes it took to lip gaff the tarpon, pull him in, take his picture, and then hold him in the water until he had recovered enough to swim away. What a thrill it was, and still is, just remembering how that tarpon felt on the end of that line and then seeing him shoot out of the water not 30 feet away. I've hooked quite a few since that first one; one in particular really gave me a whipping I will always remember.

I was fishing with John Emery, using his rod, after breaking mine on a tarpon of about 125 pounds, just as we were landing him, so he had to be let go as breaking a rod disqualifies the fish and we were in a tournament at the time. John and I were having a ball. I had hooked and lost three fish in about 30 minutes when all of a sudden right near us was a "daisy chain." For those of you who have never seen a "daisy chain," it is a group of tarpon swimming, they say around a big female, in a rather small circle. Once you see one you will become as awed as I was the first time, for as the fish turn they all have that beautiful, glistening white side that you can see so clearly in the beautiful water around Islamorada.

"Cast right back here, Harry." The fly hit the water and I didn't do anything for about five seconds, just let it drop a little before I started to strip the line. Two strips and I thought I was hung on the bottom, except that all of a sudden the bottom came to the top and out of the water came the biggest tarpon that I had ever seen, except maybe the one that hangs in Billy Pate's house. This tarpon jumped twice and two other friends of mine, Joe Hudson and Toddie Lee Wynne, who were in boats not more than 50 yards away with their guides, all saw the fish and we all started to scream at each other. John declared, "Harry, that is a big fish, I believe you must have caught the big female right out of the middle of the chain."

That tarpon then decided to head south and we went by Hank Brown and Forrest, and the tarpon was kind enough to jump for them before turning back the way it had started. John had started the boat motor, or else we couldn't have kept up at all as there was just no way I could stop that fish.

The fish only jumped once more, and that was after 1½ hours. We were in shallow water, clear as it could be, and we both thought we were going to get that fish soon. I had the fish up on top 18 times, but we could never get any closer than 10 feet to it, and we were in water that was never any deeper than six feet so we had a lot of time to watch that fish.

After a little over two hours my left hand started to cramp and then my right hand followed. I had the rod cradled in my arms, as by then my hands were just useless, and I couldn't put any more pressure on the fish. I just managed to turn the drag down as hard as it would go and the fish slowly started towing us toward deeper water. The fish started to slow down after about 10 minutes of this and came to the top, got a breath of air and then slowly went down and kept on pulling us. After a total of 2½ hours the leader finally parted and the line went slack. John didn't say anything but just handed me a beer and went back to just collapse on the deck. I sat down and managed to get the beer to my mouth and I don't think I stopped drinking until the can was empty. I didn't hurt, as I was too numb to feel much of anything. John said, "You really tried, but that fish just wasn't meant to be caught, not today anyway." All I could do was nod my head and say "Thank you, John, you did all you could do to help me, but man, wasn't that a fish!"

John and the other guides talked about the fish and they all agreed that it would have weighed at least 180 pounds. I never will be able to prove it, but just having that magnificent thing on the end of my fly line for that period of time and being able to see the fish for so long in clear, shallow water was quite a thrill. We all decided it was a big female. I personally think it was the devil in a tarpon outfit!

I have had some wonderful times fishing with the people I have already mentioned, plus a few more like Pete Krindler of "21;" Gene Hill, the famous author; Jack Samson, former editor of *Field and Stream*; and Connie Ryan, *The Longest Day* author, and all of them have been the sort of people who make it wonderful to be with in the out-of-doors.

My son has added a lot to my life, as has his lovely wife, Margaret. My two daughters Kit and Jil married fishermen. Now I have one grandson and five granddaughters who will be taught how to fish and love the out-of-doors. Two of them have already caught fish and before they were three years old! Start 'em young and like myself, here in the declining days of a life spent sometimes recklessly and lazily fishing and hunting some new spot, I wouldn't trade a day and hope the good Lord will let me do it for a while longer.

If you ever see some old man waving a 15-foot fly rod over some Atlantic salmon river, or standing in the bow of a fishing boat on some flat near Islamorada, or swapping lies at the bar at the harbor where the guides and their clients are having a cool one at the end of a day on the water—stop by—for it just might be the Ol' Gray Fox matching Murphy or Joe Hudson for the next round of drinks. We'll even let you in the game.

Adios for now.

Edward H. Boyd

Estimable flyfisher for tarpon, Atlantic salmon, bonefish, and trout and an exponent of the good life. St. Michaels, Maryland, and Islamorada, Florida.

Hot Hand

It has been said that if you cast 100,000 times you may catch a muskie. Atlantic salmon fishing is perhaps somewhat comparable. Our first Atlantic salmon experience was on the Spey River in Scotland where we stayed at a magnificent castle and the food and the accommodations were superb. But in five days of fishing and flailing the water to a froth, no one in our group got even so much as a strike, much less a fish and so it became evident that indeed Atlantic salmon fishing possibly paralleled that for muskellunge.

Arriving home, I read all the articles I could find about how to fish Atlantic salmon and, in view of the fact that my success ratio had been so poor up to now, I was anxious to try it again. A couple of years later a river in Iceland that was regularly fished by some friends of mine had a rod available and I was fortunate enough to be invited to take it. I accepted with some fear and trepidation because all of the people fishing the river were very experienced and had successfully fished it for years. It was also reputed to be a super river and, therefore, I was a little bit like a rookie joining the Yankees in the days of Babe Ruth and Lou Gehrig. Nonetheless, I went.

On the first afternoon it was rainy and blustery and cold and totally miserable. I was sent out to what was supposed to be the best pool on the river and with the leading ghillie. The young man, whose name was Foosie, I will never forget. I thought Foosie was the son of one of the local farmers on the river but I found out later he was in college and the son of a prominent banker in Reykjavik. We took a Land Rover to this pool and Foosie asked, "What do you know about Atlantic salmon fishing?" To which I replied, "Absolutely nothing." So we stood on the edge of the bank and he told me where to enter the water. I was to cast close to the pool and let the fly line swing down through it three times from the one location. At the end of that series of casts I was to move one step downstream and repeat the same three casts. From reading articles that other rookies had written about fishing in Iceland, I determined that you probably would not catch a fish for the first three days at least and then maybe the last two or three days of the week you might have enough experience so that you could catch one. I had also been told that if you felt a hit or something on your line, you should not strike the fish in the normal trout-fishing sense but just move the rod firmly over toward the nearest bank and that would be it.

At any rate I cast, and cast, and cast, and moved one step, and cast, and cast, and cast, and after about an hour all of a sudden I felt as though my hook had snagged into some object on the bottom. In order to free it I gave a mighty tug and Foosie cried, "Oh, oh, that was a fish and you snatched it right out of his mouth." Whereupon my dismay was even greater because here, on my very first afternoon, I had had an opportunity that I never dreamed of to catch a fish and muffed it. I was very depressed, but at least I now had an inkling of what an Atlantic salmon might feel like on the end of the line. I fished the rest of the length of the pool, which was not really too long, maybe 30 or 40 yards, with no more results. Looking at Foosie, with the rain running off my glasses and rain gear and the temperature at 41°, feeling very down and dejected, I asked "What do I do now?"

He replied, "You go back to the head of the pool and you start through again." There had been encouraging signs in this pool because I had seen some movement, so I pretty well knew that there were at least fish there and that I was not fishing in empty water.

I started down the pool for the second time and, after only a few casts, I felt a weight on my line. This time I had the presence of mind not to strike but to just hold a firm line and all of a sudden I saw this salmon go into the air with my fly in its mouth. After a hard but relatively short fight, Foosie was able to tail the fish for me and I had caught my first Atlantic salmon. I was excited beyond belief and anxious to reenter the pool to cast again, which I did, and within just a few minutes I was hooked to another fish. This one was far less friendly so I had to come out of the pool and, with my waders on, run about a quarter of a mile downstream trying to keep up. Again Foosie was able to tail it for me after a fight of about half an hour.

At this point I just couldn't believe my good luck and went back to the same pool again. In 15 minutes I had another fish on and Foosie declared, "Ed, this is not salmon fishing. This is not the way it is supposed to be. Nobody on their first experience gets three salmon!" The size of these fish, by the way, was between 15 and 18 pounds and I was just thrilled to death that we had caught the three fish. An hour later we caught the fourth and Foosie, shaking his head again, said, "Ed, this is not the way Atlantic salmon fishing is supposed to be. You just don't do this."

Shortly after I had my fourth fish on the bank, my host and good friend Carl Navarre came by to see what I was doing and when he saw those four fish, he gave me a good solid cussing out because even with all his years of experience and knowledge, he had not been successful that day in taking a salmon.

Carl and I both caught more fish that week and it was totally an experience that I will surely never forget. And although I live in the heart of outstanding bonefish and tarpon country in Islamorada in the Florida Keys, I still consider good Atlantic salmon fishing the most exciting fly fishing in the world.

Scott F. Ripley

A fine outdoor writer who helps Tom Pero put out Trout Unlimited's wonderful fly-fishing magazine. Bend, Oregon.

Fly Frogging

Rain came in unrelenting waves, torrential at times and unmercifully chilling. It had begun a week before Memorial Day while I camped along the Delaware River in New York. At first it was welcome, the river was unseasonably low and warm, and needed rain to bring on overdue hatches. The insects came, trout fed ravenously and fought with determined power.

The rain continued. It somehow crept into the Coleman stove, making first ignition a laborious chore. It made its way into the waterproof tent, dampening sleeping bags, pillows, and extra clothing. Protective raingear provided a bit of relief, yet water managed to slip around the elastic cuff and accumulate about the elbow. The brim of my cap turned soggy and moisture encircled my head. My shoulders felt like I had portaged a canoe 10 miles.

If it hadn't been for leaping 18-inch rainbows, good company, and plenty of Canadian beer, it would have been dreary indeed.

When darkness fell, rain *pitter-patted* a soothing melody on the canvas roof of the tent. Sleep came easily, yet always, just before dozing off, you could hear the resonating *harrumph* of a bull frog adding his bass lines to the spring symphony. On one such night, my mind drifted back to a time when life was much simpler; penny-candy, summer vacation, chasing butterflies with a cheese-cloth net, and exploring a myriad of farm ponds in the rolling dairy country of central New York.

Frogs were the No. 1 prize those ponds begrudgingly yielded. It wasn't only the succulent, delicate taste of legs fried in butter, it was also the challenge of capturing one of the slippery devils. We tried netting them, we tried clubbing, stoning. We were too young for .22 caliber rifles so we tried BB guns but found them ineffective unless fired at a close range, which was nearly impossible. Frogs were spooky.

Somewhere along the line, a wise outdoorsman (or woman) informed us that if you stuck a piece of red cloth on a fish hook and dangled it in front of a frog, it would strike at it. Sure enough, by quietly crawling on hands and knees through the muck, we would approach the frogs from behind using a spinning rod to present the cloth bait. We were in frog-leg heaven.

I awoke the next morning as a stream of water poured off the rain flap, sounding much like a cow relieving itself. A hearty breakfast took the chill off the damp morning. As I munched on a slice of bacon, I once again thought of frog legs.

Springtime wandering led me upstate, where the sun made a welcome appearance. It was shortlived. Thunderheads rolled out of the south followed by sheets of rain. Trout fed that first wet evening, becoming confident and unselective beneath the broken surface.

Rain continued throughout the night, though its sound was less audible with the tent pitched beneath a canopy of heavily branched evergreens. My angling companions and I had hoped the ground would absorb a great deal of water and that local reservoirs would hold back enough to keep the tributaries of the Chenango River at check. Driving north the next day our optimism was quickly drowned. The first small stream encountered was flooded, the first medium-sized stream was unfishable, and Chenango River was a chocolately, raging mess.

Farther along we found Oriskany Creek high and muddy; a usually unflappable Chenango Canal was off-color with not a rise to be seen. We fished nymphs and streamers in all of these waters, with little success. The trout must have gorged all night on food-stuffs dislodged by high water. We were in a desperate state of mind. None of us was sincerely inclined to spend the day at a bar, but seeing that it was just after noon, perhaps a touch of the spirits would help.

On the way to a favorite watering hole, we happened by Payne Creek. The trout portion of Payne Creek begins where it emanates as bottom flow from Lake Morraine. From there it passes through farmland before it becomes an integral part of Seven Oaks golf course. On its way to confluence with the Chenango River it gently twists through a section of the Colgate University campus. For some reason known only to those high-level masterminds controlling the big faucet at the reservoir, there was scarcely more than normal flow in Payne Creek. We parked the car.

It must be understood that fishing the golf-course stretch of Payne Creek can be productive and enjoyable. Grass is mowed right up to the bank; there are tasteful stream improvements and numerous overhanging willows. But you have to fish while occasionally looking over your shoulder. It seems there are quite a few golfers who haven't got the hang of the game and slice the ball in unpredictable directions. There is one trout-filled plunge-pool that is in the direct flight path of one hole. Needless to say, it is best fished at night.

Rain hadn't kept die-hard chasers of the little white ball off soggy fairways and greens, so we exercised due caution as we sloshed along. The appearance of the stream had deceived us into thinking that maybe the trout would be cooperative. They weren't.

On the lower end of the course is a pond, or water trap, that is semi-stagnant with just a trickle of water from the nearby stream diverted through it. As we passed, a familiar sound was heard.

Harrrumph.

I looked at my companions.

"Bet we could catch one of those bastards on a fly," I said.

Mike was the first to spot a frog.

"Here's a huge one on the bank. Do you think it will take a nymph?" he yelled.

"Sure. Ease up behind him and just wiggle it a few inches from his snout," I replied.

Mike approached slowly and offered the fly.

"It's not doing anything," he said.

"Just keep teasing the damn thing," I told him.

"I got him," Mike exclaimed suddenly. "The son of a bitch took it."

With his Orvis graphite rod bent over, Mike hoisted out a weed-draped bull frog.

"Now what do we do with him?" he asked. (You have to realize that Michael grew up in suburban Philadelphia and so missed out on some of the finer points of country life.)

"We're going to have the legs for dinner," I said. "That is, if we can catch some more."

Tom was working the other side of the pond. He had positioned himself behind a large frog that wanted the fly badly, but he was having a rough time hooking the amphibian.

I called over to him, "Don't you think a four-weight rod is a little light for these beasts?"

No reply.

The action continued for an hour. After that the frogs were severely spooked and, thereafter, probably panicked whenever a golfer came too close. We had a modest catch, yet enough for a taste, and for me a chance to re-live youthful memories. Strange as it may seem, we had forgotten about the rain for awhile.

The following week I was back on the Delaware. It was raining of course and the river had risen a foot and a half. There was a restless feeling around the campground; rained out fishermen were wandering around in day-glo ponchos looking for something to do.

As I sat under the rain flap savoring a beer, I noticed a guy walking toward the swampy area with a fancy looking sling-shot. A half hour later he came walking back, carrying a tiny frog by one leg.

"Weren't there any bigger ones?" I asked.

"Yeah, but they were tough," he said. "I couldn't get close enough for a shot."

"You should try flies," I offered. "Fly fish for frogs."

He left without saying a word.

That night as rain danced on the tent, the last thing I heard was a gutsy *Harrrumph.*

Robert H. Colson

His grandfather taught him this important truth in life: "In every body of water is a fish aching to be taught a lesson." Robert has, consequently, spent his life investigating the applications of this great truth. He can be often seen on Michigan's Au Sable or Pere Marquette, cane rod in hand, tie carefully knotted, tweed jacket cleaned and pressed, paying homage to the glorious creatures he pursues and the places they inhabit. Shaker Heights, Ohio.

Hooked on Chinook

Two days ago I received an enthusiastic letter from a friend who had accompanied me on a Michigan chinook fishing trip earlier this fall. His note was full of questions about equipment and he was ready to go after the great fish again. This morning's mail brought another letter from my friend, seeking advice about a reel he had seen advertised. The chinook experience had captured his imagination in the same way it had captivated mine several yeas ago. My friend's enthusiasm for his new-found sport was infectious and started me thinking about the origins of my love for fly fishing and the experiences that led me to appreciate its potential for exciting and challenging adventure.

Sue and I had invited friends from Columbus to join us in Ann Arbor for a football weekend during our first fall in Michigan. Scott and I had talked about fishing several times before, so they came a day early and he and I set off on our quest for a new fishing experience. Leaving Ann Arbor around 4 a.m., we drove to Baldwin, arriving at 8, and obtained information on where and how to fish for chinook on the Pere Marquette River's fly-fishing-only section from Josephine Sedlecki at Ed's Sports Shop. By 9 we had parked the car, put together our gear, and were headed toward the river.

Not knowing a thing about the Pere Marquette, we started fishing our way downstream, sticking pretty much to the river. I was thrilled by the clarity of the water and the strength of the current against my waders. The first chinook I spotted caused a shiver of excitement and near fright to move through me; its size and proximity in the stream made me wonder if I was fishing for it or if it was stalking me. That fish quickly moved downstream from me, however, and became lost to sight in some darker water.

Scott and I returned to casting and drifting our heavy, weighted streamers through the clear water where we thought we might find chinook.

"Wouldn't it be great to latch on to one of them. They must be really powerful. I bet they would really jump. Man, what a fight!"

Rounding a bend in the river, we saw a group of fishermen on the bank. All were drinking beer and watching one of their herd fight a great fish that was leaping and churning the pool below them into a froth. The fisherman fighting the chinook was a big, strong fellow and had his rod bent double as the chinook tried to take line. Suddenly we heard an awesome crack and the fisherman's rod splintered from a powerful rush by the chinook to leave the pool and flee downstream. "Holy shit! He broke my Ugly Stik," floated up to us over the roar of the river and the derisive roar of his companions' laughter. The loss of his rod didn't matter much, though. This enterprising fisherman threw down the rod in disgust and began hauling in the fish hand-over-hand! It came reluctantly, but rapidly, to the deep-water bank beneath the fishermen where one of the group netted it with a long-handled net. We could see the silvery fish lying on the bank, its gills heaving, with a large "fly" sticking in its belly. The "fly" was a large bait hook with some yarn wrapped on it and large bell sinkers suspended both above it on the line and below it on a loop of monofilament attached to the bend of the hook. The line itself must have been 50- or 60-pound test. Little wonder the man had been able to land the fish easily by handlining it after his rod shattered.

Watching that episode set me wondering. "What have I stepped into here? I have a weighted streamer, but no weight on the line. What about my seven-weight fly rod and eight-pound tippet? I'd love to fight a big fish. Am I going about this right? I thought this was a fly-fishing-only stretch of river. Maybe I'm out of my element." The episode also caused me to change to a leader testing out to a 15-pound tippet and to add some shot to it about a foot above the fly. I was new to this type of fishing and felt I should learn from my experiences.

We continued fishing, learning more about the river but not hooking any of the fish we'd begun to be able to see in some abundance. Working our way farther downstream, we came across a group of three fly fishermen who were enjoying fantastic success just below us. They seemed to have one fish on after another. Some of the chinook they landed, others slipped off, and others they seemed to be deliberately breaking off. We kept fishing but observed them intently, hoping to discover the secrets of their technique.

While we were observing this group, another fisherman approached us and began to talk about his experiences on the river. "I've been here three days now and haven't caught a thing. You know, these fish don't bite. In fact, they don't eat anything once they enter the river. I was talking to the Department of Natural Resources' guy about how to hook them. He told me you have to release any fish not hooked in the mouth. They're not legal. I've got it figured this way. You have to float your fly real close to the fish and then jerk it into its mouth before its got a chance to turn away. The DNR guy told me its' legal to do it that way. He also told me my fly's legal, too."

At this point the fellow offered to show us his fly and we looked with great interest. In contrast to the bank snagger, his "fly" was a small hook with some sponge wrapped to it and a few split-shot crimped to the line abut eight inches above it. "The idea with this fly is to bounce it right along the bottom toward a fish. The sponge keeps it floating just at the level of its mouth, and when you get the fly close to its mouth, let 'em have it! Let me show you." And show us he did for several minutes, but our attention kept returning to the group below which always seemed to be attached to yet another fish. Our new friend eventually left us, moving upstream, muttering that he didn't think it was worth all the time and effort to fish for chinook. He planned to leave the next morning.

In the meantime, the group of fly fishers left their spot and Scott and I moved into it. There were chinook everywhere, some on the clean-swept gravel, some in the dark water behind, some darting back and forth through a chute of fast water between the dark water and the gravel. We fished hard, certain that we had found the place where the chinook would cooperate. We cast our flies continuously, tried to swim them by the fish, low in the water so we had some chance of hooking one in the mouth as described by the fellow that had just left.

Suddenly it happened! I had one on! It bore upstream away from me toward a heavy snag that protruded from the water. I put every ounce of pressure I dared on the rod and 15-pound test leader I'd been using since witnessing the morning episode of the broken Ugly Stik. I turned the fish from the snag. Rather, I pulled the fish backward in the water, since I could then see that my fly was firmly stuck in the fish's back just below the dorsal.

I heard a low growl from the bank behind me, "Break it off! Foul hooked." Another angler was watching my progress and offering advice. "Break it off! Are you kidding? I've worked hard all day for the chance to catch a chinook. My arms ache from casting. My wrist feels like it's going to fall off. I've earned this fish and I don't care where it's hooked. I'm going to land it."

Land it I did. I was elated, thrilled, and thoroughly proud that I had finally caught a chinook. It was one of the most wonderful moments of my fishing life. I felt just great. Even though, two memories haunted my drive home that evening. This first was the grizzled veteran telling me, "Break it off. Foul hooked." The second was the trio of fly fishermen who had constant action in the same spot where I had been able to only snag a hen fish by inadvertently dragging the fly across its back.

My second trip for chinook came only days later. This time I was alone and headed for the place where I'd been successful before, convinced I was going to catch lots of fish and clean out the river. I'd thought a lot about how to get my fly down to where the fish were and how to entice them to take it. This was going to be a great day.

As it turned out, it was one of the most pleasant days I'd ever spent. I began to develop a love for the river and its contours and moods. I noticed the kingfishers working, the evidence of beaver, a flock of turkeys, and several deer. The beauty of the place was awe-inspiring. I was also completely and magnificently skunked. Not one chinook did I touch or feel even though there must have been hundreds within sight during the day. It was really only my growing love for the river that prevented me from giving up after that second trip.

The third day out for chinook was a carbon copy of the second. I cast my flies until the dull pains in my arm, wrist, and back told me I should stop. The sight of all those chinook in the river before me motivated me to push beyond the pain thresholds. I was dazed by the sun, the light coming off the water, and exhausted by the physical exertion of wading a powerful stream and of continously casting a weighted fly and bounding it along the bottom.

I'd been on the stream since before daybreak. Now it was evening. I hadn't stopped to rest during the day. Nor had I packed a lunch or something to drink. I was beginning to feel the effects of hard physical effort on a deskbound body that had had no rest or nourishment during the day. I felt relieved that the sun had gone behind the pines on the hill opposite me. There was a softness in the light that began subduing my anxiety over my failure. The fishermen above and below me had left. I was alone in the stream, whose flow swirled gently around my waders, experiencing one of those moments that draw me to the stream, one of those moments when the veil between my cultured city life and my identification with the pastoral elements of nature becomes particularly transparent. The life of the stream was refreshing my spirits and invigorating me physically.

I returned my attention to the narrow chute of water that connected a clean-swept stretch of gravel above and a darker pool below. No fish in the chute. Looking upstream, several silvery shadows were prominent on the gravel. I inspected my fly and was satisfied that the yellow streamer was still in good shape. I began to cast, quartering upstream of the fish and swinging the fly in front of them, hoping to get one to strike in spite of the echo in my ears from my first day out, "These fish don't bite."

Over and over I cast the fly, trying to bring it close to the chinook, and letting it swing below them in the current. After about 15 minutes one of the fish moved toward the fly slightly as it swung past him in the current. The movement of the fish caused a shiver of excitement and anticipation to move through me and I involuntarily set the hook while the fish was still yards away. Ducking the fly as it whistled by my head, I placed the next cast again in a good position for swinging it past the fish. The fly bounced off a deadfall, and began its drift over the uneven bottom, passing within inches of the fish holding above the chute.

It happened as the fly swung below the fish, gliding across the current, and straightening on the fly line. One of the chinook, a male, detached himself from the group, slowly turned in a tight arc downstream, and rushed the fly. This time I resisted the urge to set the hook and allowed the fly to complete its cross-current swing. The fish snatched the fly on a downstream run and flung himself into the air all in one motion, the yellow streamer hanging from his jaw, his eye meeting mine from a distance of no more than 20 feet. It was all over in two seconds. When the fish hit the water he wasn't hooked. But I was.

I had seen that fish turn on my fly and attack it. I knew that chinook would strike a fly, for whatever reason, and I knew I wanted to know more about how to get them to do it. In that experience I learned the immense potential of these Michigan chinook for fly fishing. Raising such fish to the fly is surely not easy; how well I know. There is something mysterious about it, a puzzle to be solved. And the puzzle requires intimate knowledge of the fish and experience fishing for them as well as reading and thought about strategy, technique, and equipment. The pieces of the puzzle are numerous and intricate, each piece fitting into the others in many and beguiling ways.

There is a group of us now who make an annual pilgrimage to the Pere Marquette for chinook. Some of us have learned a great deal about enticing these large fish with small flies with most of our fish hooked firmly in the jaw. Although our techniques and fly choices vary, we have all come to position ourselves above our quarry and fish quartering downstream to them. Fishing in this fashion reduces the possibility of an inadvertent snag to almost zero and allows good control of the placement and speed of the fly, which are critical for success.

My crowning achievement with chinook came last year. It was a clear, cool day in November back on the Pere Marquette and I was stalking elusive fall steelhead when I spotted three large, fresh-run hen chinook hanging in shallow water just at the lip of a small eddy. There were no other fishermen around since deer season had just begun and those who might have been fishing were probably hunting. As a consequence, these three late-run hens had probably made the 125-mile trip up the river without being fished over at all.

"Roderick Haig-Brown has written about fishing chinook with dry flies on their native waters of British Columbia. This would be an ideal time to try a dry fly on these fish. They're in shallow water and haven't been fished over. More important, they probably haven't been the targets of the snaggers downstream. I'm going to give it a try!"

Unfortunately, there were no large dry flies in my box since I had come equipped only for steelhead. I did have a fairly large streamer that I tied on with a riffling hitch. Each of those three chinook came up to just beneath the surface to take that riffled fly as it swung in the classic riffling arc in front of them. As the fly came in sight, the fish would back off from it, turn with it as it swung in the current, and take it while moving in a quartering down-stream direction. The fights which were played out in the large pool below were anti-climatic to the takes.

An intense interest in fly fishing for chinook has thus encouraged me to search for the pieces of the chinook puzzle and how they fit together. The quest has involved understanding the natural history and biology of these great, marvelous fish as they have been transplanted from their native watersheds on the Pacific coast to the Great Lakes, the theories for why they rise to a fly, reading the water to know where fish are holding, spotting fish in the stream, techniques and equipment for implementing fly-fishing strategies, and the construction and use of flies to lure chinook to the hook. More than this, however, the quest has centered on the traditional values of the fly-fishing angler—identifying and appreciating the humanistic qualities of the angling sport, the intellectual and physical challenges as well as the personal companionship that flow from the angling ethic.

M. B. Franks, M. D.

Buck claims to be a casual bird watcher, an Atlantic-salmon and trout fisherman of questionable expertise, and an enthusiastic spectator of both baseball and football. A semi-retired ophthalmologist, his office is frequently closed for extended periods to permit fishing and birding expeditions. Jamestown, New York.

First Things First

I've been back to the George River many times and, although the last few years have been lean, I treasure them as much as the times when six to eight rods would take over a hundred Atlantic salmon in a week.

In those golden years my daughter, Susan, accompanied me, presumably to help with the gear as I was under instruction from my physician "not to over exert myself" and it was also easier to get away if Susan was included in the party. I built up a lot of points at home by this little maneuver.

Now Susan is an indefatigable fisherman. I envy her concentration and single mindedness. When she fishes she is so absorbed by the matter at hand that she lets nothing intrude even as it turned out, a large salmon and a possible heart attack.

Susan was fishing about a hundred yards upriver from me. On my first cast, what turned out to be the largest salmon I've ever hooked took my fly. The George River at this point was over 150 yards wide and in no time I was into my backing. In order to hold the fish I began to scramble along the

141

rocky shore. At that moment I experienced the most severe angina attack I have ever had. I called to Susan, she ran to me, I handed her the rod, she saw that I had my nitroglycerine, *and then she left*. I could see her running along the banks of the river reeling in line and about 30 minutes later and a mile away she landed a 27-pound beaut.

The nitroglycerine took care of my problem very nicely and when I saw the salmon I felt a bit better about the options she had and the choice she made. After all, I know of two of my friends who had fatal coronaries while fishing and didn't even have a salmon on.

Harry M. Grinton

A retired sales, marketing, advertising, publishing, and public relations executive, Harry might prefer to be remembered best as a fisherman with a fly. Cleveland, Ohio.

Catching and Matching

To a fly fisherman, this title means being at the right place at the right time with the right fly. One of my long-time fishing companions is John Taylor of Pittsburgh. John and I fished for trout out of Almont, Colorado on the Gunnison, the Taylor, and the East rivers; the Channels out of Ennis, Montana; the Laurentide out of Quebec, Canada; Rockwell Springs Trout Club in northwestern Ohio, and many other well-known streams in Pennsylvania and New York.

One of our most interesting and really almost unbelievable experiences happened twice on the Au Sable River in Michigan. For several years, John and I would meet in late June to enjoy the excellent fly fishing on that classic trout stream with the hope that we might catch and match the caddis fly hatch.

We would stay at a most comfortable motel on the river, about six or seven miles downstream from Grayling. The proprietor of the motel acted as our guide. There were many theories among the natives about the caddis fly hatch. One that we believed, as did our guide, was that mama caddis fly laid her eggs in early spring. She chose a part of the stream considered to be still water and with a sandy bottom. The eggs then hatched in late June. To catch the hatch, you had to be there, not only on the right day, but also at the right time of day. *For the hatch only lasted for 60 to 90 minutes each year.*

To our good fortune, John and I hit the right time twice. What a thrill! Our guide would have one of his men park a car downstream from the motel for our return. John, the guide, and I would leave the motel about 4 p.m. and fish the river enroute to the hatching area selected by our guide. We would anchor in the stream and wait out the action. As I said we were lucky twice: things started, a splash here, a splash there. In a few minutes the stream was alive with trout eating flies. All you needed on your leader was a caddis fly imitation. This turmoil was to last for about an hour and then as fast as it started, complete activity changed to complete inactivity. It was over, but what a truly magnificent experience!

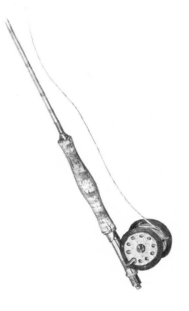

Roland S. Van Arsdale

Roland is a member in good standing of the notorious Marshmallow Gang and Trout Unlimited. Somerville, New Jersey.

Salmo Salar Sebago and the Marshmallow Gang

By now the Dam Pool was dimpling with rising fish. That magic hour before dusk was beginning to take hold. Dick laid out another easy cast. As the large white apparition drifted jauntily along, from below came the jibe "What's that you"re using, a marshmallow?" Above the splash following the salmon's take came the reply, "Yup!"

It was the fourth night on Grand Lake Stream way up north in Maine. Five sportsmen of assorted ages and backgrounds had contrived to share this week fishing for Maine's *Salmo salar sebago*, the scrappy landlocked salmon. Only two of the group, Rich and Ro, had been there before. Through their wild tales, they had enticed the rest to invest a week's vacation chasing the often elusive landlocks. The sixth, a stranger to all, had won a free trip that was first prize in a local Trout Unlimited fund raiser. The trip consisted of an all-expense-paid week of landlock fishing at Grand Lake Stream. To this point the trip had been less than memorable.

Grand Lake Stream begins at Grand Lake Dam in a very large, long pool with big swirling eddies below the dam that smooth into a moderately fast flow. As is the case with most Maine streams, the flow is dependent on the setting of gates at the dam. The gates are set, not for the comfort of the stream fishermen, but to balance the water flow throughout the drainage. Changes are ordered by some guy many miles away whose sole purpose in life seems to be that of frustrating the best-planned fishing trips. Just when the fish are starting to cooperate that guy pulls the plug and drowns everything (fishermen included) in a flood or shuts the gates and dries up the place. It's rare indeed to strike a happy medium under his watchful eye.

Leaving the Dam Pool, the stream narrows down to a very fast run for about a quarter of a mile then swings into a wide, deep S-bend to enter the Hatchery Pool. And so it runs for three miles—Cable Pool. Big Falls, Campground Pool, the Meadow, Big Eddy, and the Bridge are some of the more popular landmarks. Throughout there are pockets of holding water awaiting the patient angler.

The stream finally winds its way into Big Lake. From the bridge at Betz's camps upstream three miles to the dam is fly-fishing only. Most fishermen seeking landlocks fish the lakes and do well. Masters, magicians, and masochists fish the stream. You see, the regulations also prohibit the use of weights, weighted flies, or weighted lines of any sort. When the guy controlling the gates is in a bad mood and the water is high the fishing can be very tough. The conservation officers are conscientious and can be very touchy about how a streamer lies in the water. One distraught fisherman was overheard trying to convince a skeptical warden that *all* standard streamer patterns made in Massachusetts weigh *at least* two ounces. As the conversation went on he talked less and less and the conservation officer talked more. One can only conclude that the officer won the debate.

Lodgings at Grand Lake Stream range from camping on up the scale to a stay at Willoughby's, where comfortable quarters are provided. Meals, too, are served. This is important because it's over 20 miles to the nearest fast-food place. The food at Willoughby's is good. It is served on a regular schedule and meals are announced by loudly ringing a bell to remind intent fishermen that it's time for them to eat—or go hungry until the next meal.

The folks in our story chose to stay at Gary Betz's camps on the lower end of the stream. The camps are warm, dry, and comfortable, if a bit rugged. Food, drink, and so on are up to the creativity of the occupants. This is great if your party is blessed with a gourmet chef but every meal can be a real adventure when the experience of the cooks is limited to turning on the coffee pot or starting the microwave oven. Early in the week Ro, whose turn it was to cook, proudly announced that he would prepare his reknowned broiled salmon for dinner. Things were going well at first but then smoke began to seep from the oven. He was unconcerned but the smoke finally got so bad that Bob couldn't stand it any more, threw open the kitchen windows and popped open the oven door. In the midst of the billowing smoke sat the remains of what had once been a box of pretzels. It was not part of the recipe. The quality of the salmon was not seriously affected but the group's confidence in amateur cooks took a nosedive. Ro's reputation as a cook will never be the same.

Let's digress for a moment to meet the six members of the party. Rich has been fly fishing for 40 years. He ties his own flies, builds his own rods, and will travel anywhere for a chance at trout or salmon. To the casual observer he is just another ordinary fisherman. Wearing his favorite green hat, flat on top; rimmed by its fleece headband adorned with decrepit remains of old, used flies; a fly vest that campaigned in the Big War and Red Ball Waders that always look two sizes too small he is anything but impressive. But put him hip-deep in a trout stream with fly rod in hand and he is transformed. He becomes one with the rod, laying out accurate casts effortlessly with no wasted motion, the consummate fly-casting technician. It was he who discovered Grand Lake Stream and Gary Betz's camps. He is the acknowledged leader of the pack and one of the two "guides" for the group.

Rich, unfortunately, has a problem. It seems when he goes on fishing trips he is beset by an inordinate amount of bad luck. More than once he has waited patiently in a cold line for hours at a boat livery only to be told just when he was next to be served "Sorry. No more boats!" He was aboard the night the generator died on a bluefishing boat just after dark, completely ruining the trip since no one could see to untangle lines or to unhook bluefish (a risky game even when the light is good). This trip to Maine turned out no better. Low-hole-card-wild and follow-the-queen are beyond his ken. He won only one poker hand in six nights.

Ro, our other "guide," had been to Grand Lake Stream twice before. The last time he and Rich had shared the frustration of high water (thanks to the guy on the gates) but learned to cope with it. On a miserable morning drenched by wind-driven rain he and his '"sparse" Black Ghost had done a number on landlocks in the Meadow Run. Ro has no favorite hat. He'll wear anything that comes to hand. His vest is faded, bulging with fly boxes, and he wades nowhere without his homemade "snake killer" of a wading staff. He, like Rich, ties his own flies and makes some rods but there the similarity ends. His casting skills are rudimentary at best and often erratic. Although he prefers the dry fly, he is often frustrated in his efforts. Rather than enticing rising fish, his talent lies in the ease with which he can put them down. He's a conservationist at heart—but not that devoted to the cause. Nonetheless, he stubbornly keeps trying. He and Rich make an unlikely pair but they are close friends and most enjoy fishing when it's done together.

"Ralphie" (not his name) was christened by "Jack" (not his name either). He is Ro's oldest son. He learned everything his dad had to teach him by the time he was 14. He will never give up when the fishing is poor; he just tries harder. And when fishing is good he won't quit because, after all, that's why he's there. He has developed a reputation as a fishing machine. He is in his early 20s, a mere child among the grey and greying but with one distinct advantage for a fisherman. He's still single! His equipment is basic; an inexpensive, well-worn vest, oft-patched waders, and a couple of banged-up fly boxes. In this, his first trip for landlocked salmon, he saw no reason to bring a trout net (who needs it?). He soon learned respect. What he lacks in fishing experience he more than makes up in intensity, determination, and tenacity. He also enjoys a good game of poker—the more wild cards, the better.

Bob, the fourth in the party, is the tallest of the bunch and has to be called the Quiet One although his low-key sense of humor belies the name. He, too, is an accomplished angler, perfectly at home with a fly rod and able to reach water his shorter companions can only admire wistfully from a distance. But Bob has another talent that is rare indeed. He finds things. Ralphie lost a borrowed trout net three times—Bob found it twice. (the third time it was recovered by an attractive young lady who was wet-wading downstream from Ralphie. There is some conjecture that he contrived to lose his net in that particular case.) Bob also found the boot chains that Jack lost in a mud hole. And, to top it all, he found a complete fly-fishing outfit that had been lost the previous week in deep water. His good luck also extends to the poker table. In the course of the week he won enough to pay for the fresh lobsters he took home. However, he is the only accomplished cook and, because he makes breakfast every morning, his ravages at the card table are tolerated.

And, last but never least, we meet Dick, an artist with fly-tying materials and fly rod alike. His equipment always looks as if it just arrived from L.L. Bean because of his meticulous care. He's easy to spot by his soft plaid hat with the patch of pheasant plumage stuck jauntily in the headband. In demeanor and behavior he is always the gentleman—except when playing poker. Then he becomes a sly, devious conniver—and frequently wins at it. But because he is accurate and completely trustworthy he also keeps track of the food and beverage (spelled b-e-e-r) account. He always carries the bare necessities in the line of fly-tying essentials even on an overnight trip. This time he brought a medium-sized suitcase with enough material to open a modest tackle shop. He just hates to be caught unprepared.

Dick had been to Grand Lake Stream once before but had fished only the lake and so was looking forward to see what the stream had to offer. He began with complete faith in the two "guides" but by the time the fourth day began his confidence as well as that of the others was beginning to wane.

"Jack," as we said before, won the free trip. He is a widely traveled, well-equipped, experienced fly fisherman who reads water like an open book. In the course of his travels he has accumulated a huge store of hilarious tales. His appearance on the stream is most notable for the fly box, only a bit smaller than a foot locker, hanging from his neck. It is equipped with every fly imaginable (and some unimaginable), a magnifying glass, a searchlight, and enough assorted tools to be able to repair a car in a pinch. Jack quickly won the hearts of the rest of the bunch with his openness and his boundless store of tales of the great outdoors. The first night in camp he held his audience spellbound with a story about a bear hunting expedition he had taken out of Patten, Maine, riding the "Bombardier" into the deep woods, being posted by a heap of bear sign, the two-gun fast-draw whiz who, while showing off his skill in the parking lot by breaking bottles thrown in the air, missed one that then landed on the windshield of his car and the hair-raising outlandish roar coming from the woods the night the pickup didn't arrive to take Jack back to camp. It was a side-splitting suspense story but unsuited to this particular episode.

Jack is not easy to shake up. The first night in camp, after the stories had all been told, he woke up in the dead of the night to find Rich standing next to his bed. Now Rich was looking for the bathroom and had lost his way in the dark. (There are no street lights or traffic in the backwoods.) Rich was about to relieve his need when Jack, now wide awake and not quite sure what kind of a group this was, politely inquired as to just what in hell he thought he was doing. The predictable exchange of comments included offers of glasses, observations as to the probable low I.Q. of the marauder, speculations as to lineage, and legitimacy, and entreaties to shut up and go back to bed. Jack, the unflappable, solved the problem finally, leading Rich by the hand to the facilities but, after reconsidering his own needs, entered himself, locked the door and left poor Rich shifting from one foot to the other to endure the scathing remarks from the rest of the party who were not at all sympathetic to his plight. Jack took the whole episode in stride but kept a club next to his bed for the rest of the trip.

The dawn of the fourth day brought nothing new. Just like every other day since they arrived the group scattered, each to his own preferred piece of water. As the morning became midday they began straggling back to camp to compare notes. It had been more of the same—one taken at Cable Pool, one at Richard's Run, zero at the Meadow and Big Eddy, one at the Bridge. It had become pretty clear that the fishing was not living up to the stories told by the two "guides." Nothing they had tried had really worked all that well. The inaction was beginning to wear on Ralphie. The long drive north from New Jersey had sharpened his fishing appetite to a keen edge. While the others had seen some action, he (still without a landing net) had yet to even "prick" his first fish. To him this was a personal affront. His frustration was seething below the surface. As the talk of plans for the afternoon began once more to sound just like the day before—and the day before that—the frustration erupted. "You guys do what you want" he exploded. "I'm heading out and I'm not coming back until I get a fish!" Jack, impressed by this show of determination, decided to join him and off they roared in Ralphie's Duster, heading toward the dam area, as yet unexplored.

When they returned a few hours later they were both grinning widely. Ralphie is suddenly interested in finding a landing net he might borrow. It seems that his first landlocked salmon showed him some moves that made a lasting impression. These were no docile hatchery-bred trout like those found back home. These were the fish you read about. They spent almost as much time in the air as in the water once hooked. As to landing them without a net—well, it's not easy.

The fishing had not been spectacular in the time they had been gone, but at the Dam Pool there were fish seen lying in shallow depressions on the bottom. The standard Ghost streamer patterns had evoked some responses but the best part was that two had taken dry flies. Now this was more like it! At least now there were some fish to be seen and worked over. A rustle of excitement spread through the camp, a few brief questions and mighty preparations began for an assault on the Dam Pool. The two "guides" were completely useless at this crucial time. Neither had fished the Dam Pool. They had no idea what to expect. They had paid no attention to the water-flow patterns or even where there were entry points into the water. So much for the "guide" service. You get what you pay for, right?

The meal that afternoon disappeared in moments. While the cleanup crew was busy, Ralphie and Dick whipped up a few Au Sable Wulffs. Ralphie had had some fun with that pattern so it seemed worthwhile to have a few extra. Just to be safe. Ro, the number two "guide," expressed the opinion that only a sparsely tied Black Ghost would be dependable while Rich argued in favor of the popular Gray Ghost. While the "experts" debated, the rest of us headed upstream where the contest would be joined.

The Dam Pool is big, about 200 feet across and about 150 yards long. This year, the center consisted of a gravel bar where the water was a bit above knee-deep. With only 1½ gates open, the main flow hit the bar off center so that the predominant current was along the right-hand side facing upstream. The back pressure formed a powerful eddy on each side, with the primary downstream currents directed along the banks on each side of the pool, the strongest along the right bank. Halfway down the pool the bottom gradually deepened until it became nearly hip-deep all across the pool. The lower part then gently eased into shoals leading into the fierce narrow chute that began the river's run to the lower lake.

The Dam Pool, on arrival, was already being fished by four anglers. One was working his way into the fast water at the lower end of the pool, heading downstream. Three others, closely grouped on the near shore, were working the stronger current along the bank. One was casting to an upwelling surge of the eddy on that side of the pool. He was another named the Quiet One. The other two were plying the downstream current itself. These three were buddies, all from the Boston area. One was called Red Sox Hat after his headwear. The other turned out to be a sometimes-disagreeable fellow so his name will not be recorded here. From time to time one would hook a fish, sometimes net one. Ralphie had chatted with them earlier. They had been working the same water all day and had landed a number of landlocks. It was quite obvious that they had staked out that part of the river and in-truders would not be welcome.

After surveying the situation the assault team from New Jersey chose to split up, Bob, Dick, and Jack heading across the dam to the far shore, Rich and Ro going for the lower third of the pool, and Ralphie, with the unbridled enthusiasm of youth, setting up shop on a spot downstream from the Boston Trio where overhanging trees, heavy shrubbery, and a fast right-to-left current dictated that lots of backhanded casting would be needed to successfully fish the area. (Talk about your masochist!) And, of course, true to form, he had a fish on before anyone else had made even one cast. (Does not tradition dictate that one must carefully study the water before starting to cast? He didn't! Just went ahead, shot out a Thunder Creek pattern and *bang!* Just like that!) And, to make matters worse, he loudly announced his success at great length and in intimate detail. He did nothing to endear himself further when, having broken off the first fish, he almost immediately nailed another that, true to the reputation of the species, at once became airborne and put on one of those spectacular aerial displays that is rarely if ever captured on film. Ralphie promptly shut up and paid full attention to his landlock that by now had caught the attention of everyone at the pool. It sent the Boston Trio fumbling in their fly boxes for something that worked.

Ro, noting Ralphie's success, tried the same casting technique farther downstream. His efforts were promptly rewarded by a strike—from a bush that leaped from its position on the bank to intercept his Black Ghost. The struggle was brief. Releasing the bush to fight again another day (a true sportsman), it was only minutes before he had another smashing take. This was a much larger, voracious tree that yielded to his offering. It was only a matter of moments before the leader parted. The tree had won again and it settled back into its normal feeding position to await another tidbit while Ro searched for another Black Ghost. Grumbling at the turn of events, Ro then chose to relocate across the main flow to an area where backcasts could be made freely without interference from the carniverous vegetation that proliferated along the bank. The change of position was made but not without a few anxious moments. The slippery, treacherous rocks along the bottom contrived to trip him up and, had he not had his trusty "snake killer," he would have taken an early bath.

In the meantime, Bob, Jack, and Dick were moving into working positions from the far shore. Jack chose to work the reverse current of a large eddy. The current swept across a clean gravel bottom then, close to the shore, picked up speed and raced back towards the dam. Jack's third cast nicked a fish that splashed once and threw his Grey Ghost.

Dick headed for the middle of the pool, laying out one cast after another, searching the mid-stream side of the flow being worked by the Boston trio and Ralphie. A flash now and then but no strikes. Maybe another pattern? A Grey ghost? And the pool yielded Dick's first landlock of the evening—a splashing streak of silver that measured 20 inches.

Bob chose to explore the downstream current along the far shore. Salmon could be seen finning but none was responsive. Only a few small brook trout found his offerings worthy of their attention. But the action so far showed that there were landlocks aplenty. It only remained to figure out what those perverse fish wanted.

Rich had quietly worked into position and, casting toward the bank, it was not long before he, too, was into a silver rocket with fins. Ro had succeeded in fooling a couple of small brook trout only slightly larger than his usual Black Ghost. But things were definitely picking up. And then it began.

A swirl. A dimple, A subdued splash. A hatch had begun and the landlocks were taking notice. The bugs were showing up in th lower half of the pool just below Ralphie's position. A brief, loud argument developed as to what was coming off. There was disagreement about the size and color of the insects as well as what pattern would be the logical match. Jack quieted the squabble by netting some. He announced that there were at least four different kinds and gave us all the correct Latin names. Ro, who speaks very little Latin, was not impressed. He only wanted to know what color they were and, when given the answer, mumbled to himself as he substituted a Royal Wulff for the Black Ghost that he usually plied with such confidence.

Rich, in the best match the hatch tradition, switched to a #14 Sulfur imitation and, with long easy casts, began to work along the bank below Ralphie. It wasn't long before he was busy with a salmon that liked the look of his fly. At about the same time Ralphie also connected, having switched to an Au Sable Wulff.

It may not be widely known that fishermen from New Jersey draw comfort from the proximity of their comrades. This strange phenomenon is most notable early in trout season when they gather around holes where trout have been released. It can also be observed in summer and fall when the fierce bluefish are running. Even when occupying separate boats, they yield to the need for companionship and cluster together so close that at times one might cross half a mile of open water without getting wet merely by stepping from boat to boat. When separated they fill this need by talking back and forth. If the distance is great, they shout to each other. And so it was that evening at the Dam Pool. With each new success, or more often, near miss, detailed instructions and guidance were freely given, complete with comments on the successful (lucky) or unsuccessful (clumsy) outcome. He who hooked a fish was at once the recipient of free lectures of how to "set the hook," "let him hook himself," "give him line to run," and "keep a tight line," all at the same time. It was no secret that these guys had read every book on fishing.

All this commotion drew the attention of the Boston trio. The unnamed one worked his way down past Ralphie while grumbling about people crowding him, then flipped his streamer toward the rising fish to which Rich was casting. Red Sox Hat had switched to a dry fly. In the excitement of the splashing strike he backed toward shore and in the process stumbled and nearly fell over a big rock. (He must have been working to develop that move because the next two nights at the same place he fell backward over the same rock, soaking his cigarettes each time. It is truly said that practice makes perfect. Each fall was more graceful than the last). By this time the rise was really going strong. Dick was beginning to get action on a White Wulff which Ro also quickly adopted. Ro has often called the White Wulff his "ultimate weapon." It is his preferred pattern as the sun goes down. It's the only one he can see. At this point came the unforgettable comment about "using a marshmallow." The "marshmallows" worked! They were irresistible and the Pool was coming alive!

Ding, ding, ding called the bell at Willoughby's. That's all. No second announcement. The Boston trio faced a no-win decision—to eat or fish. The unnamed one downstream made his choice. His streamer wasn't producing so he would eat. And, as he turned to look back from the water's edge, Rich, with a long smooth cast and a short float, was hooking a fat salmon in the spot he had just been standing. Rich smiled pleasantly and said "Thank you. That's a nice fish." And the Boston trio departed.

It was an evening never to be forgotten. Jack had eased his way down to be near Rich. He needed some help and, as Rich made another cast, Jack said "Hold my rod for a minute." As Rich took Jack's rod, his own bowed under the strike of a heavy salmon. In turning to face his fish, the fly on Jack's rod skittering across the water infuriated another silvery dynamo into smashing it. Two nice landlocks at the same time—one in each hand. That was too much for Jack. He grabbed his rod from the gleeful Rich, grumbling "Who do you think you are, King Neptune?" Rich was now seized by paroxysms of laughter so hard he lost his own fish. He wound up with a beet-red face, still doubled over but with neither fish to show for his effort.

Ro, by now, was taking and releasing fish after fish, happily announcing each new success. He made sure that Dick knew that the "marshmallow" was still working just fine. Dick, casting among tricky currents, was diligently educating the suddenly gullible landlocks in the penalties for mistaking man-made for natural insects. Obviously, there was no natural insect even remotely resembling the Wulffs, but they were devastating, even in smooth, relatively slow, water.

Bob, who had moved to the lower end of the pool, suddenly found himself attached to an insane fish. He had been taking landlocks on a light colored wet fly when he got a smashing strike and the fish headed straight for him. And right between his legs! Then went into frenzied jumps and runs. Bob is tall but the current where he stood was strong and the bottom was mostly rock. He cut a fancy figure, sort of a graceful Ichabod Crane, balancing on one leg, turning and holding that crazy salmon. Through it all he never lost his calm demeanor—until the landlock did it again! Back through the legs and headed downstream. The result was inevitable. The fish won. Rich loudly suggested that if Bob really meant to let the fish go he didn't have to show off. Everyone else managed to let fish go without all that dancing around. Besides, Bob could scare the fish by splashing around that way. Bob acknowledged the advice by throwing a rock in Rich's general direction. How touchy can a guy get?

As the hatch finally died and darkness crept into the pool a spinner fall began. The action never slowed for a moment. Jack, whose fly had become useless from heavy punishment, tried to put on a new one but in the poor light had trouble threading it onto the leader. Rich called an offer to help but as Jack started through the pool toward him Rich shouted "Wait! Stay right there!" His next cast fooled a chunky 20-inch landlock that had been feeding about three feet ahead of Jack. "OK. Come on over," came the call. "I've got him." As Jack got close Rich released his fish and cast once again, saying he'd be glad to tie on a new fly for Jack—*oops*—if Jack would just hold his rod and entertain the salmon who just inhaled the fly until he finished the job.

By now the Boston trio had returned. In the dimming light it was getting hard to identify flies. The banter about marshmallows caught the attention of the guy who remained unnamed. He first tried to learn what the potent pattern was by casting a streamer across the drifting line to drag it in for examination. Now that's really not fair! He should have asked. When that didn't work he finally called to Dick "What's a marshmallow?" Dick, always the gentleman, dictated a recipe for whipping up a bunch of marshmallows—the eating kind.

The trio resumed their former positions and began to try once more. The

Quiet One struck up a conversation with Ralphie while Ralphie was tying on a new Au Sable Wulff. Since this was a really sincere guy who was anxious to learn something new Ralphie gave him another of the same pattern. As expected, it worked and in the quieter center of the eddy he connected with his first landlock on a dry fly—ever. The current was powerful and so was the fish but eventually it was landed, a fat 21-inch bright silvery landlocked salmon as pretty as a picture.

One by one the elders gave up in the growing darkness. But not Ralphie. He vowed he could still see an image of the Wulff so he kept plugging away. It wasn't long, however, before the seemingly endless feeding activity slowed, sputtered and finally stopped. It was over.

The silence was overwhelming. A short time before the air was filled with banter but no longer. As they gathered at the cars the triumphant anglers were unusually subdued. Quietly comparing notes they discovered that no one had any idea of how many landlocks he had caught and released.Once under way the action had been so intense that time became meaningless. Each had been caught up in the excitement of subduing those marvelous acrobats. There must have been an incredible number of fish at the Dam Pool that evening.

Later, searching memories, no one could remember an evening like this one. There were other evenings at the same pool with the same guys and the fish again cooperating—but it was not quite the same. Only once was the chemistry just right. We have tried time and time again to repeat that evening without success. But it is impossible to go back. It can only be relived in the minds of those who were there. Even now, when the Marshmallow Gang gets together, the memories remain vivid and in the retelling and sharing, once again it comes alive.

How do you explain what makes a particular experience exceptional? Who knows? but when it happens to you, you know it! And it is this writer's wish that every angler should have at least one experience in his lifetime that matches that of the Marshmallow Gang one night on Grand Lake Stream way up north in Maine.

BEAT FOUR
Keith C. Russell

THE TOP-SECRET SECRETS—PART TWO: TROUT

Okay, fly flingers, the preliminaries were covered in Beat Two and we have now arrived at the main event between the two leading contenders in the world for the title of *The number one fish if I could fly fish for only one.* It's trout versus Atlantic salmon, ladies and gentlemen. Let the battle (in which there are only winners) begin! Here in this first pool of Beat Four I'll concentrate on trout, and will devote the initial portion of Beat Six to the sages of salmon.

First, we hear from pro John Gierach, author of *Fly Fishing the High Country* who (not surprisingly) is the one voter who chose the cutthroat trout in the high-country lakes of the western Rockies. John goes for a soft hackle Hare's Ear, #12 or #14, with a slow to medium-slow hand-twist retrieve and says that the speed and depth of the retrieve is more important most of the time than fly pattern. He enjoys "the romance of fishing for the native Rocky Mountain trout which, in many parts of the Rockies also involves long walks, gorgeous scenery, and solitude." John says timing can be crucial for cutts: time of year, of day, weather, water temp, and so on. They fit the way he likes to fly fish: light on hatch matching, heavy on figuring out the situation. "Cutts are especially pretty fish with lots of sub-species and crosses to ponder. Although they're not often of large size, big ones are around and they are really something."

Quite surprising to me, only two votes went to steelhead. I can only believe that not many people must be fly fishing for this fine game fish. One of the two semi-pros in the steelhead's corner is Bob Herbst, head honcho of Trout Unlimited, who has led that organization to its present premier position as *The* cold-water conservation group and who likes these great fish on the Umpqua River hanging onto his Wooly Bugger fly. The other is Lani Waller, West Coast field editor for *Fly Fisherman* magazine, who prefers British Columbia, a Silver Hilton fly, and a cross and downstream presentation with either a floating or sink-tip line, controlling the fly's speed by mending. Right on, Bob and Lani.

Only two votes were cast for the redoubtable brook trout, another surprise, this time by two professionals. Pro Norman Strung, associate editor of *Field & Stream*, prefers Quicksilver Creek in Montana and a Royal Wulff fished dry and upstream. Norm declares, "The place and the fish are simply beautiful, and the fly isn't bad looking either. While they never grow to record-book proportions, there are lots of them and I prefer action to wall mounts."

The second brookie fan is Edward (Ted) Williams, contributing editor for *Gray's Sporting Journal*, who likes 'em in the northeastern U.S. and believes a dark Cahill to be his number one choice. It "resembles many insects, floats well, and is easy to see." Thanks, guys. Let's hear it for the brookie!

We're moving up the ladder rapidly now, fly fishers, for next in line is that beautiful jumper, the rainbow trout, which earned 10 ballots from four experienced amateurs and six fine professionals.

Kicking off for the now ubiquitous rainbow, the bright fish of many colors, is Dennis G. Bitton, editor of *The Flyfisher*, the magazine of the Federation of Fly Fishers. His priority location is the lower Henry's Fork, and he likes a tan elk-hair caddis, fishing dry, of course, with a drag-free drift. Dennis reasons, "The rainbow does take dries; leaps high and frequently; and *he's there*." That last point strikes home!

Silvio Calabi, editor of *Rod & Reel* magazine, steps up next proclaiming his desire for fishing southwestern Alaskan streams with a hair mouse, which he says is akin to midsummer bass fishing: hit the banks and the coverts—twitch, twitch . . . *bang*! Silvio admits, "It's a tough choice, but one that combines many of my favorite elements: stream fishing, rainbow trout, top water flies, a visible strike, a reasonable number of large, wild fish, and, of course, the Alaskan experience, something I never grow tired of."

Professional amateur Arthur T. Frey, former president of The American Museum of Fly Fishing, stakes his claim for wild bows on the Rising River in northern California on Hare's Ear Nymphs (wet) and Parachutes (dry) presented slightly upstream on a long leader. Watercolorist and pro-am Francis (Frank) Golden (whose work puts you right there) votes for mountain streams, fishing an Adams in the early morning and in the evening, and a

Carpenter's Ant during the day, especially if it's a cloudy one. Ross P. Hauck of Ross Reels prefers rainbows "anywhere" on an Adams Irresistible fished one-quarter upstream with a natural float. "After 30 years, I still get a surge of adrenaline when a big 'bow strikes." Don't we all, Ross!

From England, we next hear from does-it-for-fun Lionel Leach, a good friend and peripatetic fly angler who has fished the world over and more than once. "Bulgie" strongly yens for the rainbows of Lake Yelcho in Patagonia using a Tom Thumb fished dry. He believes "even better results could be achieved by dapping." What say, you purists? L.L. goes on to add that "Yelcho is one of the most beautiful lakes in the world, surrounded by snow-capped glaciers; the fish take like sharks and the hotel is simple, clean, and comfortable."

Now on the rainbow stage is Eric Leiser, author of, most recently, *Stoneflies for the Angler*, who opts for the Delaware River and the Chuck Caddis (with a dirty-orange body) dry fly presented on a free float and allow the drag to sweep under. Eric opines, "For some reason (it may imitate a pupa on the sweep), this fly also works after the free float and it is swept under and has the full drag of the line . . . somewhat like a wet fly." Thanks much, Eric. Octogenarian and grand (but definitely not old) pro-am Elmer Lindseth next gets the call. A practical man from Cleveland, he selects the Castalia, Ohio, area; a Gray Weasel fished wet and often deep; and he unequivocally makes the point that, "If I could fish for only one, I would fish for what I can get nearby. Salmon and bonefish are a long way off and I enjoy them. But I seldom get to fish them!"

Fish and Wildlife Service expert Frank Richardson is equally specific. For him it's the Nantahala River, North Carolina, throwing a Yellow Dog/Green Drake imitation for a dead drift, across and upstream presentation. His story: "The Yellow Dog Fly is my own creation, named for the under-belly hair of a Yellow Lab used to dub the body to match the #8 green drakes that hatch in late May and early June. They last about a week on the Nantahala. Depending on water color, tippets range from 3X to 5X. Sometimes the fly is dressed on a #8 or #10. When these flies are on the water on Nantahala, it's 'gulper' time. The big bows forget about security. There are no gentle rises. The trout lose all their table manners. The hatch will continue into darkness."

Last, but never least, we have the professional Adams specialist, pro Ed Van Put, who never (well, almost) uses or even thinks of anything else. Ed's in love with the Delaware River and a #14 Adams and advises, "Fish dry directly across or opposite fish, place the fly two feet upstream of it, and try to show the fish only the fly—no leader. Rainbows give you everything they have; quickly; every ounce of energy gets used up with leaps and long runs. They tire sooner than browns or smallmouth but are more spectacular! The Delaware is a very large trout stream with a wild rainbow population which the size of the river allows to make runs that put you into backing; even 14-inch fish. Each season I have a few take all the line and backing. These are not monster fish but 17- to 20 inch rainbows with room to show their stuff. When fish are rising I put on an Adams. I find it is all I need. If I use anything else, it is because I want to, not because I think it is necessary to catch fish." Atta boy, Ed. Presentation's the thing, eh?

Browns, you're up, front and center with 15 cheering supporters wildly applauding—including 10 pros, count 'em, and 5 ams. Let's go, team.

The lead-off brown hitter is Gary Borger, author of several fly-fishing books and Midwest field editor of *Fly Fisherman,* who singles out New Zealand as his prime brown lair and tied on, a Gold Ribbed Hare's Ear Nymph (in N.Z.). Further, he declares, "It is a one-on-one situation. Each fish must be located in the crystal-clear water and then carefully stalked. They are very wild. They are also very large; the small ones are three pounds. The country is lovely and unspoiled, and the rivers are reminders of what we had and lost in this country." Well said, Gary.

Chris Child, Fish and Game Frontiers pro, also strikes a blow for New Zealand browns—on Stony Creek in the Nelson area of South Island—using a #12 Royal Humpy presented directly upstream to visible trout. Interestingly, Chris states, "The fish take a dry so slowly that you have to say 'God Save the Queen' before setting the hook." Pro-Am Bob Colson roots for the browns of Michigan's classic Au Sable on the drag-free float of a dry Brown Drake Dun. Bob loves "the softness of the weather during the brown-drake hatch and the thrill of a good fish during daylight hours."

Dave Engerbretson, Western editor of *Fly Fisherman* magazine, urges the browns of Western spring creeks on an Engerbretson beetle fished dry, on or in the surface film. "This fishing is very challenging," according to Dave, "and requires good technique to be successful." He also likes the environment in which it is done. I second the motion, Dave! Next on center stage is Dick Finlay, contributing editor for *Rod & Reel* magazine, who goes for Battenkill River (Vermont) browns with a Red Quill fished dry up *and* cross and down with a dead drift. Dick declares, "This fly fishing is always available and consistently unpredictable."

Brown trout advocate, conservationist and author of the foreword of this book, Gardner Grant, comes on strong for the storied Beaverkill River using a Chuck Caddis (woodchuck wing) or the Henryville Special dry fly in a dead drift or with a slight twitch upstream when fished downstream. Gardner avows, "The wild brown is the most challenging for the fly fisher for trout; the Beaverkill has great charm as well as an important place in the history of American fly fishing, and the Henryville and its hairwing counterpart work very well, in various sizes, throughout the season on the Beaverkill and other streams with a good caddis population." (*Editor's note*: I'll vouch for that.)

George A. Griffith, one of the founding fathers of Trout Unlimited, votes for browns in Michigan and Montana with a Griffith Gnat in #14 to #18 and Werts Fancy in #8 to #12. George vouchsafes after "working with professionals for many years, I found out that should a brook, a rainbow, and a brown trout all be confined to a holding box in a stream, the brook dies first, then the rainbow, and the brown would be active for a time after that. The brown also seems to feed more on dry flies than the others and can stand higher water temperatures as well." Go get 'em, George.

Gary LaFontaine, fly-fishing author (*Challenge of the Trout*) and purveyor of outdoor books (the Book Cellar), has a strong affection for the browns of Clark Fork River, Deer Lodge, Montana, along with the fly, he says, to catch 'em: a Brown and Yellow Emergent Sparkle Pupa which rides semi-dry on the surface in a dead-drift upstream presentation. Gary states, "The common consensus is that brown trout are smarter than other trout species, but that is debatable. True, they are harder to catch, but it's not intelligence that protects them. My feeling, from a lot of time spent sprawled on my belly next to trout streams watching them, is that they are warier, more easily frightened, then other trout. They accept a lot less commotion. That's why I like them. They make me fish patiently, carefully. There is no rush and bluster around them—they won't tolerate it. When I slow down, putting more thought into each individual presentation, involving my self totally with a particular fish, the world around me slows down, too. For me brown trout are a relaxing experience." Nicely put, Gary!

Rancher Walt Lineberger continues the parade of brown-trout fans, opting for Western Montana and a #14 or #16 Goddard Caddis which he touts "as an excellent floater and attractor." Walt should know. Agreeing with him on fish and location is John Merwin, former editor of *Rod & Reel* and executive director of the American Museum of Fly Fishing, who prefers a dry #12 to #14 Red Quill fished quartering across either up- or downstream.

The well-known Perkins (Orvis) fly-fishing duo, pros both, Leigh and Romi, are next on tap to report (in alphabetical order to stay out of trouble). Leigh says, "Browns get the call on any flat water from the Missouri to the Battenkill. The one fly which I have enjoyed most is a Trico Thorax, #20 to #24, fishing the spinner fall. Anticipation is my reason because often one is casting constantly to rising fish, knowing that when the cast is accurate, timing is perfect, and the artificial appeals, there will be a hook-up." For Romi it's still browns but on a different continent: South America—Argentina, to be specific; the Caliefu River, to be even more specific. The fly: Panceira. The presentation is classic wet: at an angle, across and downstream. She philosophizes, "It's not flashy, but it's soul-satisfying to have a big brown take—no jumping, just the strength and nobility of the fish."

Dick Pobst, pro fly-fishing writer and Orvis dealer, puts in his oar for browns on Michigan's classic Au Sable and, at last, a vote for the well-known (*Hexagenia limbata*), the giant Michigan mayfly. Dick recommends a dead drift at about 11 p.m., which he says produces the best fish. Pete Van Gytenbeek, past president of the fine Federation of Fly Fishers, opts for browns "in the Rockies on a Light Spruce fly." and Charles F. Waterman, prolific fishing and hunting author, submits his choice for browns on Montana spring creeks with a Light Cahill.

Finally, there are those souls who simply admire *all trout* so very much that they are unable to single out just one species. So, so be it. Here is their communication on the subject at hand, from 11 outstanding fly fishers—four pro-ams and seven professionals.

Pro-am and traditionalist Charlie Farran first takes the stand and testifies in behalf of the Madison River and/or northern Quebec using a Royal

Coachman. (It always surprises me how many fishers do their thing around the world and when it comes time to select their favorite, opt for local waters). Art Flick, bless him and may God rest his soul, who will be known forever for his *Streamside Guide*, voted for trout in his beloved Catskills, and for his own Gray Fox Variant fished dry, as most efficacious. He explained his choice of fly by saying, "Because through trial, I have found it effective if tied properly."

At this point, Michael Fong, pro fly-fishing writer, marks another ballot for New Zealand trout and on a Royal Coachman. He reasons that '"New Zealand offers the discriminating angler uncrowded waters of many different types to accommodate sight fishing."

West Coast pro fly fisher and casting instructor Mel Krieger lists his preferred trout location as being a 200-mile radius of West Yellowstone, Montana. (*Editor's note*: Mel's circle—Mecca—probably, in the overall, contains the best trout fishing in the world.) He goes on to single out an A.P. Nymph on a floating line but it is, as he cautions, "the most efficient producer, not my favorite fly or methodology. An important distinction! The dry fly is my favorite presentation." Mel closes with a heart-of-the-matter comment: "The trout offers the most varied challenges—from the chess game of the selective trout through the poppers so popular for bass to the giant streamers that are usually associated with sailfish and tarpon, and on and on and on!"

That philosopher of fly fishing and sporting-book publisher, Nick Lyons, narrows everything down to the Madison River, a Jay-Dave Hopper, a "smash-it-down" presentation (honest) and exciting rises, big fish!" It's all there and in an economy of words. And now pro-amateur Mike Owen steps up to the mike with his declaration for the Rocky Mountains and a Gold-Ribbed Hare's Ear fished upstream, dead drift.

Datus Proper, author of *What the Trout Said*, boils it all down to "wild trout of any species, on the river nearest to where I am, on an imitation of the fly that's hatching or falling, and presented in the way of whatever the natural is doing." Datus explains that, "While this may not fit easily into the format, it is the only honest answer I can give." Of course, Datus. All fishermen are honest!

My very good friend, "professional" amateur fly fisherman, full-time conservationist in his retirement, fan and friend of Art Flick and now, like Art, deceased, John W. Rockwood, again like Art, was a fan of the Gray Fox Variant. John said, "The G.F.V. has taken all species of trout for me all over the U.S."

Former editor of the American Museum of Fly Fishing magazine, fly-fishing writer and historian Paul Schullery favors all trout species, especially in the Rocky Mountains. He uses different flies at different times and doesn't have a favorite.

Ken Schultz, associate fishing editor of *Field & Stream*, is also brief and definite in his opinions: "Stream trout, Catskill rivers, Adams fly, standard presentation, for the aesthetics, challenge, setting, etc." Okay, Ken. And bringing up the rear (only because his last name begins with W) is book publisher Charles Walther, who echoes Schultz's thoughts except to substitute Ant for Adams.

And there you have it, the case for trout. A very strong case, I think you will agree; a case in fact, which would be very hard to surpass. Well, we'll see soon because the supporters of the Atlantic salmon, sometimes referred to as the King of Fishes and the Fish of Kings, will get their day in court some pages hence, when we arrive at my final Beat.

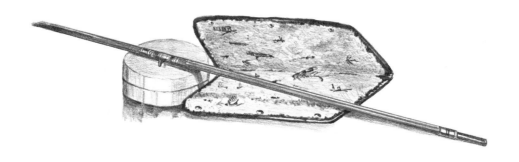

Strengir Is a Lady

Perhaps born at the time of the earth's creation itself, or at least quite likely in the distant past, Strengir is one of those oddities of the earth's crust. Located in the "land of fire and ice" in southwestern Iceland, in the river called Grimsa, "Strengir," which is Icelandic for "ledges," is a stretch on the River Grimsa which contains a deep, narrow crack of unknown depth in the river bottom continuing for several hundred yards.

Atlantic salmon, returning to the river of their birth on their annual spawning run, find this crack to be a secure and, thus, desirable resting and hiding place from predators, including those with only two legs—enlightened individuals armed with a fly rod from all over the planet who seek *Salmo salar*.

Strengir, as befitting a member of the female gender, has many moods. Most people, casual observers that they are, think of her as a rough and tumble sort. However, having been her close companion on a goodly number of "dates," I feel at least marginally qualified to report on her propensities and, as a result, wish to file the minority opinion. The fact is my experience has been that Strengir, like so many ladies, responds quite kindly when treated with friendship and respect. More: over the years Strengir has been good to me. So many others have been heard to say, sometimes to me, "That Strengir is the toughest beat on Grimsa; I don't like to fish it. I seldom get fish on that beat. If there are any at all, Strengir fish stay deep and don't take." Or words to that effect. And then occasionally they add, "Keith, how do you do it? You always seem to take fish on Strengir."

OK. I admit it. You have found me out. Strengir and I do have a little something going. Have for some time. You might call it a special relationship. An attachment, an affection for each other. Answer me this: How many times have you fished Strengir when the wind was blowing a gale upriver straight into your face? And you can't throw a fly 10 feet. Too many times you say. And so you cussed her out? Right? I knew it. And that's no way to treat a lady. The right and proper thing to do is to be nice to her. You know, try a little tenderness. Talk sweet. That's right, talk to Lady Strengir, as a friend. As a lover. And just maybe she'll respond.

She sure responds to me. In all modesty. I'm not much of a lady's man, but, Lordy, how that girl does come on. *Hooooeeee!* But you can't get over confident. Don't let down even for a second. Just keep on treating her good. As for instance, this past July on Grimsa.

That week Strengir and I had been getting along really super fine. I hadn't failed to take one or more Atlantic on every turn. No, you guessed wrong, the weather had been lousy. Heavy wind in your face, cold, rain, cloud cover and low water. But Strengir had been radiant and giving. In wonderful humor. So I was not surprised by a heavy take in Pool #3. We both went to work like a couple of wrestlers. Heavy-weight division.

With the fish on the reel and headed downstream, I knew I had to move fast. Between the twin dangers of the ledges and bowling ball-sized rocks plus no staff, I quickly admitted to needing navigational help in the form of my great ghillie, Diddi, who managed to help keep me upright for the first 100 yards. This salmon was not only big but also a *fighter.* Not all the big ones are. It looked like his square tail measured at least a foot from top to bottom and we got a good look at it as well as the rest of him several times during the battle as I had him up to within a very few feet of the leader twice.

But he sure wouldn't and didn't quit. No bull dogging it either for this senor. He just kept on moving, pulling, twisting, jumping, jerking, turning, in our give-no-quarter tug of war. And downstream we both continued. In between praying and hustling, I thought of Gardner Grant's brief bout the day before in Strengir's Pool #2 with a magnificent fish of possibly 30 pounds. Or more. If anyone should know, Gardner should. His fish, after a short get-acquainted period with the steel, took off upstream, ran out all line and backing, and may still be going for all Gardner knows. He is still shaking his head.

Now I have to admit that my Moby Dick was not that large. Actually I'm forced to do so inasmuch as guide Diddi and rod sharer, John Wheeler, were present. Diddi, a good weight estimater (guesser), flatly stated, '"In the mid-dle to high 20s." I would settle for that. In truth I would have settled for whatever, because as it turned out, I did not have the good fortune (read skill) to land that Strengir-Grimsa monster. I did play him hard. I tried my utmost to give no quarter. I was definitely on the attack, on the offensive, very aggressively giving the leaper my best shot.

But it wasn't good enough. I wasn't equal to the challenge of the biggest Atlantic to which I have ever put the steel. The fish was on for 15 to 20 minutes, maybe a little longer. I thought I was beginning to get a little control. I had had him up pretty close to the leader a couple of times al-though I knew he was still green at the time. My rod in a U, I continued to push him hard palming the reel and frequently using finger pressure against the line and rod. Then it happened. One minute he was on, thrashing wildly about on the surface, throwing spray in a wide circle; the next minute he was off. Gone. Kaput. Terminado! The battle was over. The best man won on a knockout in the tenth round. Winner and still champion!

I knew it was all over the very second it took place. But I couldn't believe it. I didn't comprehend. I was numb, in a daze, in shock. Automatically I reeled in. The fly was gone; the leader broken a very few inches above the fly. When I could think, I could only think—what happened? What *had* happened? When reality returned and Diddi and I tried to analyze what had taken place, it all resolved down to one of two possibilities. The first, and perhaps most likely, was that I had come onto the fish too strong and that in the process had, inadvertently when the fish was wheeling and dealing about, either suddenly palmed the reel too hard or put too much finger pressure on the line, and thus caused the 10-pound leader to snap at its weakest point or, as a second possibility, there was an unknown wind knot in the leader at the point of the break which, indeed, I have been known to incur, and, under heavy pressure from the movement of the fish, it provoked the leader to give way. In either case the result was still the same.

So Strengir, my dear, apparently I must have in some way unknown to me, offended you and for that I apologize. Most humbly. I hope you will, in charity, forgive me and that we can, next year, resume our well-disposed amity and regard for one another. Until then!

In any event, with respect to the 20 or so minutes that *Salmo salar* was attached to the end of my fly line, as the line goes in that fine, old song, "They can't take that away from me!" Thank you, Strengir.

Acres of Bonefish

To go from the Alberta Clipper to the Caribbean Express requires only 2½ hours. From—10° to 80°. From night to day. From white to black to technicolor. If you've lived in the northern United States, you know what I mean, and you know it's true. That fact that it can be done is what keeps you going. The act of doing saves your sanity and, like chicken soup, doctors the old bod.

Actually I like snow. When it's fresh and so white it hurts your eyes. The world looks so squeaky clean and virginal it sort of makes you feel good all over. But then after a month or more of driving your rear-wheel drive car over slippery roads and not ever seeing the sun while the temperature never goes above 20° day or night, and that's farenheit, it's no wonder that to a Yankee in mid-winter there is most definitely nothing like the bennies, make that with a capital B, to put life back into both body and soul. The Bennies being the beneficial rays of old Sol. Nothing, that is, unless to a fly fisherman it might be bonefish on the flats, acres of bonefish, bonefish absolutely everywhere, just waiting to eat your fly. Better yet put the two together, B & B, Bennies and Bonefish, along with shining flats, rum punches and plenty of succulent seafood to fill in the cracks and let's go. Thirty-four or 64, it's later than you think.

So it's goodbye Alberta Clipper with all your ice and snow and wind chill, and hello Caribbean Express with your pee wee planes, consistently undependable schedule, bone-tired pilots and beautiful Bahama Island destinations. Take us to the land of Peace and Plenty, so aptly named by its first settler for its lovely quiet and cornucopia of blue-green water and fertile coral soil supporting an abundance of fruits, vegetables, palm trees, and other verdant growth. The Peace and Plenty Hotel in Georgetown on Great Exuma Island in the southern Bahamas was our headquarters for five days of bonefishing, the most unusual likes of which, particularly on two occasions, resulted in never to be forgotten memories.

Forget for now the picture perfect, cloudless, blue, blue, sky, the tropical temperature, balmy breezes and beautiful, nubile, bikini-clad lovelies lazing about the pools and beaches. Yes, they were all there, present and accounted for: the standard travel agency brochure blandishments that attract the winter-weary the world over to more southern, beneficent climes. But forget all that nonsense and let's get down to the real business at hand: fly fishing for old Mr. Bone.

On Great Exuma, the guides and their boats and equipment are not fancy like those found in the Florida Keys, but they make up for some of that lack by their intimate knowledge of the waters, the fish therein and their behavior. The bonefish boats are not high-tech specialty fishing machines with magnum outboards capable of 60-plus mph. Rather they are mostly Boston Whalers or whaler-types powered by maybe 25 or 35 h.p. trolling motors and you can't get onto a lot of desirable flats because the water's too thin and the boat's too "thick." So? So you get out among 'em and wade and sometimes you can get a lot closer to the Gray Ghost this way than you can in a boat, and have easier casts, too. I like to wade!

The push poles are mostly a more or less straight tree branch stripped of its bark or perhaps a long two-inch by two-inch piece of lumber, not a designer pole of the latest plastic. The guides' feet are bare and not housed in state-of-the-art, non-skid, bottomsiders and there is no poling platform other than the boat itself. Yes, and sometimes, the accent and language of these black Bahamians can be a little difficult to understand. But not to worry, not to worry. They're not perfect, (who is?) and some are better than others but, by and large, they get the job done and that's what counts and all anyone should ask. You'll start understanding your guide better soon and make a new friend, too, and all that is a big part of fishing. But on to the other part. The part we all like best.

Of my two unique experiences bonefishing the Exuma flats, fittingly one took place the first day, the other on th last. Guide Clifford Dean was my man for Day One. He was an affable, gregarious sort who liked to talk with both you and the fish. Have you ever noticed that some fishermen and some guides have a habit of talking to the fish as in this case: "Good mornin', Mr. Bonefish, and how are you this day? Have you had your breakfast yet?

Where are you, Mr. Bone? Ain't it a nice day, nice and warm, and I 'spect you hungry. Cum thisaway so I can see you. Oh, there you are—I done see you now. Cum over here, Mr. Bone, we got somethin' good for you to eat. Cum' on, cum closer and we give it to you. Nice, Mr. Bone. Cum, Mr. Bone."

Early on that first morning we saw some fish but got no casts. About 10 a.m. Clifford seemed to come to a major decision. "OK, now we go to my secret hidey hole." I could hardly wait to get there and to see it. What it turned out to be was disappointing: a small bay or cove, perhaps a quarter mile across the entrance and the same distance into a small beach. Brother Dean cut the motor and scanned the area slowly and carefully obviously looking for something in particular. I wondered what it might be for we were in fairly deep water here, not the kind to wade or pole for the Silver Fox. Apparently sighting his objective he started the motor and we moseyed in a little farther toward the beach; my gaze followed his pointing finger.

At first it appeared only as a surface disturbance covering a circle of maybe 50 to a 100 feet in diameter, perhaps a feeding school of small bait fish, but somehow not quite. Then came the absolutely incredible revelation and realization. Have you ever seen a group of hatchery trout swimming as one around and around against a current of water being piped into a circular holding tank or pool? *But these were bonefish on the surface and in deep, open water!* I couldn't believe my eyes. Here were wild, wary bonefish by the hundreds, probably thousand's all swimming in clockwise fashion not only on the surface but as deep as we could see, crowded closely together just like hatchery trout and almost as tame, within 50 feet of our boat. Incomprehensible. Clifford had no explanation. I have none. They weren't feeding. There was nothing to feed on. They weren't spawning. They did move off if we got too close and sometimes when we didn't, too. We also sighted another school which we later observed moving around in the bay nearer the beach but still not in shallow water.

The fish were not all that hungry although I did succeed in interesting eight of them to take a brown, snapping shrimp fly. Sizewise estimated, they ranged from 2½ or three pounds to maybe eight. The ones I netted and released were all in the four to five-pound category. Neat, but not gaudy and, of course, a ton of fun. What a happy and fascinating time it was to witness and be a part of, what I can only now describe as a freak of nature. In this regard I would surely welcome and, in fact, invite those readers who have seen this same phenomenon or who have ideas relative to same to contact me at P.O. Box 101, Gates Mills, OH 44040. I also must report that one well-known Keys guide with whom I have spoken about this behavior, believes that the area is simply home for these bonefish and that they are just behaving accordingly. Could be.

On Day Last it was my pleasant fortune to have with me as my guide, Will Rolle, one of many, many members of the family Rolle after which a settlement on the island has been named, what else, but Rolletown. There is hardly a business on Great Exuma in which at least one Rolle family member is not involved. Will was a dandy. Anatomically speaking, he could eat an apple through a picket fence and was therefore recognizable by his toothy smile. A big, taciturn man Will really knew his onions, or rather his bone-fish, and other fish as well.

Early on that final day he filleted a small bonefish which I had seduced with one of Lee Wulff's famous Candy flies, threaded a sizable hook through one of the slabs, tied it on the end of a spinning line and flipped it to a monstrous and hungry five to six-foot cruising barracuda. The fish promptly took it without ceremony and equally promptly exploded in a boil which would do credit to a small tuna. It then proceeded to run all the line off the spinning reel, popped the mono, and continued on his way. And Will never even said "darn." As I stated earlier he was taciturn and apparently used to such a turn in events. Will was OK.

About mid-morning we motored and poled onto a new flat that was some-thing to behold. The water here was quite thin and Will's whaler-type just couldn't cut it all the way, but this flat was special in that it extended in three directions for miles and miles and, also, because it had a white sand bottom with almost no vegetation, and we had a bright sun behind us in a clear blue sky. We could see forever.

Then it happened again, to me a minor miracle. In the distance and com-ing our way were bonefish, schools and schools of beautiful bones, thousands on thousands of silver bullets whose shadows were black on the light colored bottom. This humongous flat was literally covered with bones as far as the eye could see and our visibility was as good as it can ever get for such creatures.

They would move off when my fly or our boat got a little too close for their comfort but for only a few feet and then would soon again be up right next to the boat. Once more their performance was, for me, wondrous. But they almost were impossible to seduce. I must have dragged a fly ahead of several hundred bonefish, changing flies frequently, marveling constantly and all the while talking to those fish with but three accounted for before quitting time. These were somewhat smaller fish than those found in Clifford Dean's "Hidey Hole" but when they did take their performance was second to none. Those bonefish had to have been very well fed for they were most indifferent to my offerings and we finally quit just to watch the show. And show it was, another first, with acres, and acres, and acres of bonefish in all directions, more than I had ever seen before all put together, to be enjoyed and caught, too, if you were good enough. I was happy for my hard won three but just think what if they had all been hungry. A Guiness book record for the number of fish netted would surely have resulted. I know I will never see as many bones in one area at one time again. I thought I had seen mucho bonefish in the Yucatan at Boca Paila and other hot spots as well but nothing like this. Nothing like this.

So it was back to the Alberta Clipper. Back to the real world of the northern United States where winter holds sway, stronger and longer than sometimes seems fair. As to B & B, that's more my style and I know where to find them.God willing I shall return. Soonest!

Henik Lake

Henik. When I first heard the word, it sounded like the Russian female of a species. Not so. Henik Lake was the scene of our 1981 Angling, Wining and Tittering Expedition to the area. The "area" is a recently discovered lake trout, arctic grayling, and arctic char fishing mecca, in Canada's Northwest Territories, almost a thousand miles north of Winnipeg and only a few miles south of the Arctic Circle.

I'll admit I was a little tentative about the trip. Our tour director, my great and good friend, Lee Bassett, was by way of becoming noted for the singular lack of fishing success experienced on the last several piscatorial adventures he had led. The fact that they had been definite social triumphs was, however, at least some solace. We would have super fun (make that wizard fun, I'm weary of the word super) no matter what. The presence of Sally and Bill Searle, Pringle and Ed Boyd, Pete and Bill Rose guaranteed that, along with Martie, Lee's wife and mine, Margie.

It was arranged through Dana Cole of Grand Domaine Retreats for our group to take over the entire Henik Lake camp the last week of July. (Ice out doesn't occur until early July.) Unfortunately we would be there a week or two too soon for the arctic char to have made their way into the rivers from their long winter in Hudson Bay. I just chalked that up against Lee as part of the pattern. After all, those giant lakers on the surface and those hot-to-trot grayling should prove to be sufficient. And they were and they did. In all justice, Lee said it was the only week we could get the whole camp and I guess he was telling the truth.

The master plan called for everyone to meet in Winnipeg where we would spend the night; then, early the next morning a chartered DC3 was to fly us almost due north for seven hours to a dirt strip at Henik Lake. A piece of cake, and it was. What awaited, however, was not, at least as far as the girls were concerned.

The door of the DC3 opened wide and we all couldn't wait to get out, to stretch our legs after the long flight, and to see just wat-in-ell we had gotten ourselves into for the next week. We found out in a hurry. As the first paleface exited the plane the attack began. It was not to end until the plane's door closed a week later. Our forces sustained 100 percent casualties and while it may not have exactly been World War III, it will do until the real thing comes along.

The operative word was bugs, insects, varmints, *bugs*! Headnets and closed pants cuffs became a way of life, as did deer flies, black flies, and mosquitos *and* repellents, preferably Muskol and Shoo Bug jackets *and* assorted bite and itch relievers. We learned to cope!

Our next surprise evened the score. The food was marvelous. As a matter of fact, for fishing camp fare in the boonies, it was gourmet, thanks to good management by our hosts, Carl and Marcia Moore, and a damn fine college girl cook who took pride and pleasure in her work.

So much for starters. The preliminaries were accounted for. We were ready for the main event: big lakers on top with grayling an attractive diversion plus options of fly-outs for both or using the camp guides and their power boats to fish the closer hot spots. Actually this turned out not always to be ours to choose inasmuch as weather was the final determinant.

At this point it can be said, the following week's fishing can be summed up in one word, superb, in both quantity and quality. We fooled a ton of lake trout, the largest one weighed 27 pounds, releasing all of them except a few we ate for lunch and even fewer which were scheduled for taxidermy. The grayling were a little more elusive but we got our share of these beautiful fish, too. The fly-outs were very interesting and very productive but then so was the fishing nearer the camp. The guides and equipment ranged from fair to good, in other words, typical.

Therefore, let it be recorded that a blast was had by all, a dynamite time. Indeed the expedition's title of angling, wining, and tittering proved as apt as anything could be, just as we knew it would.

Additionally, there are a couple of other matters I would like to mention. First is the table quality of lake trout. If I say that to my mind and palate they run Atlantic salmon a very close second, I am sure you get the idea.

Their pink, sweet meat was *soooo* good I never did get enough and when smoked, well, it was like you had died and gone to heaven. Simply fantastic.

Second is some comments about my own fishing experiences. The wives, except for my Margie, all fished and, in at least two instances out of the four other couples, out fished their husbands. No names of course. They know who they are and the men are already embarrassed enough and probably couldn't be more pleased. Margie did accompany me daily nonetheless as she usually does and I would here and now like to pay her tribute. She has seen more parts of the world than most while with me on fishing and hunting trips and we have her beautiful needlepoint work to prove it. In angling language Margie's definitely a keeper.

As it happened our Henik group mostly fished with hardware and they took more and bigger trout, which is understandable and OK. The Searles alternated between fly tackle and metal. Old Keith, stubborn soul that I am, went with flies all the way. Using a new Orvis Powerflex boron and graphite rod for eight-weight line, which proved just right for the constant wind conditions, I had myself a really wizard time. It didn't take long early in the week to realize that the most fun to be had was not to fish from a boat in Henik Lake, or one of its satellites because of the wind and, particularly, because the trout were down just a little and casting a sinking line all day can get tiresome in a hurry.

Rather, wading around the points of land, as well as on the bars and reefs, was more productive. My best of a great many fish was a 10-pound trout that went for a black marabou muddler skated on the surface. These fish took me well into the backing on numerous occasions, did their fighting on the surface and generally hung tough all around. Having read a number of mixed reviews on the battling abilities of lake trout, I should like to take the stand in their behalf and testify that taken in thin water, lakers need not take a back seat to any species.

From the foregoing it shouldn't be all that difficult to understand why our week at Henik Lake was a honey. Of course the outstanding fishing made it so. Plus the facilities, the food, the staff, the people who made up our group, and living seven straight days in blue sky and sunshine in an area consisting only of land and water and wind and some bent over 150-year-old, eight-foot-high pine trees.

Not too shabby!

Random Thoughts While Stalking Bonefish at Deep Water Cay

What is it that the Bahamians and others actually do to a bonefish in preparing it for cooking and eating, such as "stretching" it?

A much better and more accurate name for Deep Water Cay would be "Flats Unlimited"—200 square miles of beautiful bonefish habitat!

Why is it that on some days (few) no matter whether your cast is perfect, or lands with a fat plop 10 feet in back of the fish, Mr. Bone goes for the fly like there was no tomorrow?

And why is it that on other days (many) no matter how quiet you are, how careful of your boat and distance from the fish, the color of your clothing and, of course, your fly line, your crouching profile, and finally your cast, if you get to make one (naturally without any false casting whatsoever), Mr. Bone spooks every time, like there were a million tomorrows?

Are very large bonefish wise to have grown so big and old, avoiding fishermen's flies, baits, and nets, or are they just plain lucky never to have been confronted by same?

Are bonefish, pound for pound, as some say, the sportiest, gamest fish that swims? And why don't they *ever* jump?

The low, slanting rays of early morning and late afternoon sun, no matter how bright, seldom seem to provide as good visibility through the water as when the sun is higher, *n'est-ce pas?*

Just how important is it to know the sink rate of your fly?

Which is more important for a successful hook-up, the size, pattern, and color of your fly or its presentation?

I still get a kick out of spotting Boney before my guide.

I have never met a professional bonefish guide I didn't like or learn something from.

It seems to be a law that most casts to bonefish be upwind throws, or at best, quartering against? And with the breeze about 15 to 20!!

Another law I have observed is that on a partly cloudy day, the sun seems to be shining brightly mostly during those periods of time spent traveling from one flat to another.

Did you ever stop to think that a bonefish flat is just about the only good kind of flat there is, as opposed to flat broke, flat chested, flat feet, and flat tires?

Bonefish are almost completely unpredictable, and that is what makes bonefishing. Put another way—the more I bonefish, the less I sometimes think I know about them, and the more I admire them.

At Deep Water Cay you can always find a good flat with a good tide.

Why is it that one day you may get a hundred casts at bonefish, while the very next day, with exactly the same weather conditions, you get none?

A word to the wise—would it be a good idea to belittle bonefish and bonefishing at every opportunity, lest the word get around too far and too fast about what a good thing we are onto?

Saltwater fishing licenses should be required of all American saltwater anglers, with the proceeds put to work for the benefit of our sport through research, habitat improvement, and so on.

A bonefish is too valuable to get caught only once! Catch and release!

I'm told that on some days, a passing motorboat, 50 feet away, will not flush a bonefish, while on others, it will spook a fish from 200 yards. Why?

A bonefish is a bonefish is a bonefish. What more could anyone ask?

The "grey ghost of the flats" is a perfect description.

Someday I must try my hand at poling a boat and do some self-guiding.

I learned a new super knot today from Carl Navarre, which he calls a double nail knot—it is tied without using a nail. It is simple (very necessary for me), fast, and has many applications, such as connecting a tippet to a leader butt (what I used it for this morning). Thanks, Carl.

Is it possible that bonefishing, like alcoholism and gambling, can become a disease? If so, what a way to go!

Á la Kenny Knudsen, "Hubba, hubba, Mr. Bonefish *Jaws*, look out, cause here we come"!

How to Find Out Fast Who Are Your Really Close Friends

This story simply has to be told, for it is much too good not to share. No doubt there are those fly fishermen, hard-core cynics, who will claim it to be apocryphal. However, it is most definitely not only the truth but truth that hurt.

There lives in Minnesota an avid Atlantic-salmon fisherman, who does also pursue other fish on occasion. Our story begins one mid-summer afternoon when said fisherman, whom we shall call B. to protect the guilty, was asked by his wife to bring out to their cottage on Lake S. about 15 or so miles from town, an assortment of cocktail goodies and groceries to be consumed at a dinner party they were giving that evening at which his mother and father-in-law would be in attendance as well as a few other relatives and a small group of friends. The day was hot and humid and our hero realized, soon after he had made his purchases and was driving out to the cottage, that it was rapidly becoming a real necessity he relieve himself at an early opportunity. However, B. arrived at the cottage in good shape, deposited his

179

purchases in the kitchen, and then, being hot and sweaty from the trip on this very warm day, decided he would take a cooling plunge in the lake only a few feet from their cottage. So thinking, he jumped out of his business suit, into a pair of swimming trunks, and dove into the water for a refreshing swim.

It was at this juncture that his bladder reminded him he still hadn't taken care of a very important matter. B. also remembered that for many years he had cautioned his children and grandchildren about using the lake as a bathroom; that it was a bad thing to do and they should never do it. However, he realized, too, that perhaps he was going to have to rise above that particular constraint since he didn't seem to have any other choice at this particular time, but he did at least bow to the amenities by swimming out another few yards before the performance.

Arriving at his objective distance from the shore, he unzipped his swim trunks and took out his appendage ready to fire away. But no sooner had he done so than it felt like sticking a finger into an electric outlet. It was a great shock in a most sensitive area and he knew immediately that something important had happened to him. What, he knew not. In any event, all thoughts of relief having vanished, he immediately swam back to shore at flank speed to see what damage had been done, ran into the cottage and apprised his wife of what had taken place. At first her natural reaction was "You've got to be kidding. I don't believe it." But upon displaying three red streaks on his tally-whacker, she did indeed accept it. Then the question became one of what to do about it. Certainly it would be an embarrassment to go to his doctor with such a problem and such a story so they finally decided on self-treatment. And that was that, at least temporarily, because they had this dinner party rapidly approaching and had to get ready for it!

In any case, the dinner party came off rather well but in some manner, during the liquid refreshments, it was "leaked" that our great and good friend had received an injury that afternoon in a quite embarrassing location and what a distinct shock and surprise it was. His father-in-law was perhaps one of the more dubious listeners present and, of course, there were numerous snide remarks made by his collected friends about what had taken place. Perhaps one of the better comments was made by one of his sisters-in-law who rather dryly remarked that the damage must have been occasioned by a smallmouth bass, to which our hero's wife immediately took violent objection and stated emphatically, *"It was not!"*

Over the course of time, as such things will, the news got around even to the point of including a local TV commentary. How that was handled I don't know but I wish I had had the opportunity to see and hear it. As a result B. became something of a celebrity and received telephone calls and mail from coast to coast along with numerous comments about how, in a situation like that, you find out in a hurry who are your really close friends. In time the scratches healed without infection and our new folk hero recovered nicely. He has been enjoying his Atlantic salmon fishing and other activities with full vim and vigor, and, according to his wife, with no noticeable after effects! Meantime, over the years the story has become well-known throughout the local community and B. is indeed regarded as someone very special, or perhaps there is a better word describing his status.

In any event, the whole affair does prove up one point with respect to fishing, or I suppose you could honestly refer to what occurred as fly fishing or perhaps fly trolling, and that is you just never know what you may catch when fishing, or fly fishing, or fly trolling!

BEAT FIVE

John Russell Woods

John is quite the Renaissance man. He also is a Canadian, which no doubt gives him an advantage in the fishing and hunting department. It's a lead he has never relinquished. Quebec City, Quebec, Canada.

The Magic Rod

Father often said that Atlantic salmon fishing was very unpredictable and always full of surprises, both good and bad! After 25 years of lurching about after *Salmo salar* in some 17 different rivers I have found no reason to take issue with him.

By way of preamble, I should say that my family has had a long history of salmon fishing. My great grandfather for instance was, as far as I can determine, notable for only two things, his poetry (published privately for his friends) and the 52-pounder he hauled out of the Bonaventure at the turn of the century. My father was a great fisherman and loved the rivers, especially the Grand Cascapedia. Brother Shirley is not only a superb fly fisherman and author, but the best fly tier (amateur or profesional) that I have ever seen. (I say this, of course, totally without prejudice and with complete detachment!)

Having established the rough parameters of my piscatorial lineage, I will now try and describe my most memorable foray after salmon and also how

185

Lady Luck will sometimes ride along with you in your canoe when you least expect it.

My fly fishing really did not get into high gear until I left the Army in 1954. For the next six or seven years the most I could manage (due to the twin constraints of funds and time) was trout fishing. In 1961, however, Brother Shirley finally got me down to the Gaspé and from then on I had an acute and chronic case of salmon fever. Thankfully, the fever has not abated one whit over the years. This seems incredible, because for the next five years I had a grand total catch of exactly two grilse, which were taken on the lovely Upsalquitch River on one evening. To illustrate just how bad things were, I believe it was 1965 when I was fortunate enough to be given two weeks back to back on the Matapedia and the Kedgwick and I never had a single rise!

By 1966, although outwardly enthusiastic among my colleagues, in my secret heart I was certainly beginning to wonder if: a) there really were any salmon in the rivers, and b) if one would ever affix itself to the end of my line! Very, very few fish were getting up the rivers and pretty well everybody felt that we were seeing the end of our sport. I well remember that wonderful fisherman and author Dana Lamb ruminating about the decline and saying with great feeling that my grandchildren would probably never experience the thrill of taking an Atlantic salmon. Nets and the high-seas fishery were really cleaning up.

Preparing to set off once again on our then annual pilgrimage to the Matapedia River was always an exciting time. Tackle checked again and again, lines cleaned and greased, little brother generously filling the gaps in our fly boxes, and many calls to our guides asking about the condition of the river, catch so far, and so on. All familiar, I know, to my fellow "brothers of the angle." By now, of course, I was becoming very blase—Dame Fortune had not deigned to smile upon me so far and I was almost ready to admit that perhaps barbot fishing on the Ottawa River was more my line of work. However, as the grand old Ocean Limited snaked around the hills of the beautiful Matapedia at breakfast time we all anxiously scanned the river and hope once more sprung eternal!

Met at the station by our guides, we lost no time in stowing our gear in the Restigouche Hotel and starting up river in a modest convoy of pick-up trucks.

My guide was George Fitzgerald. George was somewhere in his seventies and his trademark was a white pith helmet, heavily varnished to the point of being almost bullet-proof. He would hunch down in the stern of the canoe and if the sport whacked him with his fly on a low cast, George suffered no ill effects whatsoever. A warm, though somewhat taciturn man, George taught me all the basics of salmon fishing, and we shared many happy hours together over the years.

Our pool the first morning was "Angus," and we flogged it diligently, without success, as usual! Fishing a wet fly on large seemingly endless pools can become very tiresome if one convinces oneself that there are simply no fish in residence. As an aside, I do not feel that fishing "blind" with a wet fly requires an inordinate amount of skill. If the unseen fish takes he hooks himself and provided the sport doesn't upset the canoe, or throw away his rod, the angler will normally bring him to net. The sun having reached its zenith, we hauled up the killick, and went for lunch.

After lunch my companions, General Roger Rowley (after whom the famous Roger's Fancy fly is named), Brother Shirley, and I took a stroll around the village. Passing Monsieur Lapointe's sporting goods store I noticed a lovely eight-foot four-inch Orvis cane rod, which I had recalled seeing in the show window the year before. On impulse, I walked in and after a great deal of palaver purchased said rod at a substantial discount as Monsieur Lapointe obviously wanted it out of the way. Rigging it up for the evening's fishing I confidently announced to one and all that this was my Magic Rod and tonight I would kill my first salmon. As they both desperately wanted me to "connect," their response was both predictable and effusive.

Back in Angus that evening I covered the pool from top to bottom—not a sausage. Coming on to 7 o'clock, with the sun now behind the hills and with about 20 yards of good water left before me, I decided to fish very carefully. On my second cast I damn near lost my new rod! A 20-pound cock fish nailed my Rusty Rat and took off in a spectacular series of jumps, eight of them as I remember (though, whoever forgets the details of his first salmon?). Twenty-five minutes later George put him in the bag and I had officially "arrived." Much rejoicing that night at the hotel and numerous trips to the icehouse to show off my fish to everyone that would come and look at it!

The next morning was beautiful, sunny, cool, and just a light breeze. We had drawn "Jim's Rock," and started our endeavors just above the rock for which the pool is named. On my third cast a fish took—not like his cousin of the night before, as all I felt were several jerks, much like a trout. I turned to George and said that I thought I was into a sea trout, George replied, "No sir, I believe it's a small salmon." Suddenly my line went smartly out into the pool at a 45° angle and then the fish took its first jump; when we saw what we had we *both* nearly fell out of the canoe! Forty-five minutes later we had a fresh-run hen fish that weighed in at 36 pounds! (This subsequently proved to be the largest fish taken in the river that year.) Home we went and more trips to the icehouse to see the "Monster Salmon." A distinct change was now taking place in my companions' attitude, the General and Shirley had obviously been praying for me, but hardly to this extent. Enough was definitely enough. It was now their turn to take fish. That afternoon, flushed with the euphoria of success, I gave my pool to the General and swaggered about the village receiving the accolades of the locals and the congratulations of the odd envious fisherman.

Next morning my luck was still holding firm and a 22-pounder again in Angus was added to my bag. Things were becoming somewhat tense now and lunch was a rather subdued affair. The only outburst came from my brother when a sport announced that he had had a rise in Mirror Pool that morning. Shirley muttered that he (pointing his fork at me) would take the goddamn thing out that evening!

Our last evening and Mirror Pool was mine. A lovely pool with a glassy surface but with a fair current beneath. We fished down to the tail of the pool with perhaps one drop left, when a doe came out onto the beach and stood quietly inspecting us. The sun had now slid beneath the hills, swallows were swooping and darting over the water, and the silence which arrives with sunset had descended upon the river. "George, I'm going to cast toward that lady on the shore." "Go ahead, sir, there's good water left." As my Rusty Rat (always stay with a winner) swung around the bow of the canoe, we both saw a huge boil of water! After the fly had completed its swing, I reeled in about six inches of line and sat down for a smoke. The stillness of the evening, coupled with the sudden excitement, reduced our conversation to whispers. "OK sir, try him again." I rose and cast once more. This time the fish was all business. He moved fast, taking the fly six feet away from his lie. Two giant leaps, then tearing around the glassy pool, more jumps with George screaming "Oh, you beauty!" again and again! (Whether he was referring to me or the fish I will never know.) Into the net, and 26 pounds of bright salmon wrapped in ferns graced the bottom of our canoe.

Suffice to say that my triumphant return was greeted with strained congratulations and outright disbelief—four fish for me and none for my collegues. The situation had been reversed for so many years that I was not feeling any remorse whatsoever, knowing that they were far better anglers than I. Simply the luck of the draw as they say.

A lot of water has rippled past my waders since those memorable two days. Many blank days, but they were all good days. My Magic Rod has been refinished twice by the maker, and despite the arrival of graphite and boron, it is still my hands-down favorite.

Though, I wonder whether the taking and landing of my son Jamie's first salmon (then age 13), with this same rod was not a bigger thrill for me than what I have just described?

You all know, don't you?

Charles Farran

An advertising man, fly fisherman, hunter, golfer, traveler to 41 countries, and, at the time of this writing, about to fish the Orinoco River in Venezuela.(Take me with you, Charlie.) Shaker Heights, Ohio.

Traveler

O the gallant fishers life
It is the best of any!

'Tis full of pleasure, void of strife,
And 'tis beloved of many.
—Izaak Walton

My indoctrination into the art of the fly rod was in the late 1940s by Harry Grinton, also a Cleveland advertising man. I was middle aged. Harry was about 10 years older and had been taught by his father, a Methodist minister, on eastern New York trout streams. Harry was a true expert, dropping a Cahill on the water as gently as if wafted there by the evening breeze. My first lesson lasted only a few minutes. After getting a dozen knots in my leader and losing two flies in the trees behind us, Harry impatiently gave up. Later on, we fished together in dozens of fishing camps in the United States and Canada and I learned much from the old pro.

Thirty years ago or so we used to go to Skytop in the Poconos. This is primarily a golfing resort, a lovely course with mountains for a backdrop. There was also a typical eastern trout stream running along the edge of the property, a branch, I believe of the Brodhead. Harry and I would get up before breakfast and fish its tumbling waters, coming back with enough eight to 12-inch trout in our creels for breakfast for our small group.

This was my first experience in fishing away from my home base, the Rockwell Springs Trout Club at Castalia, Ohio. This is a real beauty spot with its meandering stream surrounded by giant weeping willows and huge elms on the grassy banks. Fed by cold-water artesian wells, the stream has been home to a fishing club for more than a hundred years.

At Rockwell, I like to rise with the dawn as the mist hangs over the stream and cast a tiny black fly, perhaps an ant or a midge tied on a nine-foot 7X leader, with a #20 hook. The birds are starting their morning rounds. I am all alone. This is when fishing is best.

Quebec

Harry Grinton talked me into going on a trouting expedition to Belle Rivere in Laurentide Park, Quebec. It's a long drive from Cleveland. I believe we had two carloads of fishermen. The pavement ended a few miles out of Quebec City so we had to struggle through mud and ruts for another 50 or 60 miles. We made it by late morning so we agreed to take canoes and lunch and eat after fishing the river. I don't think any of us had fished here in the north country before so we were pretty excited. We walked the banks leaving our food near the canoes. I spent my time tying on new flies after being hung up in the trees or the high grass behind. After an uneventful hour we decided to go back and cook lunch near the stream. But where was lunch? Finally one guide who thought he knew English said, "Ze bear!" Sure enough, as we searched we found a can of peaches neatly punctured by big, round teeth. We located a frying pan a hundred yards away. Here and there bread wrappers. No sign of the bacon, that indispensable of French Canadian cooking. A knapsack was torn to shreds. We found nothing usable so we headed for the cottage where we were to live for six days. So went my introduction to fly fishing in the wild and as the days passed I learned a little about fly casting and even caught fish.

In later years we fished four or five different camps in the park, all of them excellent at the time. Park management furnished a cook and the food. Some of my friends ate fish three times every day!

On another visit we were staying at Gordon Blair's St. Lawrence Fishing Club in Quebec near the Labrador border. To get to this camp we flew from Cleveland to Toronto to Quebec, and then to Sept. Isles. Next a puddle jumper to Mingan, a long-abandoned World War II air base, which Gordon had leased and turned into a small hotel for his arriving and departing fishing guests. Mingan sits on the bank of the St. Lawrence, a village colorful but desolate, with practically no trees or shrubs. The small boxlike houses are painted in bright red, blues, greens, and combinations thereof.

Sept. Isles is the terminus of the railroad running north to the Frontier

Fishing Lodge. At the end of the long stream of ore cars was a lone coach which accommodated workmen going to the mines and occasional fishermen. That camp burned down a few years later, the result of an altercation between the woman owner and the head guide. Ask not for details.

Blair had fishing rights to some 100,000 acres of land and water with no inhabitants and no access except by air. He had two Norseman pontoon planes, known as "trucks of the north." They ferried in both supplies and men. A Norseman is noisy, smelly, and rough riding, but safe. Sometimes there were no seats, but for the pilot and co-pilot, except we never had a co-pilot! As long as there is a puddle of water the pilot can set it down.

It was while fishing out of this base camp that Doc Bryan and I had an idea one evening. We had learned that there was a shallow area in the St. L. less than half a mile from camp where you could always catch fish. They were mostly small brookies, but there were also some ouananiche. So after dinner we set out. No guide was needed for this spot. Our objective was to catch 60 fish in 60 minutes and throw them all back. As soon as we released a fish we made another cast. We didn't quite reach our goal but we did bring in 59 fish in the alloted time.

Another day we came in with two beautiful fish of about three pounds each neither of which we could identify. They looked like trout and yet they didn't. One of the guides at camp said they were splake, a cross between a speckled trout and a lake trout. It was new to us.

A hint of morning blushed the eastern horizon as we headed out on a long boat ride one morning to where we caught big Quebec "reds." We were fishing at the foot of a high waterfall, dropping long streamers with a *kerplonk* in the foaming water. We landed fish up to 5½ pounds which for a brookie is *big*. Unfortunately, they don't jump like rainbows but they can fight, and do. It is always a thrill when one of the big boys is netted. The colors are so beautiful. The flesh of many is red but often it is white. The taste is the same. We never found out the reason for the difference in color.

This is gorgeous country. Water everywhere. Hills everywhere. Pines and birch predominate. From the air there seems to be much more water than land. And while lakes abound, much of the water is slow-moving rivers. Rivers with misty falls make ideal spots for casting into the swirling water. Most of the fishing is from a small boat with outboard motor. Along some rocky shorelines we would get out and cast from land. There is very little wading possible.

The camp manager was a delightful guy who was called a Newfie by the French Canadians, meaning that his forebears came from Newfoundland. There are a number of "Newfies" in the area who had settled there many, many years ago, before I believe the French arrived. We had French guides following in the traditions of those famous ones who guided Lewis and Clark across the country. At one of Gordon's outpost camps, all reached by air, we caught our first glimpse of the earliest satellite streaking across the sky. We stood entranced. The sight was as startling as the aurora borealis seen in these northern latitudes. These "northern lights" would encompass the entire sky. Shimmering bands and streamers of red, yellow, and green moved across the sky. Some reached out like fingers poking at clouds. It was awesome. We were at about 52° North latitude where we saw this majestic coloration of the heavens.

Trout we caught aplenty. Caribou were common sights. Bear were there too. At times the guide would slap a paddle on the water to frighten a huge bull caribou, antlers held high, away from our boat. The trout ran big. Five and six-pounders were not unusual. Once when my wife, Irma, was there she flew with a guide to a "secret" spot. Why secret when no one could get there anyway without a plane? They caught sizeable black-caped trout which I had never heard of before.

Sometimes the fog would come in thick and smoky and the manager or head guide would get on the squawk box to home base to see if the plane could get through. In five or six trips to the area, each of a week's duration, we never saw another human outside of our own group.

Michigan

Some springs, we headed to Michigan for the early trout season driving up Route 27 to Grayling or Gaylord. Grayling was named after the fish which were plentiful in this area until the early 1900s. By 1935 they were extinct. Often it was quite cold in those early days of April. Crawford County has its roots in Michigan's lusty days of the lumberjacks. More than two dozen lakes and 600 miles of streams abound in the area—waters from which many record fish have been taken. There we saw the famous Kirtland Warbler in the Hatwick State Pines Park. There, too, are some of the tallest pines in all of the state.

On several occasions we rented a cabin for a week on the North Branch of the Au Sable and enjoyed some of the most delightful wading I ever experienced. The stream is wide and shallow, seldom knee-deep. Casting is easy and often you can throw a fly as far as you wish or can, with no chance of getting hung up in overhanging branches. There are few big trout here but it is a picture-book stream for sure.

On one outing we had four men in one car. We were fishing the Pigeon and Harry had found a favorite fishful spot. After lunch we let him out at a bridge and promised to pick him up at five o'clock. We drove away and found pools of hungry trout. At five we returned to find an unhappy, disgruntled, and soaking wet Harry. When climbing down the steep bank to get into the stream he had slipped and fallen into the water over the tops of his waders. On a lonely back road, miles from town, miles from us, he had to fish for three or four hours in soaking wet, cold clothes. Oh, the joys of fishing.

Wisconsin

Wisconsin was another area to which we returned year after year. Wautoma, in the center of the state, was our objective. We would fly to Chicago where "Parky" Parkinson, another advertising man, would meet us and immediately head north. Parky had a cottage a couple of miles outside of Wautoma. It was fairly new, well-built and most comfortable. Once I was anxious to fish a stretch of stream where I had been lucky the year before so, as soon as we arrived, I put on my waders, fishing hat, checked my flies, net, and assorted paraphenalia. I even stuck an extra reel in my pocket. One of the boys agreed to drop me off at my glory hole and promised to pick me up in three hours. The streams in Wisconsin were mostly deep cut through woods and farms. No place for more than one fisherman. The spot was about four miles from the cottage and two miles from town. As I waved the car away, I suddenly realized I had no fishing rod! Gadzooks or words to that effect! I had no choice but to walk to town in my waders. Ever try walking a couple of miles on a hot summer day in heavy rubber waders? And mine were *heavy*. I have big feet. In town, I found the local taxi to take me out to the cottage. I was disgusted, chagrined, and humiliated. And did the boys ever rib me! They never forgot the ardent fisherman without a rod.

Another memory of those days was when Parky caught a record-sized trout. What a beautiful rainbow; the largest I had ever seen. We were about ready to head for home when he decided he wanted this fish mounted. He went to see his friend the bartender at "Smokey's Bar and Grill" (also our post office address while in Wautoma) and asked him to put the fish in the freezer for a couple of weeks. "Glad to," said Smokey. When Parky returned a few weeks later for his fish it was handed to him in two pieces, neatly sawed in half! "It was too big to fit in the freezer," said Smokey, accommodatingly.

Colorado

When we disembarked at the airport in Denver, our expectations were high. We rented a car and set out for our first stop, Colorado Springs, one of my boyhood homes. Our old house on Pike's Peak Avenue was no more. But the view was the same. If you look straight west down the avenue, there in all its majesty is the famous mountain. We decided to drive to the top. What scenery! Spectacular to say the least. And here in early summer trees were full-leafed and flowers bloomed in profusion. How different from Cleveland, Pittsburgh, and Detroit where those in our party lived. But we were on our way to the fabled Gunnison. Six couples of us were staying at a fishing camp near the junction of the Slate and Gunnison rivers. Purple peaks rose all around us. The river rushed gurgling through a gully to the west. We caught a lot of nice trout but nothing spectacular. But everywhere we looked was a picture post card view of snow-capped mountains.

One day we watched a rodeo near town and visited a store that sold Western goods. John Taylor fell in love with a handsome silver belt buckle. The price was $50, a lot of money in those days. He happened to have six or eight trout rods with him on this trip so he came to me and said, "Charlie, I'll sell you my Paul Young handmade bamboo rod for $50." I said, "It's a deal." John still has the belt buckle after all these years and I still have the Paul Young rod, which is now a collector's piece.

We drove back through the Rockies, stopping at historic Leadville where the longest bar in town is punctured with bullet holes. We crossed the Continental Divide and saw men in business suits get out of cars, put on fishing clothes and start casting in rushing streams along the highway. And so, on to Denver and our homeward-bound plane.

Montana

Another time we headed for Ennis, Montana to a camp located by our mentor, Harry. Here, on the banks of the Madison, not far from Yellowstone, you get the real feel of the West. Lots of big horn, elk, mule deer, bear. In the clear air you see animals grazing on the hillside half a mile away. And lots of fish, too, brooks, rainbows, and cutthroats.

Here you truly fish in peace, far from the traffic turmoil and raucous city sounds. It is hard to know all the beauty of this land of ours but the silent fly fisherman feels akin to it as he walks over a ridge, with waders squeaking, and comes to that cold, clear, meandering mountain stream that seems to follow the sunset. As the stream burbles a little, so, too, the overhanging branches caress the current and all's right with the world.

One day the manager took four of us in a truck and drove west several miles to his "secret spot." Here we were fishing for cutthroats and I remember that each of us caught at least one. I have a 24-incher mounted on the wall of my library, a lovely fish and memory as well. I'll always have a great fondness for the Madison and Montana.

Ireland

We landed at Shannon, rented the usual car and headed south through Limerick. At Adair, we had heard there was a delightful old inn and castle nearby. And, oh, 'twas true, 'twas true. A most gracious inn, the Dunraven Arms had about 10 or 12 bedrooms and, across the street, cottages with thatched roofs. The manor house or castle, a huge, gray stone structure, was occupied by the owner, Lord Dunraven, and his wife, who lived in one small wing. The rest was open to the public—for a few shillings you could see the treasures of the past. His Lordship had about three miles of lovely trout stream on his property. This was the River Maigue. And what a joy it was to fish. You could cast from the bank or wade if you chose and had waders. It was mostly fast-running water, which harbored some fast hungry trout. I got acquainted with the gamekeeper who showed me the best spots to fish. On one side of the river there was a large herd of healthy cows. You had to watch out for fresh cow pats as you worked your way along the bank.

On one visit to the Emerald Isle our son, Robin, was along. We went northward along the coast through Galway and came to the town of Clifden. Here for a dollar a day we joined the local fishing club. We were casting in a brackish saltwater bay. We caught fish but didn't know what they were. Dark and all of one color. Two to three-pounders. Then we headed up the coast to Westport where we heard great talk of trout fishing some 30 miles away.

Our reservation was for Ashford Castle. It was all it was cracked up to be. You drive in through a gorgeous green golf course with one of the traps in the shape of a shamrock. The castle was a delight with huge gardens. If you picture your dream castle as huge, set among the tallest of trees, with turrets, gardens, and flower beds, this is it. At its feet lies the lake, filled with trout. It's a sizeable lake, four or five miles long, and this was the day of the annual fishing tournament. The entrants were all ghillies it seemed. Perhaps "gentlemen" did not compete for prizes.

We did fish the lower stream draining the lake the next day but not very successfully. But about those Irish fly fishing rods. No 6½ or seven-footers here. I didn't measure but, my guess was, they were 10 to 12-feet long at least.

On our first journey to Ireland, I had made arrangements to meet a second or third cousin of mine who had two portraits of one of our mutual ancestors and his wife. He wasn't interested in the paintings but was very much interested in a fishing camp on the River Shannon. The upshot was that we made a deal. I bought the portraits and he bought the fishing camp and we both lived happily ever after. He showed me his fishing rods. They were one-piece, heavy, and 10-feet long. Designed, I think, for dapping. No, thank you.

Bahamas

My first bonefish was caught in Bimini. In those days there were only two hotels on the island. One, the Angler's Roost, which wasn't much and another which was less. The climate was superb, bright sunny days with clear skies. You have to learn how to catch bonefish. It was not easy for me. They had many great guides, most of them black as a coal shovel. He would tell you when, and where, to cast but I did not find it easy. Finally, I caught my first, a puny little thing that was probably half blind. Years later we also fished at Cat Cay in its heyday. That was when the original owner and developer, a Chicago advertising man by the name of Samples, was still running the island. It was a fairyland with a golf course, skeet range, casino, boat docks, and restaurants for the handful of members and their guests.

Some of the best bonefishing I have ever had was on the southern tip of Eleuthera Island. There we found huge schools of fish perhaps, 200 or 300, and a skillful cast ahead of the school was often effective. It was here, too, that we learned that the natives ate the boney bonefish. They asked for the larger ones to take home and bake.

Mexico

There's good bonefishing, too, in Mexico. We found it in Quintana Roo, opposite the island of Cozumel. You fly from Miami to Cozumel, then take a local plane, which now lands right at the camp. Here they have most attractive cottages, round, with thatched roofs, a fine restaurant and bar, and a lovely sand beach sheltered by waving palms. The nearest bonefish flat is only about a quarter of a mile away. You can fish from a boat or get out and wade the shallow water. While the camp is really in jungle country, it is no longer that isolated. There is a dirt road coming down the coast from the north, up Cancun way.We saw several cars and also fishermen from another camp, at Boca Paila a mile or so away. The flats were huge, probably several miles across in each direction, and dotted with small islands. There did not seem to be other fish present except an occasional barracuda, which had come in from the Atlantic. This was a good camp, about 12 miles south of the ruins at

Tulum, where we landed the first time we visited the area. No record fish but plenty of hits and no one was ever skunked.

Belize

Farther down the coastline is the city and country of Belize, which we visited on several excursions. Just off the coast is the 175-mile-long Barrier Reef, second in size only to the great Australian reef. This beautiful coral formation offers excitement for fishing enthusiasts and skin divers alike. The Turneffe Island Lodge is a famous fishing camp which has been there for years. The bonefish flats are hard-bottomed shallow strips about 150 yards wide, located between the living reef and the island shoreline. Camp literature states, "The flats contain one of the largest concentrations of bonefish in the world. . . ." When we were there, an extremely strong offshore wind blew all week long. The Lodge record for bone at that time was 14 pounds. It didn't matter, for no one at the camp landed a bonefish that whole week. We finally gave up and fished for grouper, snapper, and so on. We never found out whether the recommended 200 yards of line on a fly reel was enough.

On another trip to Belize we fished out of the Fort George Hotel in Belize City. Just about half a mile out but still inside the reef was a rocky flat loaded with bonefish. The water was rough but it seemed that every cast was hit by a voracious bone. There was a slight problem. There were as many barracuda in that seething water as bonefish. Usually all you brought in was the head. But the action was unbelievable. The cudas would hit a 24-inch bonefish and all you would bring in would be a four-inch-long head.

Costa Rica

Costa Rica is famous for its jungle country and its fishing camps. Here is where the howler monkeys fill the trees along with snakes, three-toed sloths, huge iguanas, and ocelots, which you won't see. The jungle also holds parrots, parakeets, macaws, and toucans, to name a few. At one camp there was a tame toucan that would sit on your lap and beg for peanuts.

This is the home of the snook and the tarpon. Snook up to 30 pounds and tarpon as tall as a man. Most fishermen use heavy tackle, except when fishing for the machaca, a leaping gamester that runs four to eight pounds or the guapote which fights like a largemouth bass. When we were at Parismina, Stu Apte was there also. He was out to catch a record tarpon on a fly which I'm told he did. But then he is one of the world's great fishermen—not an ordinary mortal.

In December, 1984, at the Rio Colorado Lodge near the Nicaraguan border, George Irwin and I tried for snook. We had a problem. There had been heavy rains in the mountains and the rivers were the color of melted Hershey bars. Two young men from Cape Coral were also guests, and among the four rod cases they lugged along were two containing fly rods. We sized them up as decent fishermen but they cast and cast with nary a hit. Their objective, they said, was to catch the world record snook on four-pound-test line. The second morning George and I came in with three nice snook. "Where did you catch them?" they asked. We answered we caught them in the canal. Right after lunch we headed back to this same spot where the water was clearer and there were our new friends with spinning rods. Which just proves that in fishing, as in most ventures, it helps to be adaptable.

The entire excursion was not very productive as far as fishing was concerned but we had a great time. I have never been out fishing when I did not have fun.

Peru

On a recent trip to Peru we stayed at a jungle camp about 40 miles downstream from Iquitos. And a couple of hundred yards from the banks of the Amazon. In front of the porch was a stream about 30 feet wide. I had seen an Indian guide fishing and asked what he was fishing for. He answered, "Piranha." I asked if I could fish with him and did.

In half an hour we had four voracious piranhas, perhaps seven or eight inches long and beautifully colored with red bellies. I said, "What do you do with them"? "We eat them for breakfast." Usually it's the piranha that eats the man.

> The marlin is a mighty fish,
> Big as any you could wish.
> He'll fight until your arms give out.
> I think I'd rather catch a trout.

And so end Charlie's tails.

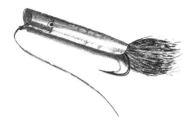

William C. Garrett

A fisherman who admits to enjoying baiting a hook, casting a plug and trolling for whatever, Bill cherishes most those hours spent fly fishing. As he will tell you, "To stalk and successfully hook a wild trout with a fly, in my mind, is the ultimate thrill!" Chagrin Falls, Ohio.

The Rocky Saugeen

I suspect that my love for fly fishing and the outdoors was spawned in 1930 when as a young lad I spent a summer on the Rocky Saugeen. This magnificent little stream, of which probably very few fly fishers have ever heard, flows into the South Saugeen River near Markdale, Ontario, about 40 miles south of Owen Sound. I was the guest of a distant uncle that summer. The Rocky Saugeen, running through his small farm, was headed by a millpond with a standing, but not operational, picturesque old mill.

Uncle Sid Roberts was an inveterate teller of tales, most of which were on the shady side. While these awakened certain latent inclinations in my young self, it was not his best trait by far. What impressed me most was his dedication to fly fishing—particularly for speckled trout in the Rocky Saugeen. He had all those wondrous accoutrements that make the young want to grow older fast; such things as fly rods, reels, creels, nets, waders, and so on, all of which were neatly hung or racked in a back room adjacent to the path running down through the cedars to the river—several waterfalls below. I would watch with envious eyes as the men suited up, collected their gear, and trudged off for a few hours of fly fishing.

Their return was even more exciting. They would never bring back a lot, but always some. The beauty of these trout was accentuated in the grass—lined basket creels as we prepared for cleaning them at the pump.

On the rare occasion, I would get to go with them, but definitely as a second-class citizen. The smallest available waders were still much too big and usually leaked. My one encounter with a trout nearly ended in failure when he went through a well-worn hole in the net. In addition, I had my first of many dunkings since, when I slipped and filled my waders. Crawling out on my hands and knees in that cold, cold rushing water was almost more than I was able to handle. But still, the waterfall from the mill, the smell of the cedars, and the clear pristine water flowing through the limestone formations of the riverbed, are all wonderful memories that I will never forget.

My productive fishing that summer occurred on the millpond above. It was here on the bank, in view of that lovely old mill, I would sit with a cane pole, bobber, and worms and generally outstrip the men below. It was more a boy's type fishing. Some of my friends these days infer I have never outgrown being a boy. So be it.

In recent years I had thought of returning to the Rocky Saugeen. This summer we decided to do it. But just where was this stream? I wasn't even sure of its name let alone the location of my uncle's old farm. Returning from Georgian Bay in July we checked into the Villa Motel in Markdale and started asking questions. The local people were most helpful. A number of old mills were mentioned, some with millponds but most without, as over the years the dams had been washed away. We visited them all and, in this effort, if I were grading, I would have given Nan (Mrs. G.) a 10 for her support. Toward the day's end we still hadn't found the site of Uncle Sid's farm.

At the point of quitting, we decided to visit just one last mill. It was decribed as an old one that had furnished power for the town of Markdale in the late eighteen hundreds. Later it had been a gristmill and this was how I remembered it. The place was difficult to locate, but as we drove in I could feel my excitement growing. There were changes all right but this was it! After all it had been 55 years since I had been there. All that remained of the old mill was the foundation. The millpond had shrunk as the dam had partially deteriorated. A grove of cedars blocked the view of the pond from the farmhouse. The farmhouse itself was better than ever. It had been restored by Tom and Marcia Hayes of Toronto.

Best of all the Rocky Saugeen had not changed! There it was in all its beauty—gin-clear water (in spite of a heavy thunderstorm the night before) flowing over those limestone rocks as though time had stood still. And the smell of the cedars still permeated the air!

We did not have time to fish that day, but you can bet I will be going back. What could be more thrilling than revisiting a place of cherished boyhood memories and applying skills learned over the years to outwit, but not kill, decendants of those trout that you had once rather unsuccessfully coped with at a very early age? We'll see.

Peg Keller

Twice Stung

Our afternoon beat was on the Flokladulur, a small river near the beautiful Grimsa in Iceland. The wind had subsided somewhat, the rain had almost stopped, and Bob and I were happily anticipating what new fishing experiences we would encounter on a river we had not fished before.

In the back of my mind I recalled hearing some interesting tales of descending to this beat by rope. Me—do this? At the site, my first response was "Oh, no." Bob's was "Oh, yes." So down we went, slowly slipping on the rain-softened ground and rocks about 50 feet to a beautiful pool—small, clear and protected by walls of stone on each side.

My turn first. What'll it be? A #10 Green Butt tied by our guide Daniel? He told me to stand about 10-feet out on the slippery rocks submerged in about three feet of water. There was a huge boulder to my left obscuring my view of most of the pool. Bob and Daniel perched on a high rock above and behind helping to direct the flight of my fly.

There lay three fish—likely takers. "Cast to 11:30," were the observers' instructions. A fish moved—a taking fish? Another cast—nothing. Third cast—*wham*! She jumped—I bowed my tip—she jumped again and wiggled, dancing strenuously on the water's surface.

In my few years of salmon fishing, I often am in awe of my feelings of friendly attachment for the fish that has taken the fly tied to the end of my line. And when I see a fish struggle to break away from my tether, I become soft of heart. So when she finally succumbed to the pressure of the drag, and had worn herself out in the play, it was with satisfied relief that I was able to release this hen and watch her swim away. The fly had been hooked in her tongue and my hook had left its two-pronged mark. Would she forget?

Bob's turn now. He decided to move downstream a bit. After all she had danced up quite a storm in these waters. He proceeded to cast his line, when out of the corner of his eye, probably about 20 feet away, he saw a shadow protected by a rock at the waters' edge. He then made a couple of casts in the new direction; the second one caused the shadow to move. The challenge grew. Could this fish, so close in those newly danced-upon waters, be a taking fish? Sure enough—it was—and after a time Bob brought this whirling dervish into a small pool near the rocky edge. The hook was well secured in the side of the fish's mouth. But on the tongue were two fresh hook marks. Could she have been twice stung?

Philip W. Orth

A businessman, conservationist, fly fisher, and nice guy. Milwaukee, Wisconsin.

One for the Money

The date is the easiest thing to remember—April 12, 1966. After all, it's on the Met citation and on the engraved plaque under the mount in our company's conference room. Actually, the tarpon wasn't all that big—70 pounds and five feet long, but it was the circumstances that made it the most memorable tarpon I have ever caught.

As I say, it wasn't the size. After all, I did have the good fortune with Billy Knowles one warm April evening a few years ago under the Channel Two Bridge to catch one that must have weighed at least 135 pounds. But that fish succumbed to a live mullet and was cut loose to fight another day.

To get back to the story, my fish most worth remembering was brought to gaff in such a high-roller way—against almost impossible odds—that the action is permanently emblazoned in my memory. April 12, 1966, began with one of those hot and sultry, breezeless mornings in Islamorada that usually typify the month of June when the tarpon are in by the thousands off the Buchanan Banks. Everything was just right when Dick Williams, my son

Jeff, and I took off for Oxfoot Bank. We knew we had a pretty good chance to get into tarpon. Dick isn't always the first guide away from the dock, as some of you may know, so when we arrived at our destination there were at least five boats in position, including some of Islamorada's best. Beside Billy Knowles, there were Cliff Ambrose, Roger Martin, and a couple of other world-class guides. One or two already had hookups, and by the time we were in position, it was about 9:10 a.m.

Until that day, I had caught a number of tarpon on bait. In fact, way back before the skiffs had started fishing the Channel Two and Five bridges, I had worked that same territory with old Bill Blackwell, who tried to do the skiff bit working out of an old inboard crab boat. I had also caught a number of tarpon on spinning equipment, my first with Clarence Lowe, on a charter that I will never forget. I had split the cost that day with a man I had never seen before, or have since, and my new-found friend did me the dubious honor of putting a tarpon plug through the septum of my nose. The results were spectacular to say the least, but somehow we did manage to finish the day's fishing.

Enough meanderings. Let's get back to the story at 9:10 a.m. on April 12, 1966. When we were ready to fish and small pods of tarpon were starting to come by, I said to Dick, "Jeff would rather fish with bait—pinfish or mullet, but I'd really like to try your fly rod, although I've never done it before." I'd had at least 21 years of fly fishing for trout in Wisconsin, Michigan, and the far West up until that day, but I had never wet a fly line in salt water. After some rudimentary instructions that had to do with the difference between saltwater casting and freshwater, and the fact that I was going to use a good, stiff, heavy glass rod, graphite wasn't in vogue in those days, plus a Fin-Nor reel with endless miles of backing, Dick turned me loose.

Just about the time I had the line loosely coiled on the deck and had started a few practice false casts, at least four big tarpon moved into range on the starboad side of the boat. Dick pointed them out and urged me to go for it, so *swoosh, swoosh,* two false casts to get some distance and then out we go without even a double haul. Now for the part that is not to be believed: my very first cast and the lead tarpon gulped it in like he hadn't seen anything to eat in a lifetime. A scream of line against the Fin-Nor and then Mr. Tarpon went up into the air for the first time. Five more beautiful jumps in succession—gorgeous arcs against the Eastern sun—then a long run straight north in what appeared to be trouble-free waters.

And so it was until my prey started to tire, when a new enemy appeared on the horizon. An immense black-tip shark started to close in on my trophy. God forbid! My very first cast, my very first tarpon on fly, and now one of nature's own to cheat me out of my prize.

Believe it or not, we held that shark at bay betwen Dick, my son, and me, by throwing a six-pack of beer in his direction—actually hitting him on two or three occasions to keep him off the rapidly tiring tarpon. At last, when the tarpon was well into circling the boat at close range, the shark left us in search of an easier meal, and in less time than it takes to tell the rest of the story, Dick Williams, who is one of the best that Islamorada has ever known, brought the fish lip-gaffed to the side of the boat. Son Jeff is a hardcore conservationist and urged his dad to release the fish, but it being my very first on fly I had other ideas involving Al Pflueger in Miami. So we took the handsome male tarpon into Bud N Mary's for the official weighing and attendant mandatory photograph.

Oh, yes! The rest of the day wasn't all that bad either. I didn't hook up with any more fish at Oxfoot, but late in the afternoon I had one in the air off the Lignum Vitae channel that must have gone over 120 pounds but eventually left us on the fourth jump. Incidentally, while this was going on, Jeff landed a very respectable 10-pound jack crevalle and, of course, that provided him with his own special thrill for the day.

I have caught many tarpon since then, and just this past April caught my first bonefish on fly. But then, how could one ever equal the thrill of catching one's first tarpon on fly *on the very first cast* in a lifetime of saltwater fishing?

Norman Hyams

An inveterate fly fisherman since he stomped through his first mud puddle at age two! He also is an expert on Michigan's famed Au Sable River. Shaker Heights, Ohio.

Relations

My finest fly-fishing experience has been a relationship—a relationship between father and son—and one which has developed into a bond which transcends fly fishing and remains strong to this day.

It began when my son was a third-grader. Our entire family—mother, father, three boys and a Rottweiler—was vacationing on Michigan's Au Sable River. Father was fishing and Mother was supervising the three boys who were doing all they could to empty the river from its banks, while the Rottweiler was doing what Rottweilers are supposed to do when all this is going on.

One evening my wife informed me that our youngest would be fly fishing with me tomorrow morning. "Even at 5:30 in the morning," chimed the bright-eyed and determined youngster.

I didn't think fly fishing would exactly capture the undivided attention of an eight-year-old, but what's fair is fair.

The next morning was perfect for the Lata hatch we would be fishing:

warm air, a high overcast grey sky, and no wind. The Latas are an early July hatch which follows the giant Michigan mayfly (*Hexegenia limbata*). The main stream of the Au Sable, not having nearly the boundary silt of the South Branch necessary for these great mayflies, offers excellent Slate Wing Olive fishing. The fly is a #18 with a deep olive stubby body and dark smoky grey wings. Their emergence usually starts after 8 a.m., so 5:30 was fortunately out of the question.

Next morning, hand-in-hand, my son and I waded into the water: I, in my felts, fishing jacket and Orvis hat; he, in a bathing suit and bare feet. We stationed ourselves just downstream from a quiet riffle that had, at its head, a log jam and a cedar sweep—absolutely classic Au Sable conditions!

We waited. Soon the mayflies started to show. Small trout began rising in the tail of the riffle. Then the larger fish came out from their cover within the log jam and joined in the feeding.

We commenced fishing, Well, *one* of us did. My son's fly casting was not quite to the point where he could deliver a fly to the proper vicinity.

One thing for sure about a mayfly hatch—when it's over, it's over, so after about an hour, it was over. The trout disappeared. The sky began to brighten. The river resumed its quietude, the tail water of the gentle riffle unscarred by the feeding frenzy, which had occurred just moments before.

I took my young son's hand. We trudged from the water and sat on a damp log near the river bank. I waited. Son stared at the water, his lower lip quivering, then tears started to flow.

"What's wrong?" I weakly asked.

"I want to catch a trout," he said and sobbed.

"Is it important to you?" I asked timidly.

"Yes!" he wailed.

"Well, then, I'm going to work with you until you can cast, and then we're going to come back here, and you're going to catch a trout," I bravely stated.

"You will?" His face lit up, and off we walked.

Shortly thereafter, I purchased one of Lee Wulff's Fly-O's and started my young son on a casting program, which he enthusiastically enjoyed. Evening would find us in the family room where, as an eight-year-old, he was doing tight loops, open loops, curves right and curves left.

For the rest of that year, the two of us ate, slept, talked, and breathed fly fishing and trout. He watched me tie flies and started acquiring bits of equipment of his own.

That fall, while fishing with Cal Gates and Doug Swisher in Livingston, Montana, I found a pair of extra-small vinyl stocking-foot waders which I knew he could use. Boy was he getting ready!

Early May of the following year found us back on the Au Sable. Through happy coincidence, Doug Swisher was there, too. Introductions were made, and the three of us bounded off in Doug's black Volkswagen Beetle. We got into the main stream about one mile down from Pine Road. I tied my son into his waders, his older brother's red basketball sneakers on his feet.

We found a shallow place in the river to stand where the current flowed over to one side and under some trees, affording the protection that the trout were seeking. This time the day was bright. The sun warmed the water, and the subvarias—better known as Hendricksons—started their own regatta beneath the overhangs. Early-May hatches over winter hungry fish are a fly fisherman's delight—even if that fisherman is now only nine years old. His casting stroke was beautiful! He sent his fly to where instinct and intelligent observation told him to fish.

Two unsettling events then occurred. Those vinyl waders started to develop pin hole leaks at each crease point and, more seriously, he started to catch more fish than I did! Both problems had a common solution—he had to leave the water!

This time, however, I took a wet, cold, but happy, youngster off the river; the fingers of his hands white and shriveled from the water, his teeth chattering, but his eyes bright and a grin from ear to ear. The problems were repaired by a hot shower and one of Mary Gates' steak dinners which he devoured in the company of his father and his new fishing "pal," Doug Swisher. The excitement, glow and enthusiasm on his face were all I could have hoped for.

We continue to fish and backpack together. This past summer he canoed the Yukon Territory, Alaska, and British Columbia. The rod I made and the box of flies I tied for him represented my presence on that trip.

He will shortly receive his degree in engineering, and his interests are in keeping with those of a young man now. Perhaps some day he'll repeat this experience from a father's perspective, but I know we will continue to save time for one another—time which will always reflect a relationship that began on a trout stream!

David Kolbert

David is currently learning to tie flies with one hand while he works a steering wheel with the other. Once this goal is accomplished, he'll be able to perform both tasks during his 2½-hour drive to trout water. For fast relief he works out with cantankerous smallmouths in the Shenandoah and Potomac rivers. In addition to all depressions wet enough to hold fish, he is known to frequent jinxed duck blinds, poison-ivy infested grouse covers, and unstable canoes. Professional TU'er. Washington, D.C.

Welcome

When I first saw him, I swore he was the largest carp I'd ever seen. That his rich browness was detectable through the watery depths was only half my logic. It was, I surmised, his sheer size that made my conclusion irrefutable. Fly-fishing spring-creek trout was new to me and that should have been reason enough to cast the cloud of skepticism across my casual observation. Novice or not, a trout that size could never make it in such a small creek—of that, I was convinced. I was younger then and just beginning to understand trout fishing and how it would affect my life. For all I knew, it was just another Saturday, and Saturdays were for fishing. A rendezvous with a few willing trout was all I had on my mind as I headed the old rust-green VW out of town that afternoon.

Summer was in the midst of August's long and humid dog-days. Stifling heat, lethargic trout, and head-high nettles had left the creek corridors oddly

208

barren for the first time since opening day. I knew Art and I could enjoy our choice of any run or lie. We would easily work through Al's Hole, the Box Dam, and then the Rainbow Hole before dark settled into the cool, back-road valley. No need to hurry now, patience, thoroughness—seeing beyond the obvious, that is, would be everything, as Art, the gentleman who lived no more than a modest cast-length from this fertile, limestone jewel, would often advise.

A mentor and friend, I had met Art that spring. On my knees casting in utter frustration to a pair of handsome, but skittish, risers, I had stepped back to rest them when he approached to offer encouragement. Complimenting my cautiousness he handed me a fly he'd tied to match the hatch of pale buff mayflies, a strategy I was just beginning to grasp. I introduced him to my girlfriend, who had accompanied me and who was patiently waiting a few yards downstream. His good humor and charm were readily apparent as she smiled at his comments. The three of us talked for several minutes. He spoke with reverence of the creek and its wild trout. And, before excusing himself, he mentioned his extensive library of trout fishing books and how I could stop in for a look whenever I liked. "Welcome to the world of trout," he said in parting.

I was elated at our meeting. Finally, I had discovered someone willing to share their knowledge of this mystifying art/sport. While my friend could not understand the significance of this event then, she was to learn. Her patience has worked well, as we are still fishing together.

The iron gate was tied back and I pulled into the driveway of the small white cottage. Nestled against a truck-sized limestone protrusion, Art had built a modest wood-framed home for he and his wife. Nothing too big—by this time in life one tires of cultivating appearances and other mundane tasks. Stretching, I stood in the sun for a moment. It was hot, too hot. Damn hard to keep cows out of a cool spring creek on days like this. Glancing at the time, I looked up. From the open window came the dull buzz of a fan. Art would be taking his mid-day catnap, conserving energy for the evening fish. No need to disturb him, I quietly slipped the rod from its case, closed the car door and headed off downstream.

I had walked three-fourths of a mile, through the pasture and into the woods. The canopy of spidery willow, maple and dying elm produced a tunnel, trapping the moist water-cooled air and blocking all light, save a few peepers—slim beams darting across riffles with the overhead breeze. That summer was the year the Henryville Special caught on in our region. We referred to the fly as the Lady Greenkill—the perfect impostor. In her feathery vail she danced high and light along the currents easily mezmerizing all but the most astute observers. I worked the fly with meticulous caution into pockets, under banks, and across riffles. But her magic had waned with the August heat and I was fishless.

Working back upstream, I had come to an abrupt right bend with a huge hole carved out by the grindings of spring snow-melt floods. At first, I simply stood there, calculating the flow, staring silently into the pale green pool. Mirrorlike at first, I was gradually able to penetrate the surface. Slowly, a long, dark, shadowy shape became discernible. "Carp?" I asked dismissingly. Has to be. No trout that big has been reported here for a long, long time. Damn big carp though!

I listened and watched as the undulating torpedo took on a distinct brown hue before slipping downward into the lightless depths. Though they didn't seem to bother the trout, the thought of even an occasional carp or sucker in this lovely creek marred my thoughts—much like Jethro Tull's Aqualung, a derelict in the garden of Eden.[1]

Having fished for nearly two hours, it was time for a break. Must be alert for sundown: the sorcerer's hour when anything is possible. Glancing over to the bank, I spotted a large rotting elm branch and sat down to wait. Perhaps a sipper would take advantage of the pool's Lazy Susan-drift, a smorgasboard of assorted spinners, ants and stillborns.

Upstream a hen woodduck was chiding in her nasal, *pee-pee, pee-pee-pee-peet*. Flight training commands, no doubt, for the fuzzy youngsters she kept hidden away beneath the grass-covered banks, whenever I approached. Her splashy, broken-wing antics had both annoyed and amused me throughout the summer, as I made futile attempts to fish her pool. Strange how a tragic plague like Dutch elm disease could be responsible for a much replenished woodduck population. Combine dead trees, insects, and Mister Woodpecker and you have a resourceful tree-duck's answer to community development. How is it in her disasters nature seizes such opportunities?

My thoughts followed the currents, and it was some time before I noticed the shape again. It was rising, slowly rising, nearly imperceptible, but up it came. I could not believe its size. A huge vegetation-devouring leviathan. What perversion could elevate such an evolutionary mutant to the status of delicacy in any man's culture, no matter how it was prepared, I could not comprehend. And in a slight masochistic way, I watched. I wanted to see the beast's scales. They must be the size of silver dollars.

Up he came. Another foot, maybe two and I would see the vacuum snout, the bulging eye. I was Captain Ahab and this was my Moby Dick about to blow. Bring on the harpoons, ye lads! The scales—where are its damn scales" Where are . . . Oh my God!

The mind and senses collide, and Castaneda's Don Juan tells of the Nagual and the Tonal and the struggle of each to dictate reality. The Yaquai warrior learns to "see," therein discarding casual observation and common-sense interpretations. Why in hell is it reading such wisdom is never enough? It must be lived.

Almost to the surface now—my grotesque, thick-finned carp has transformed and now bears black marbles with brilliant rings of orange, the snout is a gaping mouth, which has just sucked a struggling carpenter ant from the translucent film.

Live it? Absolutely, because life's insights are rare—glimpses of what lies

---

[1]Jethro Tull is the name of a British contemporary rock group highly popular during the 1970's. *Aqualung*, the name of one of their most popular songs, refers to a highly despicable derelict.

beyond one's own mirror. Let's face it. How often did Moses see the burning bush? How many times does Francis Macomber face the charging buffalo? And how fast can one regain control of trembling fingers and ever-so-cautiously knot-on the lone Black Ant pattern in his fly box? Perhaps in every moment-of-truth there is the absurd touch of comic relief. The great trout was cruising now, as I, on hands and knees, sneaked along the bank to reach a casting position. I watched for several tense minutes as he patrolled the circumference of the pool. At times, I would lose him in the depths, but again he would drift slowly upward to take in some hapless bit of drifting protein with all the finesse of a true epicurean and not even a ripple.

I timed my cast to intercept him on his swing past the nearer side. One would be all. But at the moment of release I felt the strange and exhilarating feeling one perceives when instinctively tracking and folding a flushing, twisting grouse. You know, the instant the gun butt touches your shoulder.

My wind-blown ant now lay on the pool. I could see the great fish and he was close—now closer, closer, and then, as if vaporized, the fly was gone. Reflexes are a wonderful thing. They come into play just when you most need them. The great trout who had drifted so slow, now lunged toward the dark bottom, his sudden speed freakishly out of character. Holding my rod high, I watched as the line shot through the guides. Luckily, the fish halted and I leaned back on the rod, almost timidly, attempting to judge his strength and mood. Had I not known, I might have guessed the fly was snagged; the resistance was that absolute. Now and then the massive head would shake, sending vibrations up my arm into my mind. With little effort he could snap the frail leader. A few quick belly rolls and it would be over. I had suited up for bantam-weight action only to step into the ring to greet the heavy-weight defender.

The fish had been still for seconds, getting his bearing, sizing me up. Now he sensed it was his move. Up from the bottom he raged, slashing wildly from one side of the pool to the other then back, the line ripping the surface with a sinister hiss. I followed him, stumbling along the bank, picking up slack, then dropping the rod tip to prolong the inevitable. He sulked momentarily. He was humoring me—light jabs and punches, sparring practice actually, setting me up for the count.

Keeping the line tight, I began pumping the rod with determination, working, the reeling line inch by inch. He was nearing my side and beneath the surface I could see him clearly, bronze-gold flanks of rippling sheet metal and the aged jaw of a veteran. For a second I allowed a sliver of optimism to creep in. Reaching back, I carefully pulled my landing net free. Easy, easy, slip it through the surface gently. At the instant the net touched water the great fish paused. Then, in one explosive movement, he was airborne! My heart was now nudging upward. I was certain it was done. But no, the tenacious furry ant stuck true and, over and over and over, the trout flew skyward only to fall back still attached by a mere thread to a world he cared not to know.

Deep again now, he had forfeited his advantage, but he was not finished. Seven times he'd cleared water. His strength was noticeably diminished, but not so his cleverness. I almost knew it was coming and started toward the tail of the pool. But he still had great speed and slipped into the tumbling rapids downstream. Running and reeling, I fought to work around him. I could see below us a large stricken elm had dropped crown-first into the stream, its earth-leaden roots solemnly skyward. No way to clear it. He had stopped just yards above the mass of branches, there was no choice—jump in and work back to the pool.

The pounding current made walking treacherous, but my plan was working. I could see the line reluctantly retreat as I approached. Almost there now, three maybe four yards at most. But in his probing, the fish had discovered a hidden ledge. Beneath it he buys time, conserving strength, knowing what lay ahead. But I must push him, make him work. And as I neared the ledge the tiring fish dodged up and into the pool.

This was the crucial turn of the tide and I was about to congratulate myself when the trembling rod in my hand went abruptly still. In desperation I pulled the handle back, hoping to pick up slack. But the rod was lifeless. In his retreat, the great trout had sliced my leader across the hidden ledge and he was free. I gasped, the air having suddenly left me.

Staggering to shore, I folded on the soft grass bank. My legs had somehow turned to rubber. My heart jackhammered violently, while the adrenalin rush consumed me. The body is an astounding manufacturer of mind-altering drugs—potent yet legal. My thoughts flowed clearly in a hyper-motive play-by-play and I was transfixed.

Later, as the sun brushed the tallest pines on the valley ridge, I stood. The pool was still now and breathing deeply, I left to join Art. He would be on the water, a heron, silent and patient. That night I told him of the great trout. Listening intently, he smiled, his white hair glowing in the light of the fireplace. Then softly he repeated, "Welcome to the world of trout."

Henry P. (Rip) McIntosh, IV

Rip leads the life most of us wish we could.
Palm Beach, Florida.

A Very Good Year

Having learned the art of sailfishing with the fly from no less a master than Billy Pate, and with a modicum of experience under my belt, I was delighted when Joe Hudson called me in late December of 1980 to say that a previous commitment prevented his participation in the first International Invitational Sailfish Flyrod Tournament to be held in Islamorada the following January. Joe had booked Alex Adler, skipper of the *Kalex* out of Bud N Mary's, for the tournament, and would relinquish the booking to me. Hearing I would be competing against Billy Pate aboard Rick Defeo's boat as well as against a most impressive list of world-class fly rodders was not particularly comforting, but I counted on having a good time even if all else failed.

I arrived in Islamorada to be greeted by leaden skies and 25-knot winds which had not let up when we left Bud N Mary's for our practice day Wednesday morning and ran out to the Alligator light. The mate, Billy Noll, had assembled a fluorescent pink squid, daisy-chain teaser with numerous bubblers, hula skirts, and other assorted elements which shortly after noon produced the first looker in the form of a five- to seven-pound sailfish. Billy's excellent work with the teaser rod holding the hookless bonito belly bait lit up the mini-sail, who boldly came within a few feet of the transom, giving me a short cast. As the white saddle-hackle bedecked 7/0 hook, equipped with a ridiculously large cork laughingly called a fly, reached the end of the backcast, Alex took the boat out of gear and Billy yanked the teaser out of the water. When the fly hit the water, the sail was on it in a flash, but he was so small he couldn't get it in his mouth. Each time I felt tension on the line and tried to set the hook, it would fly from his mouth, and I would fumble around trying to get it back to him. Alas, the tiny sail—which I would have loved to hang on my trophy-room wall—finally tired of the fun (?) and departed, leaving me in a hopeless tangle of fly line.

The bad weather did not abate, and the first two days of the tournament produced nothing more than the completion of a couple of spy thrillers aboard the Kalex, with nothing different aboard the other boats. At two o'clock in the afternoon of the final day, Billy Noll's cry "Fish!" bolted me from the chair in the *Kalex's* cabin, and with near mechanical perfection the fly was presented to and eaten by a 25- to 30-pound sail which within three minutes had been fought to the boat, billed, the fly extracted, and promptly released—thereby earning us the first hundred points of the tournament. Following tournament rules, Alex had radioed the hook-up and release, eliciting at least half-hearted groans from other boats within sight. Then began the radio vigil. Any other released fish would have put us in a tie for first place, but a boated fish larger than 40 pounds would have earned enough points for a win. The two hours to time for "lines out" seemed an eternity. About 30 minutes before the deadline, the radio came to life with Rick Defeo's pronouncement that Billy Pate was solidly hooked to a fifty pounder. Groans from the *Kalex*. Billy's boat was out of sight, so we couldn't watch the action, and I had my nose back in my book trying to act nonchalant. Fat chance. Evidently, Billy's potential winner gave him quite a tussle because it was not until almost the final moment of regulation time that the radio proclaimed us the winners. In the rough water, Rick's mate had blown the gaff shot, and the sail had been lost.

During March, April, and May, 13 flyfishing days were logged in Marathon and Islamorada, guided by Dale Perez and Hank Brown. Mainly our quarry were bonefish and tarpon, which because of bad weather that year were in short supply. Nevertheless, sufficient fish were eked out to make the trips worthwhile if for no other reason than the pleasant company of the guides.

For me, one of the great pleasures of fishing the Florida Keys is the caliber of the guides. While it is often intimidating to know that the chap pushing the pole can see, cast, hook, fight, and boat fish several orders of magnitude better than his angler (myself definitely included), these guides are, with a few exceptions, genuine gentlemen. It is good fun sharing days on the water with them even when few or no fish are to be found. Perhaps it is their sense of humor that keeps them from knocking an angler overboard when he blows a shot for which the guide has worked so hard against wind and tide to maneuver the boat into position. I think it was Jimmy Albright who quietly remarked one morning at Nine-Mile Bank, "Rip, if that tarpon had had teeth in his ass, you'd have a hell of a fish."

In May, Jack "Bigeye" McCulloch, a friend from San Francisco, and I journeyed to Tropic Star Lodge in Panama to saturate ourselves with fly fishing for sailfish and dolphin. Jack earned his nickname two years later at Tropic Star on a Club Limited trip by catching a world-record bigeye trevally on fly. Neither of us had previously fished Panama, but had heard excellent reports about both Tropic Star and Club Pacifico. On arrival in Panama City on Saturday, May 9, we were puzzled to find no other anglers bound for the fishing resort. It seemed we had arrived a day late, and were forced to charter a plane to fly to Jacque the following morning, missing a half-day of fishing in the process. Arriving at Tropic Star, Jack and I dropped our bags, grabbed our tackle, and went straight aboard our assigned boat. We had previously fished together for sailfish with Rick Defeo aboard the *Flying Fisherman* in Cozumel, and had watched Rick's mate, Mark, tease enough fish so we felt comfortable undertaking that task for each other.

While Jack caught skipjack to make the belly bait teasers, I set up the rods and tied some 15-pound Bimini-twist leaders with 100-pound shock tippets and flies. Arriving on the fishing grounds near the small offshore islands, I manned the teasing rod while Jack stood ready amid coils of fly line on the deck. Within a minute and a half of the teaser hitting the water, the first sail came up. I teased it into position for Jack, who made a perfect cast and hooked solidly into the 50-pounder which he boated and released in handy fashion. That set the theme for the remainder of the week, during which time Jack and I caught 19 sails and seven good-sized dolphin—including three doubles on sail and two on dolphin.

Home in Palm Beach for only a day, I departed for five days of tarpon fishing with Dale Perez in Homosassa. Dale was on a roll that year. His previous angler, Tom Evans, had bettered Billy Pate's tarpon world record on 15-pound tippet, and had tied Billy's 12-pound record. The fish were there, but I had not been prepared for the sight of such huge schools of tarpon cruising down the flat. The first few times Dale had me in position for a good shot, I had difficulty selecting a fish at which to throw the fly, and by the time the decision was made the fly usually landed in their midst, spooking the lot. With time and many opportunities, the technique was learned, and numerous nice fish were lip-gaffed and released. The best was estimated by Dale at 165 pounds, and took 45 minutes to subdue. It stands as my biggest tarpon to date, but I hope to return to Homosassa for an improvement.

The Gold Cup Tarpon Tournament, held in Islamorada each year in mid-June, attracts 25 world-class fly fishermen and an equal number of the Key's top guides. While fishing conditions and the number of fish taken vary greatly from year to year, the common denominator of the event is an abundance of good comradeship and good sportsmanship. I was privileged to be counted among the field in 1981, and while my luck in this tournament did not hold as good as in the sailfish tournament, I nevertheless contributed to the count of fish released. My guide for the Gold cup in A Very Good Year was "Dirty Ernie" Chapman, who put me on quite a few good fish, and, had it not been for several cases of angler failure, we might have had a better showing.

A most pleasant fishing lodge in the Bahamas is Deep Water Cay, at the east end of Grand Bahama Island. Quickly and easily reached by twin-engine aircraft from Palm Beach, the resort until recently was ably managed by John and Anne Dickinson. The stated purpose of my trip was to catch my first permit on fly, and John had said they should be showing at Burrows Cay on the tides at that time of year. The permit were where John said, but try as I would with every fly in the book, I couldn't get one to eat. Near Burrows is a long mound of sugar-white sand totally devoid of aquatic vegetation which seemed to attract permit in their search for food. At low tide the water on the mound is barely calf-deep and makes for excellent wading. As the tide floods, the water over the mound is moving with such velocity that putting a fly on the bottom to attract a permit is difficult at best. Trying various combinations of lines, leaders, and flies, I was able to get the fly down while my guide was teasing the fish onto the flat with a hookless crab on a spinning rod. Several times large permit broke off their pursuit for the teaser to come to my fly, but always just as the fly completed its swing across the sand it was snatched off the bottom by the current, and they would spook. One critter that did eat the fly and was finally beached and released was a five-foot nurse shark. Another hook-up involved a large string-ray. Both were a lot of work, but not much excitement.

August found me back in Islamorada for a couple of days with Hank Brown in pursuit of tarpon. Hank loves the Keys, and there are few guides whose skills equal his. Many are the tournaments where Hank's anglers have carried off top honors. August is usually not the best time for tarpon in the Keys, but Hank knows where fish are to be found at almost any time of year. Within 30 minutes of leaving the dock at the Islamorada Yacht Basin, we were out near Buchanan Key with a 60-pounder in the air, and within another 30 minutes another of about the same size was airborne.

Later, running back toward Flamingo, we experienced one of those rare moments that make fishing the Keys so magical. There was no wind, and the water was like a mirror, with a patina of burnished steel matching the overcast sky so exactly that distant keys seemed to float in the air. Close by, a school of porpoise broke the surface and briefly maintained a parallel course in their pursuit of mullet. Except for the sounds of wind and outboard motor one could easily get the impression of flight. We saw roseate spoonbill, snowy egret, and rare wood ibis, which number among the plentiful bird species inhabiting the Everglades Park. If ever there was a place deserving of the respect and protection of sportsmen and nature lovers, Florida Bay and Everglades Park should be at the top of the list.

Hopeful of breaking Billy Pate's near absolute monopoly on billfish fly-rod records, in September wife Susan and I ventured to Venezuela with another Palm Beach couple, Donna and Jimmy Clarke. There in La Guaira, we joined Alex Adler and Billy Noll, who had chartered a Venezuelan boat to fish several of their U.S. clients during the white marlin season. The first day produced a decent sail for me on fly, and a couple of nice dolphin for Jimmy and Donna on spinning tackle. The following day was a bust. Nothing showing for either my teasers or Jimmy's baits.

The third day, with the boat rigged for fly fishing, Billy's alarm call got me to the transom pronto, and I agonized while he tried to light up a blue marlin that was investigating the squid teaser. "He's not hot, Rip," said Billy. "You're going to have to throw long." I had already stripped all 50 feet of my three-weight running line plus a goodly amount of backing off the Pate reel. The wind was right, the backcast sufficient, and the fly went where intended. Brother blue seemed interested. To heighten his ardor I attempted to make as much commotion as possible with the fly's popping action. By the time the fish lost interest and sank from sight, nearly all the cast line had been retrieved into the cockpit, where it had wound itself into a frightening rat's nest. Guessing the fish would not reappear, I allowed the fly to stay in the water, and waited for the boat to get under way to assist my efforts in unscrambling the line.

With the rod under my arm, the fly trailing 30 feet astern, and ten fingers enmeshed in the rat's nest, the blue came up again and ate the fly.

Alex's cry from the flying bridge made me look up to see what was happening. What I saw was a damn good-sized blue marlin going away from the boat with my fly down his throat. I dropped what remained of the rat's nest, grabbed the rod, fumbled to grasp the line, and set the hook.

It took. The fish was solid on. The next few minutes are still a dream.

I remember seeing the fluorescent orange running line with its garish tangle passing cleanly through the guides, and wondering how the hell I'd ever get it back on the reel.

I remember getting the fish on the reel, and his getting deep again into my backing.

I remember that the fish seemed to be continually in the air, and when he did go back into the water momentarily he never seemed to go deeper than 10 feet.

I remember the shouts of encouragement.

I remember turning the marlin and gaining line.

I remember the fish swimming straight at the boat, and the Venezuelan mate leaping to the gunwale, gaff in hand, and his being tackled by Billy to get him out of the way.

I remember seeing the marlin so close to the boat that I felt I could touch him with the rod tip.

I remember the fish turning away from the boat on seeing it, and I remember frantically trying to recover the slack line his rush at the boat had left in the water.

I remember the jolt as the blue took up the slack.

I remember the line going slack. Terminally slack.

Upon later examination, we discovered the line had broken where the running line was joined to the 20-pound Dacron backing. The break was not in the knot but just behind it where the line had hinged from its heavy use earlier in the year. My failure to heed Billy Pate's lesson about retying all knots before each outing had cost me the fish that would have blown his record out of the book—probably forever. I remember it well. So, I'll bet, does the marlin. He must have caught a load of flack from his buddies as he trailed that hideous orange line behind until the hook worked itself loose.

The World Invitational Bonefish Flyrod Championship was held in Islamorada September 21 through 25, and I had signed up knowing that I would probably have to cut short the final day in order to make my flight to Alaska. For this, my final tournament of the year, the weather was as it had been for the first. Lousy!

The wind blew constantly at 10 to 20 knots, and frequent rain storms had the temperature hovering in the low 70s. Still, Dale Perez and I set out each morning with high expectations, and oddly enough found bonefish. We had good luck. Not good enough to place in the tournament, but good enough to avoid embarrassment.

That year, the tournament committee had decided an extra 100 points would be awarded to anglers successfully releasing fish after being brought to the dock for official weighing, and the boats had been equipped with large white Styrofoam coolers to be used as live fish wells. Dale had equipped ours with a pump to keep the water oxygenated, and we were confident that any large fish we took could be kept alive and healthy for hours, let alone the time needed for the run back to the Islamorada Fishing Club.

Just before noon on the final day, we were near Whale Harbor using the cooler for a purpose probably not intended by the committee. Seated back to back on the cockpit deck, we had the cooler upside down covering ourselves to mid-back, seeking protection from the torrential deluge being dumped on us by a nasty thunderhead. When the rain abated and we came out from under our makeshift shelter, Dale spotted a large bonefish tailing nearby. Quickly and quietly we made our way to our respective ends of the boat for the stalk. Dale eased the boat upwind of the fish, and I cast the eight-weight line, dropping the fly a few inches from the bonefish's snout. As he pulled his face out of the marl, he spotted the fly and grabbed it without hesitation.

Despite the pronouncements of Joe Hubert in his lovely book *Salmon, Salmon with a Chapter on Iceland*, I don't think any Atlantic salmon can touch the blistering first run of a large bonefish. Aside from elevating the rod to keep the line from fouling, there is nothing an angler can do to break, slow, or direct that first run, which can literally turn an inferior fly reel to scrap metal and will test the design merits of the finest. The bonefish's second run is of similar fury although somewhat shorter, and can be followed by two or three more before being brought to net—if ever.

Our beauty safely in the large cooler with Dale's pump functioning nicely, we returned to tournament headquarters for weighmaster Warren Felton's verdict. 9 pounds 12 ounces—the biggest for the tournament. We were elated. Now, if we could earn the additional 100 points for a successful live release. Back into the cooler went the fish, and we sped to the outside of the yacht basin where I proceeded to go overboard to nurse our prize back to his former active state. Sinking to mid-calf in the marl, I moved the bonefish back and forth to force water through his gills. A couple of times the fish gave signs of recovery by swimming off a short distance, only to stop and float belly up. unfortunately, we lost that fine bonefish, but only after a valiant effort lasting 15 minutes of more. With another thundershower starting to unload on us, we returned to the Fishing Club to eat our sandwiches in relative although somewhat soggy comfort, and perhaps wash them down with something more substantial than Coke. Sitting at the bar, we watched as another boat produced a 12 pound 3 ounce bonefish and then released it unharmed. Thoroughly wet, cold, and defeated, and with only a few hours remaining to plane time, I bade farewell to Dale and drove home to Palm Beach.

That same evening, after a hasty repacking job, I boarded a plane for the first leg of my journey to join Dr. Ernest Schweibert, architect, bugologist, author, and fly fisherman extraordinaire, for nine days of trout fishing in Alaska. I had fished Alaska on a couple of occasions, but Ernie had enthralled me with tales of 36-inch rainbows which are best taken during the last week of September, and I had found his tales irresistible. Of course, Ernie had prepared me well with eloquent narratives regarding tackle and clothing, and I was almost well enough equipped for the weather. If memory serves, Ernie's description of the temperature possibilities contained the statement, "If it gets cold, you'll discover where winter goes to rehearse in summer stock." He sure had that right. Several mornings it was necessary to pause every few minutes to break away the ice which had accumulated around the guides on the rod, and we usually had roaring bonfires nearby for frequent warm-ups.

Our first week was at the Kulik Lodge on Nonvianuk Lake in the Katmai area, south of Illiamna on the Alaskan Peninsula. Kulik is one of several lodges operated by Katmailand, Inc., in Anchorage. It is basically a fly-out operation with small groups of anglers flying out daily with excellent guides to fish the famous and very productive American, Brooks, Grosvenor, and Upper and Lower Tularik rivers which are short flights distant. A favorite feature of Kulik is that in non-flying weather one has only to step out of the lodge to fish the Kulik river which, while short, is full of large rainbows at that time of the year. I had fished Kulik Lodge on a Club Limited trip several years before, when it was owned and operated by Wein Airways. Since then a single-hook, no-kill policy had been implemented, and the rainbows in the river had increased dramatically in both size and numbers.

Normally, one might expect that at the end of a lodge's season the personnel would be burned out and perfunctory in their duties. Not so at Kulik. During that final week the guides were as cheerful and enthusiastic as any with whom I have ever fished. They were constantly moving up and down the rivers, checking on their charges and keeping a watchful eye for the myriad Alaskan brown bears picking up free fish dinners streamside. Our own streamside lunches of char were always delicious, and the hot food and warming campfire were welcome breaks from the Alaskan chill. Flying back into camp in the evenings, our pilots would radio ahead our preference in beverages. Drinks would be brought to the beach on a tray by a smiling young lady, and served to us as we stepped off the plane's pontoon. Leigh

Perkins often remarks how easy it is to recognize an owner-operated lodge.

The fishing that week was nothing short of spectacular. Schweibert demonstrated the art of loading a leader with bits of fuse wire wrapped behind the knots of a leader to keep the #2 black Wooly Bugger flies on the bottom even in fast water. All hands got into more five- to seven-pound rainbows than they cared to count. Even driving snowstorms did not dampen our enthusiasm in areas where it was almost impossible to make three successive casts without being into a large rainbow. Some rivers fished better than others, and species varied from place to place, but all outings were memorable.

At the end of the week, most of the Kulik gang departed for home. Ernie and I flew to Illiamna to join Andy Puyans at Cliff Pulis's camp on Slop Bucket Lake. Cliff also runs a fly-out camp, but he is sufficiently far from Kulik so that anglers can fish different waters. One day the weather gave us a break, and we felt it safe to venture as far away as Kodiak Island for some excellent action.

The weather in the afternoon after our arrival at Cliff's was too poor to fly, so we drove through the town of Illiamna to the New Halen river to test ourselves against the big lake trout. Most of us caught several of these large silver fish which put on fine demonstrations of acrobatics when hooked.

At Ernie's and Andy's request, we spent two of our days with Cliff fishing the small Tularik rivers, which flow into Illiamna on its north shore. These rivers do not host large salmon runs, but are nevertheless the sometimes homes for trophy rainbows which come up out of the lake. These are the 36-inchers with which Ernie had enticed me, but catching these lunkers is far easier said than done. They are very cagey fish, and quite selective in what and how they will take a fly. That time of the year they are feeding on "caviar rouge," as Ernie calls the occasional salmon eggs floating down from upstream where a few salmon are spawning. Those trout take an egg-imitation fly so softly, and discard it so quickly, that hook-ups are few, and nymphing techniques must be near perfect to discern the proper moment for striking.

Andy spent a few moments nipping the barb off a fly with a spun deerhair head, and then trimmed the rest of the fly so that only the head remained. This he threaded onto his leader between knots a couple of feet above the egg-like fly, allowing it somewhat free travel. With this strike indicator in place, Andy managed to stay hooked up most of the day, and count was lost at 26 of the big rainbows. Andy swears it was necessary to continue catching fish as it was the only way he could keep warm in the minus -10-degree (with wind chill factor) weather. I found it necessary to spend long breaks huddled by a fire. Ernie, on the other hand, was being a purist and refused to stoop to a strike indicator. Consequently, and for the first time in my memory, Ernie was out fished. Of course, Andre Puyans can hardly be called a novice. He is the owner of Creative Sports, an excellent tackle shop in Walnut Creek, Califonia, and has fished all over the world. If a body is going to be out fished, it's no shame to be bettered by the likes of Andy Puyans. It's a pleasure just sitting on a bank watching either Ernie or Andy. Their work with a fly rod is sheer poetry.

That was, for me, the year 1981. Seventeen outings encompassing 72 days with a fly rod of one weight or another in hand. Shared experiences with family and friends. Making new friends. Continuing to learn about fishing, its equipment, techniques, and quarry, and improving on previously learned skills. Perhaps best of all, being abroad in some of nature's finest handiwork.

It was a very good year.

Tom Mertens

Another dedicated trout fisherman who finds summers getting shorter as he grows older; he also splits fishing time with the "boys" with fishing with his wife. No dummy is Tom. Green Bay, Wisconsin.

Conservationist

Some fly fishing experiences are soon forgotten, but others last a lifetime. I won't soon forget a trip my friend Jack and I made one rainy autumn Sunday.

We planned to meet another friend in Iron River, Michigan, who would guide us to some Upper Peninsula hot spots for a final fall trout fishing fling. The rendezvous was set for dawn. As we neared Iron River, we saw a heavy storm approaching from the northwest, but we figured it would pass quickly.

As we approached our guide's red pickup, we sensed something was amiss. He had no fishing gear and as he emerged from the truck, it was obvious he was in no shape for fishing, much less guiding. Being the life of the party at a night-long wedding reception had taken its toll.

Jack and I then made a considered decision to backtrack to Wisconsin and try our luck on the headwaters of the Reshtigo River. During the 20-mile drive back from Iron River, the storm caught up with us. The winds were fierce and driving rain cut visibility to zero. At one point, popple trees were being toppled across the road and rain was blowing in the air vents of the car. We waited out the storm on the shoulder off the road.

Once we reached the Reshtigo, everything was beautiful. Fall colors sparkled in the hardwoods along the stream, the air had the fresh scent of rain-soaked forest and, best of all, fish were feeding.

I took and released several nice browns on a wet fly while Jack was getting even more strikes, but couldn't seem to hook a fish. Time after time, heavy trout would sock his fly, only to get off which was unusual, for Jack is really a skilled fisherman. Exasperated he finally took a close look at his fly and discovered the hook was completely broken off. No matter how hard the trout hit, there was nothing to hold them.

We've relived that trip many times, chuckling over the wayward guide, the terrible tempest, and the trout fisherman who took barbless flies one step farther by fishing hookless.

John E. Drotning

The good professor has waded trout waters from New Zealand to Ireland to Labrador to Quebec, not to mention the United States. During all this angling, along with sailing and shotgunning, he claims to have enjoyed varied fortune. (Fishermen are so modest.) Shaker Heights, Ohio.

Taupo Trout

It looks like glass; only the broad eddy currents indicate that the river is moving steadily through Delatour's Pool down a long flat stretch to the narrow Groin Pool where the Waitahanui River empties itself into Lake Taupo. From the bridge on the main road between Taupo and Turangi one can estimate the fishing prospects by the number of rods on the stream and in the rip formed by the river forcing itself into the ice-blue lake.

The Waitahanui begins about 20 miles east of Lake Taupo and flows in a northwesterly direction through land populated by deer, pheasants, and wild pigs. It joins this 240-square-mile inland sea just eight miles south of the village of Taupo. This isn't a brawling river like the Tongariro, the Yellowstone or the Bitterroot in early June, rather it is a river that can be fished easily throughout most of its length. There are numerous good pools between the lake and the upper reaches where the rainbows spawn.

However, my interest is centered on the stretch between Delatour's Pool and the river mouth. Every inch of this water holds trout, but fishermen seem to congregate at the pool below the bridge, the Groin Pool, and the rip at the mouth. In fact, when the run is on, there may be 20 or more rods in the rip forming what is known as the "picket fence of the Waitahanui."

I had been put on to Tom Wall, an expert Maori fisherman, who suggested that I move into Delatour's Pool just below the bridge. He noticed my thin leader, or cast as the New Zealanders call it, and my floating line and told me to switch to a sinking line and a nine-pound tippet. I thought this size tippet a bit heavy, but why argue. I waded into the pool and cast directly across the current, letting the sinking line sweep downstream. Then I began a very slow hand retrieve. I repeated this procedure again and again. This, as opposed to dry fly fishing, can get tedious, but there are always fishermen to chat with on this river. The smooth flowing, easily waded Waitahanui attracts many older fishermen who naturally reminisce about the size of the fish this stream gave up 20, and even 50, years ago. While I was fishing, a woman on the bridge called to me and pointed out a spot where she had hooked and landed a 13-pound hen rainbow about 50 years ago.

While talking, I hardly noticed the line, but suddenly I felt a strong pull, much stronger than I had been used to on Eastern brown trout water, and a big rainbow catapulted himself into the air. Instinctively, I brought the rod tip up and tightened the line. Nothing happened for about three seconds. I took this opportunity to move out of the pool onto the stream bank all the time trying to get the fish on the reel. I didn't want a loop in the line, to stop abruptly at the first guide when the fish made its initial run. I was set. The fish, perhaps remorseful that he hadn't moved more quickly, rushed downstream, and my reel sang. I hadn't heard that song often—in fact only three times, once on Montana's Georgetown Lake, another time on the Anne Marie River in Labrador, and lastly while losing a salmon on the River Blackwater in Ireland. The run stopped and the fish started upstream and I recovered some line. I couldn't see the fish. The Taupo rainbows, running up the rivers in June, don't jump like resident stream rainbows in the United States. They may make an initial jump, but then they stay down like big browns. I kept plenty of pressure on—after all I had a nine-pound-test cast. The fish ran again and this time I moved the fish and slowly recovered line, always keeping plenty of pressure on the trout.

I had a light (by New Zealand standards) 4³/₈-ounce Orvis Battenkill and it was well flexed by the unseen rainbow. The fish started upstream, but I had no worries because the pool bottom was clean and its wasn't like trying to hold a brown in Michigan's South Branch of the Au Sable away from undercut banks. This fish was really strong and cruised back and forth in a small area before a swirl on the surface indicated that he was tiring. The next minute he was on his side and I beached him. Most New Zealand fly fishermen beach trout because the stream banks make this more efficient than a landing net. This was a fresh-run jack rainbow—a typical Taupo trout— tuna shaped, short and deep, weighing about five pounds.

This wasn't my first Taupo trout. I had landed five others, two or three in about two hours of fishing, but it was the best conditioned fish I had taken. The others were spawning females and they weren't as strong as this male.

This fish may have been what New Zealanders call a maiden fish—that is, a first-run jack rainbow.

I tried other rivers along the east shore of Lake Taupo as well as Maori-owned Lake Rotoaira, where I claimed a nice 3½-pound brilliantly colored rainbow.

I cannot claim great success on the Tongariro, but it was exciting simply to fish the Red Hut, Dutchess, and Island pools. Moreover, I also spent a delightful Sunday afternoon on the upper reaches of the Turango–Taupo. This is a beautiful and easy-to-fish river running through meadowlands or paddocks.

I hardly skimmed the surface of North Island fishing. The smelt runs in December, January, and February provide something like dry-fly fishing, whereas spawning rainbows in May and June behave much like Atlantic salmon. This lure fishing (really streamer-fly fishing) as it is known in New Zealand, while perhaps not quite as exciting as stalking a rising brown, still gave me the biggest trout of my life.

The experienced Taupo fisherman knows where the fish lie in the pools, and they were more concerned about helping me get a good position than they were about themselves. What surprised me was fishing closely with other fisherfolk without getting annoyed. The humor, wit, and cameraderie of the Taupo fisherman added to the fun. All the men on the stretch of water between the bridge and the mouth knew "the American" had landed one and they seemed as happy as I.

Fall rainbow fishing in New Zealand was quite an experience and some of my fishing dreams were realized. How could one end an evening better than with talk of trout and a wee scotch overlooking this lovely, deep green pool on the Waitahanui?

Woods King, Jr.

Woods is perhaps noted more for what he can't do: He is a self-styled potential reverse role model for Orvis. Unable to double haul or tie flies, he uses chewed up flies with rusty hooks, wears a disgraceful sweat-and-grease-stained cap, and is a charter member of the dying "How Not To" School. Placido, Florida.

Railroaded

September 10, 1962

Canadian National Railroad Company
Montreal, Canada

Dear Sirs:

Your letter and claim of September 1, 1962 is acknowledged. I feel that you're acting like a big bully bringing the wrath of the entire Canadian Government down upon a poor little country boy enticed into your country by advertisements broadcast on our radio stating how friendly all of you are (or were as the case may be). Demanding immediate payment of $300 or return of a well-worn silver carafe from your train seems a bit overbearing.

Perhaps I can put the matter in perspective for you by relating a few facts surrounding the situation.

Liz, Frank, Beverly, and I drove into Montreal from the northwest at the height of rush hour traffic. We reached the central square and became stalled in the middle of eight-or-so lanes of non-moving vehicles. Immediately behind us was an ambulance with flashing lights, blaring siren and dinging bells. Liz thought a mother was having a baby and Frank figured someone was dying. Beverly told me to do something and I became nervous.

When we were able to repair to the Ritz Carlton, I opened the traditional cocktail hour somewhat early. In my case, I found their bar well-stocked with an assortment of gins. My best recollection is that they were all passable with one brand of note being named Focker's, which particularly appealed to me. We proceeded to have dinner accompanied by fine wine in the lovely courtyard amidst the ambiance of the baby ducks settling into their quarters for the evening. All was tranquil, and I arose to thank and tip the maitre d' for a fine repast. Unfortunately, I had tucked the linen tablecloth behind my belt along with the napkin. Unlike the magician who pulls the tablecloth and leaves everything in place, there was a tremendous crash as crystal, silverware, and china struck the stone patio floor.

We then repaired to our Pullman car on your late evening train headed for Chicoutimi. The several porters from the station plus the one on the Pullman were able to arrange our considerable baggage such that we were able to sit down in the drawing room attached to the bedroom by laying our legs lengthwise across the baggage. At this juncture your carafe was put into service.

We were bleary-eyed, when the porter awoke us at 4:45 a.m. to detrain at Kiskisink, a whistle stop on your Chicoutimi route. Somehow, your carafe found itself in one of Liz's many bags and detrained with us. It was not until after we portaged via Fargo truck and canoed down the Metabetchouan River to Blueberry Island that the carafe resurfaced. We were not in position to make immediate return, and so we once again placed it into service.

In the old days, my favorite combination for the local brook trout was a Montreal at the end of the leader with a Parmachene Belle as a dropper. On this occasion I had come armed with Woolly Worms which had bred success in the West. They were mostly red with grey hackle.We discovered a spawning area in an estuary of Lake Metabetchouan that teemed with brook trout. I did so well with my Woolly Worms that Frank begged to borrow one. Although Frank did will with the borrowed fly, I did better, and it took Frank considerable time to figure out that I was using the weighted variety. Frank determined to get even for the injustice, which he did; but that presented other problems which I suspect were related to your letter.

Voyaging back upstream in a heavy rain, the guides were unable to get the Fargo started. Lacking appropriate rainy-weather clothing and being very uncomfortable in the wet cold, I managed to make it run and instructed our local friends to "Voulez-vous knockez on the window when we get there," using up a good bit of my French patois in the process.

At the clubhouse we cranked up the old player piano and proceeded to "walk the dog" to the accompaniment of ancient jazz. Here again your carafe was indispensable.

So as soon as we boarded your train for the return to Montreal, Liz placed the first carafe alongside the one already there, and we proceeded to ignore the whole matter until your letter arrived. In the interest of maintaining peace between our two great nations, we pray that you will put this matter aside and allow bygones to remain bygones, at least with respect to the matter of the carafe.

Reference earlier to problems with Frank and my suspicion regarding your mailing related to what Frank had undertaken upon our return to Ohio. While camped out at Blueberry Island, I had bathed in the nearby rapids. The water being swift I clung to the rocks with hands and feet leaving my backside prominent. Frank surreptitiously took a photo, developed it, enlarged it and cut the enlargement into pieces of a puzzle. Frank thereupon distributed the pieces to friends, foes and unknowns all over the world, who in turn were instructed to mail me the pieces with whatever commentary seemed appropriate. You may understand that I am quite occupied sending out threats of libel suits without having time to properly prepare an adequate defense versus whatever action the Canadian Government intends to file against me.

Very truly yours,

Woods King, Jr.

Romi Perkins

An Apt Simile

It was pouring when we landed at Keflavik Airport. It was 7 a.m., and I was just glad that I had worn a raincoat and that I was getting out of that sardine can of an airplane. I had no idea how important that rain was. It was my first salmon-fishing trip.

While we had breakfast, a shower, and a nap at the hotel in Reykjavik, the water was steadily rising in the rivers and spilling into the fiords, where the salmon were milling about, just waiting for enough water to swim upstream.

We arrived at the lodge in late afternoon, and after tea the 10 of us climbed into about a ton and a half of rubber, collectively. Underneath the rubber we were wearing quilted down pants and jackets. By the time the fishing vest went on over it all, one was lucky to be able to waddle outside and string up one's rod.

Our guide was a very good-looking Nordic type who held my arm when we were crossing the rocky stream. His smile was dazzling, and from time to time he would quote snatches of poetry he had written during the endless nights of winter in Iceland. I started thinking, "Well, this won't be all bad."

We splashed across the bone-chilling river and the guide said, "See that rock out there with the white patch on it? Cast just next to it." Popping quite a few threads in the armpit of my down jacket, I did so. Immediately after it sank, something grabbed the line and started towing me toward the fiord. Wow! This wasn't at all like the Battenkill River trout. After running downstream several hundred yards and finally backing up a small hill, I brought the beauty in. It hadn't taken very long. Since I was sharing the rod with my husband, Leigh, I looked up to see where he was. We had agreed to change places after getting a fish. He was way upstream, so it didn't take much persuasion on the part of the guide to get me to cast again. Presto! Another fish on, another exciting scramble around on the rocks, and salmon number two went into the bag. Snowbear smiled his dazzling smile and said, "Cast again."

I looked upstream to see Leigh just in the middle of crossing a difficult place in the river, and cast again. We didn't want to waste time and leave the rod idle, after all. I had hooked a third fish and was happily playing it toward the beach when Leigh huffed up and threw several rocks at it. Who could blame him?

I landed the fish anyway. When Leigh rather testily demanded to know why I had caught three in a row, I airily explained that it was just like eating peanuts; when you ate one, you just had to have another one and another one. Such a ridiculous answer made him almost smile, and when he made a cast and hooked into a 13-pounder, his sunny disposition returned.

The next year, with a 40-mile-an-hour wind blowing the sleet into my face as I ended the eighth straight 10-hour day of casting without even a touch on the line or the sight of a fish, I remembered that first day the year before as if it were a dream. I staggered up the shale cliff to the car. The guide was passed out in the Jeep with his dazzling teeth lying on the floor beside him, smiling up at me. I smiled back, and took a leftover airline bag of peanuts out of my vest pocket and started eating them, one by one.

Michael N. Greco, Jr.

The president of the New York State Council of Trout Unlimited and a director of the parent organization. The very kind of hands-on conservationist who is the strength and future of T.U. Bethpage, New York.

High-Low Tech

A weekend fly-fishing trip to New York's Catskill Mountains found my close friend Sal and me fishing rivers rich in angling history. These famous rivers, the Beaverkill, Willowemoc, and the Esopus have always provided the charm and peace a trout fisherman seeks. Further, although heavily utilized by an angling population from metropolitan New York, New Jersey, and other surrounding areas, they still can provide excellent sport if one pays his dues in time and patience. These freestone gems flow smoothly and majestically through mountain laurel-shaded slopes. Moreover, they are home to a fine population of trout and abundant aquatic insect life. For all these reasons this region has earned a secure place in the hearts of all fly fishermen. Hatches of mayflies, caddis, and stoneflies remain dependable even today as the plague of development creeps slowly upstate from New York City, about 100 miles away.

I look forward to these weekend excursions with Sal, not only for the angling potential but for the all too infrequent time spent with a good friend away from the daily grind of business, the telephone, and the normal rat race of everyday life.

You must understand that this friendship, of which I speak, has the added wrinkle of seeing who can enjoy the most laughs at the other's expense. Mutual friends enjoy looking upon us as a constant floor show: a straight man and his partner. As would be substantiated by our circle of acquaintances, I am the straight man of this team. Characteristically a realistic, practical businessman, who is conservative by nature, I dismiss (publicly if possible) every liberal, artistic, imaginative comment that Sal makes as easily explainable and having an obvious answer. This is further followed by a display of complete shock that he thought a particular subject worth bringing up in the first place. Thus the stage is set for a particular afternoon on the Willowemoc.

Approaching evening on a stretch of river on which we have usually enjoyed some measure of success, Sal and I were experiencing an excellent hatch of March browns. The brown trout in this pool were responding cordially to our drifted imitations. This perfect evening hatch continued as darkness approached and we strained our sight to extend our fishing. The fall of darkness on a trout stream not only brings forth trout and insect activity but another of God's creatures as well, the bat!

Now Sal, city bred and born, would rather climb into the ring with Muhammad Ali and go a couple of rounds than have a one-ounce bat innocently buzz him in its pursuit of an insect dinner. More than once Sal has proven that water depth, rate of flow, and a slippery stream bottom, are no deterrent to escape when a man is scared stiff!

From my fishing position the evening's peacefulness was shattered by much splashing and foul language. Looking downstream for the source of this disturbance I was able to discern Sal's hastily departing form. After a few more casts mixed with chuckles and devious thoughts, I decided to leave the river and meet him back at his four-wheeler. On my walk back, I planned for our meeting, for I knew why he left his position with such lack of grace. Arriving at Sal's old Chevy Blazer (which, for the record, was painted a shade of yellow G. M. had no right to produce), I leaned on the front fender, foot raised onto the tire. It was now time for my planned verbal attack. Looking across the hood sarcastically at him as he approached, I began, "What the hell are you doing splashing around in the water like a moose in rut? Congratulations, you were successful at scaring every trout within a mile; more, you ruined a sexual encounter for every mayfly in the river— and their time is so limited!" "The bats, The bats! The damn things are all over, one almost flew into my face. There should be open season for those," he replied.

Having set himself up perfectly for this straight man, I commenced my lecture, "Sal, how can you be so ridiculous; bats have a highly developed radar system. In fact, their radar is so technically advanced that they are able to catch an insect in the air in total darkness even though the creature is totally blind! Moreover, scientists for years have marveled at this natural phenomenon. Why, many of NASA's early space studies involved the bat.

Satellites hurtle through space at incredible speeds yet radar such as the bat's is able to track their course both accurately and efficiently. Therefore, Sal, a bat will never fly into your face!"

Then, as if on cue, at the precise moment I decided to step off my soapbox, a bat, this high-tech rat with wings, flew between our faces, across the hood of that 6,000-pound yellow Blazer, and slammed into the windshield. As the animal lay unconscious in front of us on the hood, the silence was deafening, for I knew this straight man had run out of answers.

Edward C. Medves

One of the finest gunsmiths around when he isn't trout fishing in season, which is his true passion. Euclid, Ohio.

Memoirs of a Love Affair

Thirty years have gone by since our first meeting, but it still seems like yesterday. The years have been good to her and she has changed only a little, which is more than I can say for myself. When I first met her it was a case of love at first sight, and from morning till night, I wouldn't and couldn't leave her alone. Oh sure, there were other guys who tried to win her over, but she was difficult to understand. She was stubborn, fickle, and proud. But treat her with respect and take time with her as I have and she will reward you with everything any fly fisher could ask for: lemon-bellied browns and moss-back carmine-flanked rainbows. Her name is Tionesta.

The year was 1955. While I had always been a Lake Erie fisherman, it was rapidly becoming a cesspool. The blue pike were gone and the yellow pike would soon follow. Factories were dumping pollutants into the lake almost as fast as its water was flowing over Niagara Falls. The Lake Erie mayfly hatch used to cover sidewalks, windows, and streets, but now they too were of the past. It was time for "greener" water. My close childhood buddy, Tony, and I began asking and reading about trout fishing in Pennsylvania. It was quite by chance we heard of a small mountain stream that began near Kane and meandered through the lush Allegheny Mountains before helping to form the big Tionesta.

It was a big day in April for us when we headed east to find this so-called East Branch of the Tionesta and we felt we were well-equipped for any trout we might encounter. My rod was a True Temper glass of about six ounces and my reel a push-the-button and zingo in comes the line, leader, and pop-off-the-fly-type. The only kind of flies I was familiar with at that time were the self-propelled kind found in a garbage can. We had a box of worms that must have weighed 20 pounds, plenty of hooks and good strong eight-pound-test monofilament to support the weight of those hefty night crawlers. Freeways were unknown in those days so it was two-lane roads for 170 miles. The final leg of our journey was an old mud and gravel road that would have been tough for a four-wheeler much less an elderly loaded down Mercury wagon. Finally while driving across an old bridge, we realized that flowing underneath was the stream for which we were looking.

With the headlights directed toward a small level spot in a stand of cherry trees we set up our fishing "lodge," which consisted of a length of rope strung between two trees and an old tarp flung over it. It was a foggy night, wet and cold. We slept on a mattress of leaves and pine boughs and our sleeping bags were paper thin and about as warm, but we were thrilled to be there. Our ears were filled with the music of the stream as it rushed past boulders and log jams, and the hooting of an owl voicing its disapproval of our trespassing. What a switch from city life only five hours away.

Next morning we hit the stream early and I had my first meeting with my life-long love. I even caught several trout which were nothing like I had seen in full-colored pictures. They were eight or nine inches long, pale, and had faded orange spots. We guessed they were hatchery browns. Half of them swallowed both hook and worm and were almost dead when brought in. I wasn't too pleased with myself and, on the way home, I tried to evaluate my first exposure to trout fishing and the way I had killed those fish.

There was a tackle shop near my home whose owners, the Liotta family, were fly-casting champions. Back in the late 1930s and early 1940s, father, mother and son Sib Liotta, were well-known for their fine split-bamboo rods and after World War II they pioneered in fiberglass. So I then spent many hours talking with and listening to Sib and his father and the knowledge acquired was priceless. Sib fitted me with my first properly balanced fly outfit. It was a 7½-foot 3-ounce two-piece rod and Bronson Royalist single-action reel topped off with a double-taper five-weight line, some tapered leaders, and some flies, total cost $40. I used this outfit for several years on my favorite little stream until a friend of mine, who was a walleye and northern pike fisherman, gave me an aluminum tube four feet long and 1½ inches in diameter; it's contents bamboo. It was an Orvis 7½-foot Battenkill rod in pristine condition. He insisted that I accept it as it was useless for his type of fishing. I had never really examined a cane rod closely before and was amazed at the skill and workmanship involved in producing such an artistic implement for the sport of angling. A fine cane rod is to angling as a beautiful, double-barreled, side-by-side shotgun is to upland bird hunting. Since that first cane rod, I have fished with nothing else. For me they are poetry in motion and nothing else feels quite the same.

In early spring the East Branch gets a lot of attention as it is well stocked, but after a month of heavy pressure she settles down and becomes her natural, beautiful self again. This is my time to hunt the shy and wary. I say hunt because I know of no animal that must be stalked as carefully and where one must be so completely hidden in order not to spook it. The deer hunter, with a modern, scoped rifle can take his game at several hundred yards. A bird hunter spooks his game before he shoots. But with wise trout on a small stream, you've got to be in his front room and still present your fly as a natural. This calls for light tackle and one of my favorite rods is a seven-foot rod-wrap Leonard for three-weight line and a Hardy feather-weight reel. This whole combo weighs only a trifle over seven ounces and can lay out a fly about as naturally as humanly possible.

Tionesta and I had been seeing each other for about two years when I introduced her to my wife and baby daughter who at once were taken by her sparkling splendor as she sashayed down and through the lush emerald green mountains and forest. We camped by her side in our new lodge, which was a very used three-man Boy Scout tent, the kind that forever smells of waterproofing. It wasn't long, however, before our little family of three blossomed into two lovely young ladies, two young men and Mom and Dad. The three-man tent had to go. It served us well, but if Mom and Dad wanted to sleep under cover, we needed something bigger. The year was 1964 and we purchased a Nimrod tent camper, which would sleep four, my girls on one bunk and my wife and I on the other. The boys found the floor to be great as they were rugged woodsmen at ages two and four. Every summer we camped, hiked, fished, and played by my beautiful stream and I watched my family grow.

We were camped streamside in a small valley called Pigeon, the month was June, and the water was perfect. I had been working a pool that I named Rainbow and daughter Linda was fishing about 100 yards downstream. This was her first real attempt at fly fishing so I almost jumped out of my hip boots when I heard her crying and screaming at me. As I looked downstream, I could see her running and stumbling toward me with rod in one hand and something in the other, stopping every so often to dip whatever it was into the water. As she got nearer, I could see that she had a trout in her net which she apparently was unable to unhook. There she stood, a grown woman in hip boots and fly vest; holding her rod and net with trout inside, tears running down her cheeks and sobbing as if her heart would break. Later after calming her down, I took her picture standing by the stream with her 13-inch lemon-bellied brown trout that she had wanted to release but couldn't. The trout, of course, had died, victim of a barbed hook. That evening I cooked the fish just for her and since that time, we have used nothing but barbless hooks. It was on that same trip that my children presented me with a beautiful wild cherry landing net while we sat around the camp fire. It was Father's Day!

Spring of '73 was a time to be remembered, as was the spring of '75. These were the years when my two sons, Mike and Jeff, were introduced to *Arundaria amabilis* from Tonkin, China in the form of 7½-foot Orvis Madison medium-action cane rods. Mike, the eldest, was 13 and had fished for several years now with my old Liotta glass rod. With his new birthday gift in hand we headed upstream together toward a few fishy pools of my acquaintance where we stalked a lovely 12-inch brown which was taking terrestrials next to the left bank. There were some overhanging roots and branches so after putting a #20 Black Ant on the business end of a 7X tippet, Mike fed his rod out over the bank and dabbed. No sooner had it dimpled the surface than the water erupted in a maze of lemon, orange, and bronze. How he kept this fighter from entangling itself in those roots is still a mystery to me. His line shot out upstream, tippet cutting the water, and the new rod flexing itself for the first time. After a courageous battle this little gem was carefully landed and released unharmed. Mike and his new rod had been baptized in my Tionesta.

It was late spring of another year and I was again dreaming of my charming little brook and her colorful inhabitants. My youngest son, Jeff, and I gathered up our gear and food, kissed my wife good-bye and were off. We arrived at our favorite camping spot late in the afternoon and set up our dining fly with our sleeping bags under it. Someone had left an old picnic table nearby so we figured we might as well use it for what it was intended. Placing our box of food on one end of the table, we sat down at the other and had some hot chocolate. What a beautiful evening it was to be with my son, the only sound reaching our ears was from my lovely burbling brook not more than 20 yards from our campsite. As we were making our plans for the next morning's angling, Jeff was alerted to footsteps on a low ridge behind us. I asked him if it sounded like some fisherman walking in the woods and he said no. With that I said how about deer? Again no was the answer. Next I suggested in jovial mood that the only thing left was a bear. No sooner had I uttered the "*rrr*" in bear, when this big, black, furry critter came tumbling end over end down off the ridge and landed not 30 feet from our table. Having had several confrontations with bears in the past from Canada to the Carolinas, I told Jeff I was going to give this guy the old bang-the-pots-and-pans trick to frighten him off, but I guess this brute thought the banging was his dinner call. Seeing that he wasn't about to miss out on a free meal, I told Jeff to swing his legs out from under the table so as not to be trapped if the bear decided to rush us. I picked up the box of food and we walked gingerly to the car. As we got to the car, the bear walked over to the table, took a bag of apples from it, laid in the grass and munched them down. He then climbed up on the table and lapped up our hot chocolate without spilling a drop from our plastic cups. I did manage to set up my Nikon 35mm camera and get some shots of him on the table, but they came out somewhat darker than I had hoped. After getting off the table he went to our sleeping bags and pawed at them, messing up the bags and ground cloth. Not finding any more food, he walked over to our Volkswagen, stood next to the right door, and looked straight in at us. I started the engine and this really startled him. He took off like a race horse. I was astounded at his speed as he ran down to the stream. If this animal was bent on attacking an angler while in the stream, there was no possible way to escape. After all this action and brother bear gone, we found a perfect footprint which I measured. It was six inches across and 8¾ inches long, which made this baby a pretty large black bear. My son didn't sleep out under the moon and stars with me that night. All six feet of him slept in the little V. W.

At Bear Valley (so named by me after the foregoing experience), several years ago, I lost a close fishing buddy. Eddie and I shared streams together for over 20 years and almost exclusively on the East Branch of the Tionesta. Eddie was an angler's angler and on the stream he was Abercrombie & Fitch with a heart of gold. If you ran out of Gordon Quills, Eddie would have a dozen at hand. If you needed a Red Bodied Waipahi, he only had to dig a little deeper in his fly box.

It was around the first of June and at the time I was making my yearly pilgrimage to pay homage to the Beaverkill in Roscoe, New York and also to rekindle my friendship with Winnie, Mary, and Walt Dette.After a week of fishing, I returned home to find that my old friend had cast his last fly. Eddie and my other inseparable friend, Tony, had ventured to Bear Valley on the Tionesta for a long weekend, but it wasn't to be. As they were setting up the campsite, Eddie had a coronary and the good Lord made him a member of the Heavenly Trout Club on the spot. From that day on, whenever Tony and I camp there where Eddie left us, after the fishing is over for the day and we are relaxing with a Cognac, we toast our friend and wish him tight lines forever. We know he still casts his favorite pool just below our campsite. We named it Eddie's Pool.

Several season had gone by since Tony and I lost our good angling partner, Eddie, and the month was October; the place again was Bear Valley and we were closing the trout season for the year on our Tionesta. We set up my old Nimrod trailer overlooking Eddie's Pool, and spent the rest of the evening relaxing with some munchies and a little Courvoisier to combat the cool fall mountain air. Drowsiness takes hold awfully fast when inner warmth and outer cold meet. Morning came, and we were hungry as bears, to coin a phrase. A pot of coffee was first on the menu followed by fried corn meal and bacon drenched in pure honey. A second cup of strong coffee and we were ready for some serious trout hunting.

Fall trout hunting calls for one to think small, #20 to #24 midges and ants tied to a 7X tippet, a light leader and a three-weight double-taper floating line. My favorite rods for this type of micro fishing are a 6½-foot Leonard Catskill, a seven-foot Leonard Letort, and a midge rod made for me by my good friend Bob Summers of Traverse City, Michigan. You have to see and feel and cast this 6½-foot Stradivarious of cane rods. It is dark brown, heat treated, and cane dressed in clear silk trimmed in black, while the handle and reel seat are of one piece with a butt cap of black walnut. The exquisitely slim ferrules are also hand-made by Bob and over this masterpiece is an impeccably perfect varnish finish that accentuates the positive of this splendid cane rod. All three of these rods balance nicely with a Hardy feather-weight reel.

As we walked to the water, one would have had to be blind not to be aware of the fall colors of the hemlocks: the most gorgeous hues of red, yellow and dark green, and of Eddie's Pool with its tapestry of leaves on the water like little sailboats busily bent on their downstream course.

I walked upstream to where several large boulders created good deep holding water throughout the season. The first two had no surface activity. The third one, about a quarter mile upstream, had a good riffle flowing up against its right side. As I was standing back away from it taking some pictures of the area, I noticed a slashing rise behind the boulder. I put my camera back in its case and was assembling my rod when there was another good rise, but this time at the head of the boulder. At first I figured these trout were feeding on ants that were falling off the boulder, so I tied on a #20 Black Ant. A couple of false casts to measure the distance and I dropped the ant above the rise and into the riffles. As I made cast after cast, but with no interest evidenced, they still continued to rise. Since I couldn't see anything these beauties were taking, I sat on a rock and watched. After several minutes of observation, I thought I saw some midges above the riffles, so I tied on a #20 Black Midge. As my first cast floated from the riffle to the boulder, a salmon sided rainbow struck and it was on. My little Summers rod flexed and strained. After several runs and a few jumps, I finally netted it, gently removed the fly and put it back home where it belonged. All in all I caught three rainbows, the largest being 13 inches. It was a nice day.

The next day equalled the previous. I went back to the same pool, only this time with my seven-foot rod-wrapped Leonard. Again the trout were cooperative, and I caught two. On my way to our campsite for lunch, I saw something black moving about 30 yards in front of me. I stopped and was standing by a tree when I saw a large black bear walking toward me. A moment later, and walking behind this bear, were three more bears, two second-year cubs and a very large male. They were coming straight down the path that I was on. When 20 yards from me, they changed course and passed me, all four of them, walking in single file. They never sighted me and, if only I had my camera with me, what a fantastic picture that would have been.

The October wind was coming down off the mountain across from Eddie's Pool blowing leaves and cold air all around us, a reminder that leather hunting boots and a shotgun would soon be replacing our hip boots and fly rod. "Gosh it's getting cold, one more snifter of cognac, Tony, and it's into our sleeping bags. We've got a lot of packing to do in the morning and it's a long drive home."

Robert K. Keller

Fishing, hunting, and other outdoor activities are Bob's high priorities. He also has the good sense to live on Maryland's Eastern Shore and to marry his wife Peg, a fellow Atlantic salmon fisherperson. Wittman, Maryland.

Trophy

When asked about an outstanding fishing experience, where does one start? I can't remember the details of those great fishing days back in the 30s, in particular Jackson Hole country or fishing the streams and lakes of the Mt. Assinaboine area in the Canadian Rockies. But the memories of beautiful virgin forests and streams unspoiled by the pressures of modern man will never be forgotten. Thus the telling of a fishing experience from those days might be subject to the stretching of the truth, or just another fish story! Therefore, let me tell you of a recent experience about a "trophy" fish in my life.

It was late morning on a beautiful day with a slight breeze blowing as the water left the flats of the lagoon on Christmas Island. There I was reviewing the failures and successes of the morning. What is there to be done on a dry bonefish flat, waiting for the boat, and thinking of that cool relaxing drink back at camp?

The deep blue channels on the edge of the flats piqued my curiosity. Yes, no doubt there were fish there, trevally, barracuda, and others. I had no fine wire leaders and, therefore, had to take a chance with coral and teeth. I went to my odds and ends flybox and chose a light pink narrow bodied #1/0 streamer. The breeze and the weight of the fly created a slight problem with the casting, but all I was doing was checking the water. After three or four casts a bonefish came out of the deep, followed the fly to the edge of the shelf, and took. I landed and released a four to five-pound bonefish. The prospects for the remaining time on the flat looked interesting.

After a few more casts, another fish struck at the edge of the shelf. Out went the line with a nice bonefish at the end. After a relatively brief argument with the fish, there was a coral release and I never saw the fly again. With all this action why even think of going back and having a cool drink? During this latest encounter I noticed movement of what I thought was a piece of dark coral about 75 feet to my right on the sand shelf between the flat and the deep.

I investigated and, oh my, yes, it was a very large bonefish! There was my trophy bone sunning itself and relaxing on the beach. Whoever heard of a bonefish lazing on the beach? All kinds of thoughts ran through my mind. Can an almost senior citizen get nervous and excited about a fish? You better believe! There were no more pink streamers so I settled on a white one about the same size. It was necessary to sneak up on this fish keeping a very low profile (difficult for me). I started casting to the outside and stripping past him at an angle. On the fifth cast, a slight movement—a taking fish. My fisherman's adrenaline was building up rapidly and I was thinking about all the things I should not do to mess up this opportunity.

I cast again, stripped, my trophy made a run for it, but missed the fly. My immediate reaction was that I had messed up my only chance. What a beautiful fish! Taking his time he quietly swam back to the same lie. This was not a wild, hunted bonefish. It reminded me of fishing for a taking salmon. What a break. I was going to have another chance. My anticipation level rose. After waiting about a minute, I cast again—action! My adrenaline put a little too much excitement into my retrieve and before I knew it the fish was on the shelf in front of me. I mean *right in front*! We met, and with a mighty swirl, Mr.Bone took off into the deep.

How big was the fish? Usually those that get away do so only after a great battle of runs and leaps. Mine didn't do any of that but I would guess it went about 15 pounds, give or take a few ounces. He surely would have looked nice on my wall.

I will never forget that big "got away" trophy bone that never even touched my fly or gave me the thrill of having had my line and reel sing as he went off into the blue space of water. It is an experience that I can put near the top of my list and dream about for many a year. Thus it is not necessarily the fish you hook and lose or land but the exciting experiences of the fishing process which make a fish a trophy!

Harvey O. Mierke, Jr.

A fly fisherman and hunter, Harv is in the best business possible—he owns a travel agency. Shaker Heights, Ohio

Gentleman Jim and the Lord

Be prepared! Why the hell not? So into the suitcase went Topsider boots, a pair of old Levis with a battery-acid hole in the knee, my favorite Wright and McGill fly/spinning combo in an aluminum tube, and fly and spinning reels. Trout fishing in Ireland? Was it too much to expect that such a fantasy could top off what promised to be—and was—an unforgettably unique travel experience.

It was late April of 1977, and Herb Strawbridge, CEO of Cleveland's department store chain, The Higbee Company, had asked me to tag along for a week's visit to Dublin, Kilkenny, and Waterford. Among the eventual results of the trip (in addition to the piscatorial adventures related herein, the veracity of which I swear to on my father's fly box) was a visiting artist-exchange program between the Cleveland Institute of Art and the Kilkenny Design Workshops, the Higbee suite in the renovated Kilkenny Castle Manor House, a Higbee storewide Irish Import Fair, and a mid-life career change for the writer—who has owned and operated Higbee Travel since February, 1978.

But I digress. Ireland and I hit it off right from the start. Though I lack even a drop of Irish blood (to the best of my geneological knowledge) the period after my middle initial was quickly dropped, an apostrophe added and I became "O'Mierke!" I receive Irish mail to this day so addressed. I became so wrapped up in the scenery, hospitality and character of the people, history and marvelous food that my fishing gear and dreams were virtually forgotten until I was at a dinner party at the Kilkenny Design Workshops hosted by its director, Jim King.

As is often the case when those suffering from the fishing disease gather, discourse on the subject becomes so all encompassing that even the non-fishermen, who circle enviously on the fringes, are loathe to bring up such mundane topics as history, art, business, politics, religion, and sex. Among the more enthusiastic piscatorial commentators were Lord Freddie Teignmouth, Richard Eckersley (an English graphic designer on the Kilkenny staff), and Jim King himself who spoke at length of fishing adventures with Joe McCullough, director of the Cleveland Institute of Art and admiringly of Joe's legendary fly-tying skills.

By the time coffee was served in front of a pungent peat fire, I had not only gotten the details of how Lord Freddie's ancestor had acquired the exclusive rights to fish a half mile of the River Nore banks, which border his estate outside Kilkenny, but also had an invitation to walk those banks the next day and learn the rudiments of handling a 14-foot two-handed salmon rod. I accepted the invitation and found it was something like surf casting with a much longer wait on the back stroke.

Upon learning that our travel plans called for a Saturday return to the States, Richard expressed regrets as he was looking for a companion for the season's first brown trout expedition on Lough Corrib. Being of quick mind and blessed with an uncanny ability to sort out priorities, I assured him that my affairs could be quickly rearranged—as they were via a call to Aer Lingus and a hasty note to my wife.

Dawn on Friday found us heading toward the fishing village of Cong on the border of Counties Mayo and Connemara in Richard's Morris (very) Minor, which rode like a Cleveland taxi and, with flapping fenders, looked as if it had seen 15 Cleveland winters. We stopped in Galway to pick up an Aran Island sweater and my fishing wardrobe was completed with a moss green ghillie hat from Millars in Clifden to properly set off the borrowed O D British Army field parka.

A late afternoon arrival in Cong gave us time to explore the ruins of the thirteenth century Augustinian friary with its unique roofed stone pier permitting the monks to obtain fresh fish from the local river without getting wet. The clever monks also designed a fish trap in which each salmon rang a bell as it entered! Across the town square, with its ancient Celtic cross, was our spartan, but immaculate, fishing hotel where we had a hearty home cooked meal, traded fishing lies with a couple of English priests on a trout fishing holiday, and enjoyed a good night's sleep.

It was grey, cold, and damp as the tiny blue and white boat came sputtering toward the dock where Richard and I sat clutching our assembled gear.

The boatman, a sprightly man with ruddy cheeks and gnarled hands, tied up quickly and introduced himself as Jim Maloney. "Gentleman Jim," as Richard and I came to call him, was a soft-spoken man who, although he was to entertain and educate us constantly for the next two days, did not waste words off the water. "I've spent my life fishing for the brown trout with the wet fly and that's what we'll do today—let's go!"

Jim's old, heavy duty, nine-foot bamboo rod looked cumbersome as it lay in the boat, but in his hands it became light as a maestro's baton and he handled it with equal artistry as he instructed me in the intricacies of casting a three-fly, four-foot "lead" from a seated position in a round-bottom 12-foot boat on a choppy lake. While the ghillie called a leader with more than one fly a lead, the English term was "cast," according to Richard. Jim selected three flies from those donated by Jim King, a Sooty Olive, a Fiery Brown, and an intriguing little black number. These, Jim explained, were intended to match the duck fly hatch.

With the boat broadside to what Jim called a "bad wind for fishing," we spent the day drifting over shallows where the brownies might be feeding.

Although we never had a strike, I learned more that day than during the first month of law school. Richard, an experienced and knowledgeable fisherman, and Jim kept up a banter about spawning and feeding habits, acid versus alkaline waters (Corrib is alkaline), local entomology, and, of course, yarns of fish and fishermen. My shipmates showed me flies they had tied themselves which imitated not only the duck flies, but sedges (with marvelous names; for example Green Peter and Silver Horn), caddis flies, and nymphs.

The backside of many a corporate, political, and church leader had graced the seats of Jim's home-crafted boat and as he spoke proudly of his "clients" it was clear that many had become good friends.

With patience, and some gentle ribbing, the two coached me to the point where the flies were landing more or less in front of me as opposed to lodging in heads, ears, jackets, the boat, and so on. Thank goodness there were no overhanging branches! Each time I made a cast Jim and Richard tended to disappear down inside their jackets and it became evident that Jim's heavy leather cap with storm flaps was not worn solely for protecting his neck and ears from the chilly spring wind.

As he instructed me in the technique of coaxing the flies through the water, Jim told us of the giant brown trout called Ferox which had been caught in the deeps of Lough Corrib. Those big chaps don't often rise to a fly, but seem to be bottom feeders taken with deep trolling techniques. Occasionally a monster in excess of 15 pounds is caught!

Our time on the water the second day, a Sunday, was substantially shortened by a morning rain storm and increasing afternoon winds, which tossed our little craft around like a cork, causing the prop of Jim's antique Sea Gull kicker to come screaming out of the water. With ice-blue fingers and a perpetually dripping nose, I watched my line sink and was about to start to retrieve when I heard: "tight line!" Jim saw that a brownie had sucked in the Sooty Olive just as I felt it. We were jolted out of the doldrums and I was instantly barraged with helpful (?) and conflicting advice from my companions: "give him more line," "tighten up on him," "look out—he's going under the boat," "don't stand up" (who could stand up on a cork?), "bring him to the net." Before I knew it a fine brownie of about 2½ pounds—a dark golden brown with large black and bright red spots—was brought aboard.

After pulling into the lee of a small island to inspect the catch and eat a sandwich, Jim loosened his parka revealing a handsome tweed jacket and matching tie. When I remarked about his sartorial splendor he allowed that he and the wife had been to Mass that morning and he'd talked to the Lord about the weather and the possibility of his American friend catching a brown trout. Although he didn't seem particularly surprised at my "luck," his broad grin suggested that he was almost as pleased as I.

I'll long savor the memory of our brown trout feast the next morning and my introduction to "fishing for the brown trout with the wet fly" by professional ghillie, Gentleman Jim, who, for me, reflects the worldwide image of Ireland of the Welcomes. The three-fly lead still adorns my Sooty Green ghillie hat.

Leigh H. Perkins

For the record Leigh has been a fly fisher-
man for 50 years; president of the Orvis
Company 21 years; and has fly fished in 27
states, seven Canadian provinces, and 26
countries. He is a former national director
and Executive Committee member of Trout
Unlimited; treasurer of the American Mu-
seum of Fly Fishing; director of the Nature
Conservancy; and director and past presi-
dent of the Ruffed Grouse Society. Some
misspent life. Manchester, Vermont.

Concentration

What is a fly fisherman? We fly fishermen consider ourselves a superior group, several cuts above other sportsmen, generally highly intellectual, extremely perceptive, with an uncommon sense for the aesthetics. Now to be a bit perverse, let's dissect this elite faction and see what else they are made of. In my 50 years of fly fishing, I have run across all kinds; the perfection-ist, the laid-back, the naturalist, the technician, the snob, the detailist, the conservative, the liberal, the artist, the intense competitor, and other various combinations of the foregoing.

Most of us would agree that fly fishing should not be a competitive sport. Fly fishing is best enjoyed where one might only compete with one's own past, taking smug pride in the fact that some newly discovered knowledge or skill has enabled one to succeed in deceiving a fish that he or she wouldn't have caught the previous year. Any fly fisher knows enough not to ask how many fish another angler has caught and despises being asked himself (ex-cept on the rare occasion when he has really had a magnificent catch). Tournaments such as the "Good Ol' Boys" and "Bass Master" are sneered at by fly fishermen. Something else that gets a fly fisherman's goat is some damn fool stating that they don't have the patience to fly fish. As we all know, fly fishing has nothing to do with patience, it requires intense concentration. This intense concentration leads to another attitude a few of us have been accused of. That is, *greed*. Here are a few episodes that I have witnessed and participated in. You be the judge—was it intense concentration or was it pure *greed*?

One experience, I'm not infrequently reminded of, occurred during a summer vacation where I was being hosted at a marvelous lake in northern Ontario by a college mate, Jerry Tone. Jerry was rowing and I was standing in the bow of the boat with rod in hand as we approached some shallows. We had had good fishing that week, but hadn't taken any smallmouths over 2½ pounds. Anyway, I spotted a string of mammoth bass (snob fly fishermen don't use the word "lunker") and the second fish in the string was the biggest bass I had ever seen in my life. While casting, I became aware of an unpleasant noise in the middle of the boat and something tugging at my foot, but it didn't disturb my intense concentration. The streamer landed two feet in front of the lead bass, who charged it. I skillfully slipped it away from the first bass enabling the much larger, number two bass, to take it. I set the hook and was into an unbelievable smallmouth. At this point my concentration relaxed and I realized my host was referring to my mother as a dog and requesting rather vehemently that I get my — — foot off his rod. The smallmouth was just under six pounds. Was it concentration or *greed*?

Episode II. Shortly after acquiring Orvis, I had the opportunity to fish the famed Alta River in Norway and to take a partner to share the rod. My mother had introduced me to fly fishing and I had been her guest and companion throughout my teens and early twenties on various, marvelous fly-fishing trips, so this was the perfect opportunity for a turnabout. The Alta, of course, is the premier of all Atlantic salmon rivers, lying north of the Arctic Circle in the land of the midnight sun. Salmon average over 20 pounds with 40-pound fish not uncommon. The 28-foot canoe-like craft that one fishes from is manned by two gargantuan, autocratic Norwegians who make it quite clear what you shouldn't do. Two of their don'ts are casting and using a rod under 15 feet long. Their idea of salmon fishing is for the angler to let his line drift behind the boat while they harl, that is swing the stern of the craft from side to side while slowly backing down the river. In other words, the boatman maneuvers the fly and the angler is simply a rod holder. Enjoying casting and enjoying Orvis cane rods of 9½ and 10 feet, I broke the rules. After losing a salmon, the two guides started making guttural, mutinous noises. Mother, much to my horror, joined in with them. They rowed to the bank and abandoned me on foreign soil and proceeded back to the middle of the river where Mother followed their instructions with a 15-foot rod and proceeded to fish the rest of the day an unshared rod. Her concentration produced only one 20-pound fish that day, while I sulked on the bank.

Episode III. Wife Romi and I were fishing the Maigue River in southern Ireland, a nice flat-water stream with good hatches. The water is tea colored, so one can't see the bottom. I was in deep concentration on a really nice brown that was rising to a tremendous hatch of iron blue duns. There were so many flies I had to time the cast to catch the cadence of the rise. Romi was working her way up and apparently intent on getting in on the action. With barely enough survival instinct to not totally ignore my wife. I suggested she step in, just as the ghillie rounded the corner and cried, "My God, no, madame, it's eight feet deep there." Moments later, Romi managed to break my concentration. I never did get the cadence right—or take that brown.

Last episode. Good friend and life-long fishing companion Dick Whitney and I were floating the Bow River, south of Calgary, Alberta. It was rainy and gusty and there hadn't been any surface action. The weather finally broke and we came around the bend to see our first rising fish. As we approached, we could see there were more than three or four with noses at least two inches wide. There was only one vantage point to fish from, a small ledge where Dick and I had to stand very close to each other. In our haste to cover these rises, we got on the wrong side of each other, me being left handed and Dick being right handed. On about the fourth false cast our leaders tangled on the back cast. I pointed out the error of our ways and we changed positions. While doing so, I offered to untangle the line, having the younger, sharper eyes. Apparently, in my intense concentration, I snipped Dick's leader off at the fly line and then cut the rest of it in short pieces, disengaging it from my leader. When I released the first 21-inch rainbow that had gone well into my backing I realized that my good friend Dick was a little less mild mannered than normal and making threatening gestures. Apparently I lapsed into another spell of concentration, hooking three more nice rainbows and landing another of about 19 inches before I generously offered to loan Dick my rod. At this point, he declined my generosity. I ask you, was it concentration or was it *greed*?

BEAT SIX
Keith C. Russell

THE TOP-SECRET SECRETS—PART THREE: ATLANTIC SALMON

Forty in all, including 11 professionals, 24 "professional" amateurs and five half-and-half'ers, await the call to testify in behalf of *Salmo salar*, the trout's top rival in my poll of top fishermen. And away we go.

Semi-pro Roger Baikie, a Director of the Atlantic Salmon Federation, is the first witness. He steps into the box, raises his right hand, and swears that he prefers the Grand Cascapedia River; his fly would be an Upsalquitch or a Bomber, depending; he would be wading whenever possible and casting over a slick pool above rapids or heavy water. Roger concludes his testimony with the statement: "There is no greater thrill than watching a fish over 30 pounds rise in a fast-water slick and create a 'hill of water' as it approaches the fly." That should set the pace, Roger.

The next big hitter is half-er Duncan Barnes, editor of *Field & Stream*, whose idea of fly-fishing heaven is *salar* on the River Grimsa, Iceland, throwing a Blue Charm in the classic across-and-downstream fashion or possibly using a riffle hitch. Dunc's summation: "The gameness of the salmon, the Icelandic countryside, and, most especially, to be with my Icelandic friends—these are the reasons for my presence. Oh yes, the gravlox and the skyr with sugar, cream, and fresh blueberries ain't all bad either!"

Another laborer in *Field & Stream's* vineyard, Jim Bashline, associate editor, next testifies to his admiration of Atlantics in any river where they happen to be because all salmon rivers are beautiful. He likes a Black Bear (green butt) riffled across and downstream on a "Portland hitch." Jim reasons, "the method catches salmon and, as the fly rides on top of the water, the strike it generates is visible."

Texan pro-am Perry Bass is strongly inclined toward Iceland's *Salmo salar* cast to with a Black Eyed Prawn fly tied by Peter Dean in England and fished wet in the classic manner. He declares, "The salmon attack it." Right on, Perry.

Col. Joe Bates, Jr., fertile fishing author, names the Atlantic salmon as his number one fish (as you might suspect) but does not otherwise wish to be quoted. S'all right, Joe.

Anthony Bisgood roots for Glovers Pool on the Matapedia River in Quebec flinging a #6 Royal Wulff and using a 9-foot, 4½-ounce fly rod and a 9-foot platyl leader tapered to OX. Tony enthuses, "When the sun is 'right' this is the ideal dry-fly pool for salmon. One can see the fish, see the rise and take. There is plenty of water to play fish and good landing areas."

Do-it-for-fun-er Roy Chapin, Jr., selects either New Brunswick or Quebec as the place to fish for *salar*, a Rusty Rat as the fly, fished traditionally (i.e., wet), and concludes, "Nothing in my mind can match the thrill of an Atlantic salmon taking a well presented fly—or the surroundings in which this event usually occurs." Indeed!

The first choice of Len Codella, of Thomas & Thomas, is the Gaula River in Norway and a Green Highlander presented in classic fashion. Len raves, "Beautiful country, magnificent water, easy to wade, majestic, large salmon, a challenge!" John T. Dorrance, Jr., pro-am and a director of the Atlantic Salmon Federation (U.S.), cheers for the Grande Romaine in Quebec and a #6 Green Stonefly. Why? "Memories." What better reason!

The author of *Salmon Talk* and Atlantic enthusiast Jean-Paul Dubé dreams of the Matapedia and Bonaventure Rivers on the Baie des Chaleurs on the Gaspe Peninsula. He favors a low-water Blue Charm and/or dry flies. Jean-Paul declaims his preference for fishing "the low-water fly barely below the surface and/or a dry aimed at the fish as opposed to long drifts." He also favors the late part of the season as opposed to "blind fishing." Interesting! Compadre Dave Egan (at least with respect to salmon) casts his vote for Iceland and/or (there seem to be a number of these "qualifiers") the Grand Cascapedia. He favors a Butterfly/Black Bear (green butt)/Cossaboom (more and/or's), fished classic. Dave remarks, "Iceland for the scenic beauty and numbers of fish. Grand Cascapedia for the size of the fish."

Jack T. H. Fenety, president of the Miramichi Salmon Association and longtime friend of *salar*, pleads guilty to his prejudice (of course) for the Atlantic salmon and for his favored geography: the northwest Miramichi River, New Brunswick, Canada. Jack is equally prejudiced in behalf of the

Brown Bomber fly with a white nose and tail. You all pay attention now. He says get a lot of line out in order to get the longest possible float, in both slow and fast water. According to Jack, the Bomber is the "greatest attention-getter yet devised for Atlantics. Even the non-takers will show their presence when the Bomber drifts by!" Thanks for the tip, Jack.

Apparently speaking for the Iceland Chamber of Commerce (maybe he's considering a branch there), pro-am Marshall Field likes small tube flies, wet, (how can you fish them dry?) and continues, "The North Coast country-side is lovely and the fishing is excellent."

Immediately following in the same footsteps is Susie Fitzgerald, of Fish and Game Frontiers, casting her ballot for the Big Laxa: Laxa i Adaldal, wading with a #8 Hairy Mary Brown on a floating line fished mended dead drift." She too has some salmon ideas, starting with "noble fish (1); gorgeous river (large Laxa) in lovely valley of beautiful clean and green country (2); dramatic take (3); powerful fight, long runs, great leaps, marvelous endurance—salmon, not angler (4); heart-thumping drama of missing a fish several times before maybe inducing a take (5); ideal balance of big, 10- to 25-pound fish versus light tackle and small flies (6); and the challenge of so many variables in weather, water temp, etc." Sounds like you've been there, Suz!

Play-for-fun'er Buck Franks almost wins the brevity, if not the information, prize. (The good doctor obviously took me at my word with respect to a "one-minute" poll. He still has 55 seconds coming.) "Atlantic salmon, George River, Black Bear," sums it all up for Buck. Summing it all up a little more is Jack Hemingway, the pro son of a pro and avid *Salmo salar* admirer. He'll take 'em wherever he can find 'em and favors "a #8 double Moise Cock Teaser on a greased line either hitched or normal." His point list follows: (1) spectacular fight; (2) tenacity, they don't give up; (3) beauty; (4) beauty of places found; (5) excitement; (6) feeling that the proportional rate of luck to skill can be improved with knowledge and application; (7) when species is abundant, it's a gastronomic delight; when scarce, fish can be released un-harmed." Truly said, Jack!

Fine fishing and hunting artist Tom Hennessey not only paints beautifully on canvas but with words as well. He goes for the King on the Grand Cascapedia tied to a Lady Amherst and using the conventional wet-fly sweep. Tom also goes lyric with, "This is salmon fishing as it was meant to be. The river runs so swift that it strums the anchor line holding the canoe. Veils of mist shroud towering hills perfumed with spruce and pine, and your bones feel brittle as your fly sweeps over the slick where, several casts earlier, you raised a salmon which would easily weigh 30 pounds plus!" Amen, Brother Tom.

Bardon Higgins, a very professional amateur and Iceland fan, hedges his bets, claiming a tie among best-producing flies: the Black Sheep, Blue Charm, and Bulldog. His recipe for success is a "floating line (sink tip only when water is very cold—47° and under); a straight line, no belly, from rod tip to fly and jiggled constantly. The salt-shaker action on the fly gets their attention." Agreed, Bardo.

Next is the Atlantic salmon-fishingest amateur, Joseph P. Hubert, author of the magnum opus *Salmon, Salmon, With a Chapter on Iceland*. His loves: Iceland and all of the British Classic Patterns. Joe's preferred presentation is wet, just one or two inches under the surface of the water. His answer to the why is inspirational: "An unobstructed view of the salmon at the fly—once experienced—is the most emotional event in the blood sports."

Now David M. Lank, half-and-half-er, to the platform and welcome. Dave has authored more than 300 articles and 17 books. His preferred locales are Quebec's North Shore and the Pyrenees. (The Pyrenees?) Wet, with a Cosseboom. Dave observes, "The spectacular scenery of both, plus the thrilling contrast of basically virgin waters with waters where Caesar's legions named the mighty fish they discovered represents the two extremities of great fishing and great traditions." Something to ponder and remember, Dave.

Salt Water Sportsman editor Hal Lyman admires Atlantics anywhere and everywhere "I can afford to go." His special fly is a Hairy Mary, fished traditionally. Hal feels that "locating the fish is half the battle. Presentation is the other half. The fish is a challenge since it doesn't feed in fresh water." And succinct *salar* supporter and your basic professional amateur, Carl Navarre, Jr., states his choices: Galtenes Pool, Vididalsa River, Iceland, pitching a #6 Pate Diablo, and skittered with a Portland hitch. Why? "Most fun!"

Hot wildlife sculptor, A. J. (Tony) Obara, Jr., is hot for "Labrador, hairwing fly patterns, classic wet presentation, and the King of Fish." Alain Prefontaine believes Quebec's Moise River to be number one and a Green Highlander wet or a White Wulff dry to be the same, cast down and up in that order. "Does-it-for-fun" W. Hardy Prentice heads for Norway and, based on experience and advice of trusted ghillies, his flies would be a Black Bear (green butt) in North America and a Blue Charm in Iceland or Scotland. (Wonder what he prefers in Norway?) Hardy also leans toward small sizes.

Frederick C. Pullman, who has already caught more trout than most of us amateurs ever will and who can cast to them from his front porch, has turned in a unique ballot. His particular liking is for Atlantic salmon on the River Dee, Banchory, Scotland, on a fly presented across and down, but he lists no fly and answers as to why all of the above, "I have never caught one." Did I say unique?

Artist, fly fisher, waterfowler, "half-er" Chet Reneson seconds the motion for the George River and Black Bear (green butt) because of the few people fishing the neighborhood and the quality fish. I'll third the motion, Chet. Next to the podium is fly-fishing author and innovator Carl Richards, announcing his number one pick is the rivers of Quebec, a Muddler fly, *dry and dragging*. See what gems of inside information you're getting? Carl says modestly, "They hit it best that way and it's a spectacular strike."

On to the "Squire of Speakeasy Hill," founder of Amwell Press, the "Old Soldier," Jim Rikhoff. He orates for the Helen's Falls Camp on the George (again), a black fly with green butt (again), and with a riffle hitch (again). Jim, who by the time he departs for those salmon rivers in the sky will probably come as close as anyone to doing it all (if the man hasn't done it already), thought he died and went to heaven on the George in '84!

The tributaries of the St. Lawrence and the Jock Scott, fished dry or wet with a double hitch, get the nod from Willard F. Rockwell, Jr., who declares, "It's the best all-around fly for high or low water." Who's to say nay? And then there's El Viejo, *Yours Truly*, KCR, who will not be denied, standing on top of an Icelandic glacier (have you ever tried 10,000-year-old ice with your 20-year-old Scotch?) proclaiming his love affair with the River Grimsa, hurling a #10 Black Sheep double at a 30° angle downstream with one (or more) upstream mend to straighten the line and leader to fly and using a salt-and-pepper wrist shake on the swing. "Grimsa and Iceland are beautiful. The fly and presentation are most effective."

Pro-am Bill Searle aspires to *salar* in Iceland on a Blue Charm and says, "It works!" while Roger B. Smith, of GM and another pro-am, is also in the corner of the land of fire and ice but using a Hairy Mary. His tribute: "The Atlantic salmon is the greatest fighting fish in the world—pound for pound [there we go again]. It takes great skill and a lot of luck to be successful!"

Now for something a little different. African hunter, founder of Game Conservation International, and "professional amateur" fly fisher Harry Tennison recommends the Gaula River in Norway. He also offers the following: "Use a dark brown or black tube fly with either a double or triple hook and several Flashaboo streamers, blue and white with a little red, approximately 2½ to 3 inches long. Casting from a boat 90° to right or left, give the fly short, five- to six-inch jerks or strips as its swings in the current. This causes the Flashaboo to flare and then to come back flat, giving the impression of a swimming object. It really works for me. Basically what you are doing is teasing the salmon. Sometimes they take the fly very gently. At others they will hit with enough force to almost jerk the rod out of your hand.

"It was hard to decide between tarpon and Norwegian salmon, but then I'm getting too old to fight a tarpon for several hours and then lose this majestic fish. Climate has a lot to do with my choice also, for it is usually cool for salmon fishing and/or cold and wet, but the rewards are there. The contest for salmon is not as much a test of strength as a tarpon and you may have to be a bit more skillful, although casting a big fly with a heavy rod after tarpon is not the easiest thing in the world to do. That first jump of both fish is worth the trouble to go after them though and it was a tough decision, but *Salmo salar* won. It might be because they get bigger in Norway. Besides all that, my wife likes salmon fishing the best." Harry always tells it like it is.

The brevity prize goes to a man who believes more in deeds than in words, the Splendid Splinter (and author too) Ted Williams, whose poll answer read: "Atlantic Salmon, Black Dose!"

A thoroughly professional "am," Philip M. Winslow, M.D., takes us back to the George with a wet and hitched black Bear (green butt). He says, "It's hard to describe; almost any fish that will take a fly on the surface is a tremendous thrill. The strength of the fish, its size and acrobatics all contribute to that thrill. The air-borne jumps magnify the pleasure. I remember one fish on the George that took me down a small but white and rapid chute, and then shortly went back up and in the process jumped 19 times. Another quality includes the possibility that on presentation of a dry fly the fish will come up and out of the water near the fly and take on the way down. When this happens it's sure hard not to pull too quickly."

Canadian John R. Woods, a pro-am fly fisher from a long line pro-am family, favors the Ste. Anne River in Quebec, a Rusty Rat, wet, and/or a White Wulff, dry. John's reason is, "Just because!"

Joan Salvato Wulff, who needs no introduction, turns on for the Grand Cascapedia and presenting a Black Bottom fly quartering downstream, covering the water carefully, adjusting the speed of the fly as necessary to improve on the current's movement of the fly. Joan says, with feeling, "Atlantic salmon are large for the tackle and require my best efforts in presentation and playing skills. They will take dries, wets, hitched flies, and skaters—three of which methods produce exciting fishing!"

Lee Wulff, legend and master on the salmon, also is strong for the Grand Cascapedia and puts his vote in the ballot box for the Surface Stone Fly fished dry in the surface film. When it comes to *Salmo salar* perhaps no one is more knowledgeable or has had more on-the-water-experience than Lee, so when the Surface Stone Fly is his first choice, I'm paying attention. Thanks so much, Lee! He goes on to say, "Back in 1950 when I discovered it, no one else was using a surface-film dry fly." A lot are now, Lee.

And now to Exit, not Laughing, but still with Ed Zern who is "sent" by Scottish Atlantics. Ed says, "No one fly has produced best for me but if forced at gun point to name one, it would be a Rusty Rat." He further reports, modestly, that he presents a fly "ineptly" and that he likes "Scotland, its fishing, the whisky, and the people." And concludes: "Keith, this was a toss-up with bonefish, and was predicated on a hope that the salmon make some sort of comeback even if I don't!" All the best, Ed. We all share your hope and must continue to work toward that end.

There you have it: perhaps the most informative package of fly-fishing information every assembled; hard-won facts regarding the best geographic location, most productive fly, most productive presentation, and the why of all this for 14 of the most highly prized species of fish of over 100 of this planet's most experienced fly fishers, professional and "professional" amateur. The results speak for themselves. There were no losers in this exercise, and no winners except for you, the readers. I hope you will use your winnings to advantage.

My Health Is Always Better in Iceland

It was definitely not my best year—1984. It was, in point of fact, a ballbuster, to put it in proper perspective. Following medication for a back injury I had incurred 18 months previous, and continually reinjured every time it got halfway decent after weeks and months of pelvic tilts and swimming, a reaction developed which devastated my digestive system for the next five months. Finally, specialist number three did come up with the right answer so, in appreciative response and without even trying, I managed to acquire a virus which laid me low for another month. Then I reinjured my back for about the seventh or, was it the, eighth time. How stupid can you get? Plus another reaction to the antibiotic prescribed for the virus. And I didn't win the lottery.

All the while my Margie was forced to suffer along with me as the biggest event of the year approached on the wings of fleeting time: G-Day or more accurately G-Week; my annual, anticipated for the past 12 months, pilgramage to Atlantic salmon fishing mecca, the Grimsa River in southwestern

259

Iceland. Now it's Friday the one-three of July and I am at last on a TWA flight from Cleveland to JFK. The pills and liquids are all packed for both back and tummy, which are still on the knife edge of disaster. But I'm going. I figured I can feel lousy just as well in Iceland as I can at home and besides I have too much invested in friendships and love of salmon fishing. Anyway, my health is always better in Iceland.

And so it proved, even though the salmon were scant for some of us, if not for others. As an avowed Atlantic salmon "expert" (anyone who has fished Atlantics two or more times) and in my inborn infinite wisdom, I have come up with some observations (read that excuses) relative to our success in '84 or lack of it.

I fished the week through with my host and Atlantic salmon mentor, Gardner Grant. Now I simply find it hard to believe that G.G., when determining the starting beat assignments for all rods, which in turn establishes the sequence of beat changes for all rods throughout the week, would deliberately select for us a poor initial beat on day one, however... Even more important, this unseemly lack of productivity would continue as we moved upstream changing beats every fishing session.

What happened was this (I think): the salmon which had entered the Grimsa shortly prior to our arrival had moved upstream by the time our group hit the river so the beats where Gardner and I began our week were empty or almost so while the middle beats prospered. As we rotated beats upstream the salmon continued to move farther up, too, so we were behind them all the way. Then as those original upstream rods made the turn and went back to start to fish the low beats in progression, fresh new fish had arrived and their gravy train continued as before. At the same time when we got to the top, *salar* had already moved on. It was a difficult sequence to break and all together a tough week.

There were, however, some redeeming occurrences which made Grimsa '84 quite special indeed!

It was our fifth day on the river, our next to the next to the last day. Gardner and his good friend, Charlie Loveless and I were attacking a pool and beat which I do not care to name and number. Here the Grisma is relatively narrow and quiet with some excellent small, deep, holding pools from which a number of larger-than-average Grimsa Atlantics are taken annually. I was fishing downstream a hundred yards or more ahead of Gardner when I had a nice take by what felt like a good fish. Fifteen minutes and 200 yards downstream later Siggi Fjelsted, the very knowledgeable head guide on the Grimsa as well as river and lodge manager, netted a 16-pound hen for me. It is my largest fish from the Grimsa to date. A #8 double-hook Black Sheep did the job. I was thrilled. The trip was made. The fish was placed in a holding box for later transportation to our Grimsa hatchery where, with others of over 11 pounds, she will do her part in producing large, strong salmon for future river stocking. This worthwhile effort has been pioneered in Iceland on the Grimsa.

It next became Gardner's turn, and quite a turn it was. Twenty-five minutes after my fish took, maybe 10 minutes after it was netted downstream, on the self-same pool which I had so recently vacated connected to my love, Gardner's turn and salmon both arrived with a vengeance.

Salar accepted his single hook Lady Ellen offering and they were both off to the races. This time it was 25 minutes and 400 yards downstream later when Gardner was finally able to beach a very handsome 26-pound cock fish. It was the mate, I like to think, of my 16-pound hen and it, too, now reposes alive and well in the Grimsa hatchery producing fish for the future.

Gardner was elated, as well he might, for his salmon was not only the largest of the week but the largest he has ever taken on the Grimsa in the some 18 years of his love affair with the river. Adding to the thrill was the fact that it was caught on a fly of his own design and named for his wife.

And to think only those few minutes separated the two fish. The Big One just might have been mine but the fishing gods decreed otherwise. Oh well, a really good fisherman helps make his own luck and Gardner is not only a fine fly fisher and very experienced on *Salmo salar*, he also is our host on the Grimsa *and* a very good friend. Besides I was there to witness, which is next best and I had taken my largest salmon ever.

Thus Grimsa '84 was a major success providing, as it did, another reason why my health is always better in Iceland!

Lee Wulff: Legend

What do you say about a living legend, the Chairman of the Board of fly fishing, that hasn't been said already? Over and over. What *can* you say? Why even try?

I'll tell you why: Because he is my friend. And because this is the best way I know to tell my friend how I feel about him. And because I want to tell him while we're both still around.

Like you, maybe, when I was a young kid still wet behind the ears, I did my share of hero worshipping. In those dead days, it was the baseball stars of the era who drew my adulation. Today, in my vintage years, as my friend Ed Boyd is kind enough to put it, I have no heros. Over time and experience too much cynicism has set in, and so now, I guess, I'm too old or think I know too much to be able to indulge myself as I once did. Matter of fact, on those rare occasions when I do think about it, I feel a little sorry for myself and others like me, rather like something important is missing in our lives. And it is then I think of Lee Wulff!

Lee made a statement to me one time that "I didn't go to work until I was 60." Think about it for a minute. What a grabber! So it may be a small exaggeration, who cares? It's the idea imbedded in that statement; the idea of spending all those wonderful year earning a living doing something which you didn't really consider to be work.

The fact is that whatever he chooses to call it, Lee Wulff has been, throughout his four-score years, one of the most active of men. More than that, in his chosen profession, no one is more thoroughly professional. What makes this man tick? I'll take a crack at the answer. But before I do, I want a disclaimer clause in our contract. And a lot of liability insurance, too, just in case.

Lee Wulff is, of course, many things, but primarily he is a pioneer in the classic sense, a person who has led the way in the field of inquiry and progress with respect to game fishing and fish management and conservation.

Lee Wulff is also a contrarian of the first water. Saying that something can't be done a certain way because it's always been done this way has been responsible for many of Lee's breakthroughs in fishing technique and technology. Probably, however, the Chairman will best be remembered for his creation of the Wulff series of hairwing dry flies. Perhaps he *should* be best remembered for his countless major contributions to the welfare of the magnificent Atlantic salmon.

Personally, I feel rather strongly that his major contribution to the sport of fly fishing is his very early-on and consistent—ever-since advocacy of catch and release. His statement that "a good game fish is too valuable to be caught only once" is historic and has led the way to the quality of game fishing today equaling that of the so-called good old days.

What *I* will also remember about Lee Wulff is the shock of white hair, the craggy visage, the piercing eyes, the still nimble fingers which can produce a #28 fly, hand-held, almost like magic.

More than anything, however, I think of Lee Wulff as Teacher, an ever and always eager sharer of his vast wealth of information, ready and willing to be helpful to beginner and veteran alike in any way he can. As a result, his disciples are legion, and the legend lives on; the great world of sport fishing so very much the better off for it.

Well done, Mr. Chairman, and God bless!

The Fifth Annual Spring Invitational Bonefish Fly Tournament

This was to be the big year; my third of participation in the above titled tournament held at Islamorada in the Florida Keys. Fishing with Capt. Mike Collins, pre-eminent bonefish and tarpon guide, my first year, 1983, was for the experience, period. No fish were netted although a number were thrown at, some poorly with predictable results, some respectably but without subsequent cooperation by the fish.

Year Two, 1984, saw some improvement with an 11-pounder brought to net the first day. It was a very nice bonefish, my largest ever on a fly and led the pack until the next day. Actually no fish were seduced on either the second or third days, by me that is, but I really did feel good about the tournament and my fishing which made a contribution to the winning team. I looked forward to the next year with anticipation. Now it was here.

The tournament, during which all fish are released, runs for three days in April: a Thursday, Friday, and Saturday. 1985 was it's fifth year and all chaired by Dick Pope of water skiing and Cypress Gardens fame. All fish under eight pounds are not counted for weight. Those over are. Prizes are awarded for most fish caught and released under eight pounds and most weight caught over eight plus an overall grand champion on a combined basis. There are also team prizes along with awards to the winning guides.

The Wednesday before the competition starts is generally termed Practice Day. A lot of good fish and thus a lot of trophies are left on the flats that day when, after a good Practice Day in size/and or numbers, there is little or no follow through the next three days, to the frustration and disgust of those particular anglers.

OK, now you've got the picture and the scene is set.

I arrived in Islamorada on Tuesday afternoon to stay with close friends Pringle and Ed Boyd for the rest of the week. Ed, a veteran bonefish and tarpon angler, would be fishing the tourney, too. We also would be on the flats on Practice Day, Wednesday. It turned out to be quite a day!

Ed was fishing with Capt. Cecil Keith. "Cousin" Cecil is one of the old-time Keys guides in the mold of George Hommel, Billy Knowles, Jimmy Albright and others, old not so much in years, but in experience and knowledge of the ways of skinny-water fish and fishing. "Cousin" because Cece's grandfather on his mother's side was last named Russell and what with his own last name of Keith, Cecil and I figure we just have to be cousins.

Mike Collins was once again my main man so off we went early in the a.m. of Practice Day heading north full-bore on the outside. Mike had a new skiff this year, a 17-foot molded fiberglass Dolphin Boat named *Snafu* complete with stabilizers, a 150 h.p. Yamaha on the stern with poling platform above and a special casting platform on the bow. It was some bananas, a real sweetheart that handled and rode like a dream.

We pushed about 15 or more miles north against a north-northeast wind and a rough chop past Rodrigez and a little short of Ocean Reef. After poling a couple or three empty flats, late morning found us on another, still and always continuing the search for the Holy Grail, the Gray Ghost. Mike remarked that there had been few bonefish around for the previous week or 10 days. Early on nothing much appeared of great interest here either except for the odd ray. Light and bottom conditions were really excellent, however, and we could see almost forever in a northerly direction. It was about then when it all began to happen. First it was a group of maybe half a dozen bonefish swimming out of the north and heading south directly toward our staked-out boat. I cast but I had waited too long, just as I have done all too often on driven birds both in Scotland and in Spain, and although the fly was at least reasonably well-placed in front and ahead of the on-coming bones, they were too close to *Snafu* and spooked. Tough noogies. What a good chance muffed that may be not repeated that day or for who knows how long. No castigation surpasses that of an angler of himself for such errors of omission and commission, not even the harsh and colorful critical harangue of a Keys back-country fly-fishing guide. The fires of hell pale before self guilt.

But wait. What comes? An opportunity for retribution? A chance for redemption? Another small school of fish appears at the top of our visual screen to come ever closer in a direct line toward our waiting, self-appointed, welcoming committee aboard the *Snafu*. Once again I cast, this time early and far off, and strip, strip, strip. But they no eat and once again hurriedly depart at the sight of our boat's presence. An unexpectedly soon second chance down the drain. Why me, oh Lord, why me?

Capt. Mike answers for Him. "You're not stripping properly," he declared. "Your rhythm isn't right. It's too regular and the strips are not long or fast enough. You've got to move smartly and give better action to the fly to heat up that bonefish; in other words, jig that jig, make it dance a little to get Mr B. to turn on."

Live and learn is fine. I appreciate the advice and hope I live long enough to benefit from it, somewhere, sometime. But look, what's that? Black spots before my eyes. I definitely and desperately need to see my opthamologist and, perhaps, look up a shrink, too. It is most difficult to live through such highs and lows, such joy and despair.

No, my God, it is for real. Incredible but true and this time in quantity, in bulk, in very large numbers. Would you believe 500 strong on parade? This time it's too much of a good thing. The mind has its limits and this time fails to direct the body into action. This time is for looking, for awestruck, for thank you's for the privilege, for wondering what in the world is going on that we are so privileged to witness. They pass us by on both sides of the boat, paying no heed whatsoever to our presence, then gliding off southward into eternity. Something big's afoot, folks. We speculate on what because Mr. Bone had made himself scarce of late.

Our discussion of the subject is quickly interrupted by more bogies on the screen which eventually turn into more bonefish, this time perhaps a hundred. Have you ever seen or read or heard of the fantastically large annual animal migrations in Africa? It soon dawns on Mike and me that we are privy to observe one of the world's finest gamefish participating in a similar routine. And the band continues to play on as wave after wave after wave, some small, three or four, some huge, 500 up and many, mostly in between, schools of bonefish appear, approach and file past our front row center seats. They have to know something we don't. Where did they all come from and where are they all going and why. Unanswered questions, destined to remain so.

Have they just spawned and are now returning to their permanent "home area?" Personally, that's my guess in view of the recent paucity. Or have they just gathered and are on their way to an unknown destination to spawn. Or what? Or what? Our minds are boggled. But we do remember we're here to fish and not just to watch as these waves of fish continue to lap our shore.

My fly is frequently not cast well. Too soon and they change direction; too late and you know what; too left, too right; the wind interferes; the line in my great excitement, is tangled—the casts are perfect and the strip definitely seductive and the damned fish won't eat; they simply will not eat; they ignore.

We do notice more, and a better reaction, to a fly from the small groups of less than 10 *vis-a-vis* the large schools, but don't know the significance of this. Also, some fish are now straying off from the arrow straight path to our boat, mostly to seaward, but continue to come they indeed do and our eyes and our souls are the gainers.

During a brief lull in traffic I decide to grab a sandwich and a cold beer; all of this expected activity has taken its toll. I hand the rod to Mike for a minute who fools around with the fly, watching its action in the water as it is stripped. Naturally I'm only two or three bites into the turkey on rye and a couple of gulps of beer when once more on the horizon appear those telltale black specks. "See what you can do with these, Mike," I said. "Show me the way."

With perfect timing and grace, he flips the white jig fly to the lead fish, strips rapidly, the fish darts forward, wriggles, tips down and takes the fly pretty as you please. Ten minutes later Mike releases a nice nine-pounder. One cast, one bonefish. I congratulate him, thank him for the lesson and then warn him never ever to do that again, at least when I'm fishing with him.

More schools follow and finally it's my turn. Everything goes right like it's supposed to do and the result is an eight-pounder put back into the water to grow older, and wiser, and bigger, perhaps to please another angler sometime in the future. I hope so and wish him well. The fish, that is.

Eventually, of course, the parade ends. It has gone on for the better part of two hours. Mike and I again agree we have been privileged to witness a sight for the books. Perhaps 5,000 or more bonefish have passed before our incredulous eyes. Coming from where or going to where or why, we know not. All we really know is that we were at the right place at the right time and saw them. We saw them!

And thus we also know one other thing: the area is most definitely not fished out of bonefish.

So much for the good news. Tournament days one, two, and three came and went, uneventfully. We found a goodly number of fish to which I cast, unsuccessfully. I did not catch another bonefish. I did not win the tournament or a prize for anything, except perhaps the booby, if there was one.

But for me this 1985 bonefish tournament was a huge success.

Grimsa '85

All was well on Grimsa this past July. *Salmo salar* was present both in numbers and in size and what a very great pleasure it was to be sure.

Actually our week was one of contrasts. While the fishing was definitely excellent, the best in several years, the weather was the worst in Gardner Grant's 20-plus years experience. After the first 24 hours of typical partial sunshine and moderate (50s) temperature, the sun abandoned us never to be seen again, the air temperature plummeted into the middle forties, the water temperature hovered between 38° and 42°, the wind came up, hitting from 40 to 50 mph in gusts, while blowing most of the time in the 30s throughout the week, it rained, and low water conditions prevailed. But forget all that, *salar* was in good humor! Which was really all that counted, of course.

We arrived in Reykjavik on the usual early Saturday morning. Our flight from New York was over two hours late leaving Kennedy, this time was spent in the plane on the tarmac, the only saving grace being the able ministrations of Iceland Air's chief steward, Birgir Karlsson. A few hours to recover from travel is always most welcome. That night, it might be worth-while to note for the benefit of future Iceland bound travelers, our group enjoyed the finest dinner I have ever experienced in Iceland, in a private dining room at the Hotel Holt.

The next afternoon, now, finally, on Grimsa, the fishing got off to a fast start, and kept up the pace throughout the week. Also, for me, the fish averaged larger than in years past. And quite happily so, I might say. I followed up a 14-pounder with one of 17, my largest not only of the week but ever on Grimsa, to my great delight. The rest of our group of 10 rods were also doing well despite the inclement weather conditions.

This year we enjoyed the added fillip of having an opportunity to fish the River Flokadalsa as a fifth beat along with Grimsa. The Floka, a small river which flows into Hvita, is less than 20 minutes drive from Grimsa Lodge. This three-rod river (we fished only two) was a charmer and engendered 27 salmon on the week including my 17-pounder. I understand it provided fish to 20 pounds in 1984. Floka has a variety of small, but quite attractive, fishable pools ranging from meadow pools to one at the foot of a lovely foss (waterfall). Flokadalsa was fun!

There was another first for Grimsa fishermen in 1985. For the first time on Grimsa, perhaps in all of Iceland, perhaps for the first time anywhere including Canada, the U. S., England, Scotland, Ireland, Norway, Sweden, Spain, France, in all the world wherever sport angling for the leaper is or has been carried on, *all* Atlantics, salmon *and* grilse alike, were released. For those who wished to take something home, smoked, commercially caught salmon were available. I did not hear the first word of complaint. Grimsa, I think, I feel confident, is the wave of the future! Who knows, you may even grow to like it. Feel good about it. Be proud of it!

Any way you look at it, the week of July 14 to 21, 1985 on Grimsa was historical. A week to be remembered!

BEAT SEVEN

J. Leon Chandler

*In addition to being the guiding light of Cort-
land Line Co. for many years, Leon is a
former national president (and still a guiding
light), of Trout Unlimited. He and his company have contributed a great deal to fly
fishing's present and future. Cortland, New
York.*

Austrian Adventure

Red Fisher and I have been friends for a lot of years. The acquaintance
began back in the early 1950s when we were working at the large outdoor
shows—or sports shows, as they were called—in some of the large Midwestern cities. Then, as now, it was a part of the late-winter–early-spring ritual
for outdoors oriented people to attend sport shows set up in huge arenas like
the International Amphitheater in Chicago, Keil Auditorium in St. Louis,
and municipal auditoriums in Kansas City, Cleveland, Minneapolis, and
Milwaukee. Always there was a water filled "tank" with a stage on one end.
Twice daily, a "tank show" was presented, with log rolling, archers, sharp-
shooters, seal-balancing acts, retrieving dog demonstrations—and always,
one or two of the acts would involve exhibitions of bait casting and/or fly
casting.

Surrounding the pool or '"tank" were dozens of exhibit spaces containing
displays set up by manufacturers of fishing tackle and other outdoor gear.
Manufacturers' display booths were manned by sales representatives or fac-

tory personnel on hand to "pitch" and answer questions about their products in preparation for the fishing season ahead. The shows were of 10 days duration, with doors open for the public from 11 a.m. until 10 p.m. To help tolerate the long hours of standing in a booth answering questions and passing out literature, we usually chipped in a few dollars and rented a room to serve as a lounge and a quiet place to take a few minutes break for a beer and a sandwich—then as a place to socialize after the day's work was done— with a couple of drinks—and a lot of conversation. The same cadre of reps and factory personnel moved from show to show over a period of eight or 10 weeks each spring, and we got to know each other pretty well. A lot of fast and lasting friendships were formed.

Then, as during the years since, I was a "factory man" working for the Cortland Line Company in Cortland, New York. Cortland introduced the "333" fly line in 1953. It was the first commercially successful floating fly line featuring a new, tough, non-porous synthetic finish coating that would float for hour after hour, and it represented a dramatic improvement over the oil-impregnated fly lines of that period. The sport shows provided an important vehicle in the introduction of this new product to fly fishermen. To help dramatize the performance characteristics of 333, we appeared regularly as a part of the tank show production. Some old timers will remember the Unison Fly Casting routine we did with Eddie Wood—two fly rods cast synchronized fly lines through intricate casting maneuvers, all in timing with soft music from a live band. I like to think we helped to introduce the grace and pleasures of fly rod fishing to thousands and thousands of people during those appearances.

Red Fisher came into the sport show circuit from a different direction. During the late 1940s, the fixed-spool spinning reel made its first meaningful appearance in the United States, after having been used in Europe for a number of years. The Airex Division of the Lionel Corporation recognized the possibilities of the new fixed-spool reel and began importing the Airex Master Reel, produced in France. At that time, Red ran a sporting-goods store in Cleveland, Ohio. Red was a pretty perceptive fellow and when he first saw the new Airex Master Reel he immediately recognized that there was a new reel system that could solve the problem that plagued most fishermen of the day—the inevitable backlash problem in using the revolving-spool baitcasting reel. So he stocked a few of them, showed them to his customers, and quickly sold out. He bought some more and moved them out. The gregarious redhead was a born promoter, a pitch man who enjoyed people—especially people receptive to his spiel about all the things they could do, and all the fish they could catch, with the new spinning reel. He started organizing spin-fishing clinics—first on the sidewalk in front of the store—then branching out to vacant lots, parks, high school gyms—any place he could gather people to listen to his spiel and watch his demonstrations. And did he sell reels! He did so well that he attracted the attention of the Lionel management group in New York. They went to Cleveland to find out how one small retailer could be moving so many Airex reels. The answer was an enthusiastic super salesman who believed in the product and had the ability to project his enthusiasm to fishermen. So they hired him and set up a schedule of personal appearances in other Eastern and Midwestern cities. He became the Airex promotion man and, sort of like the Pied Piper, he infected people with the spin fishing craze and helped to make the Airex Master Reel the dominant spinning reel on the U.S. market during those early days of the spinning revolution.

This was the vehicle that brought Red into the sport show circuit. When he wasn't appearing at in-store promotions or clinics, his talents were utilized to work the Airex booth in the large seasonal shows and to help the regional sales representative promote the product.

Red and I had a lot of good natured arguments about the respective merits of spin fishing versus fly fishing. He maintained he could catch more fish with his spinning reel and "hardware." I maintained that the fly rod was more appealing, especially for trout, because with fly-rod equipment I could effectively present imitations of the flies and other aquatic insects that make up the principal diet of trout. We never settled the argument, and he continued to act out the role of the "hardware man" and I was the "fly man."

Red completed his contract with Lionel Corporation and stopped attending the shows. I lost track of him for several years and we had no contact until one day in the spring of 1970 he telephoned to tell me he had moved to Canada and was involved in producing his own television show, known as the Red Fisher Show. He told me he scheduled filming of fishing and hunting footage for 13 half-hour weekly programs each season—broadcast across all of Canada. The telephone call was to tell me that the Ontario Bureau of Indian Affairs had asked him to make a show on the Sutton River, which flows out of Hawley Lake and runs east to Hudson Bay. The objective was to publicize Albert's Fishing Camp, a new business enterprise of a young full-blooded Cree Indian. He explained that the Sutton River was reported to be one of the real blue-ribbon brook trout rivers in northern Ontario. He said "I'd like to have you go along—we'll have some fun and maybe we can settle the old question about whether the fly rod or the spinning rod is the most effective on trout." Never one to back away from a challenge—especially one that promised the prospect of fishing over four and five-pound wild brook trout, I accepted the invitation.

Mid-June found us on a commercial airline flight from Toronto to Timmins—then a transfer to a bush plane into Moosonee at the bottom of James Bay for a brief stop before continuing farther north for the 300-mile flight across the tundra, which was pock-marked with thousands of small muskeg ponds and numerous well-defined lakes. The float plane circled the camp before landing on the river in a spray of water and taxiing into the makeshift dock immediately in front of the small camp. The camp consisted of two small, but comfortable, cabins, each of which would accommodate four people. We had arrived—and I'm sure my blood pressure jumped a few notches as I looked out over the Sutton River as it flowed past the camp. Big brook trout aren't found in many places anymore—and here they were, practically at my doorstep. It was an exciting moment!

Working out of big, sturdy freighter canoes, we fished the Sutton River for three days with only a minimal amount of interference from the cameraman who was constantly moving his canoe for the best camera angles and who had his eye on the sky waiting for the sun to break through the clouds. The reputation of the Sutton River had not been exaggerated. I have been blessed with a lot of memorable fishing experiences through the years, but few can compare with the thrill of catching—and releasing—those big, beautifully colored brook trout—with their bright red and blue spots on their orange flanks, and the distinctive white leading edge of their fins. Even the most talented artist cannot come close to capturing the remarkable coloration of a brook trout fresh from his natural surroundings.

I'm not sure we completely resolved the spinning rod versus fly rod controversy—but I succeeded in demonstrating, and I'm sure, impressing upon Red, the versatility of the fly rod. During the long twilight period toward the end of each day, we would get sporadic hatches of aquatic insects and, by using a reel filled with a floating fly line, I could present dry-fly imitations to the rises and take good trout on the surface. During a hatch, they weren't much interested in spoons and spinners. Then, during mid-day when little insect activity was evident, I could switch to a reel with a sinking line and fish nymphs and streamers in the rifts and the deep holes. The range of fly-line types—from full-floating to sink-tips to different-density full-sinking lines gives fly fishermen a great range of capabilities to meet different situations.

After editing the raw film footage into a half-hour television show, the program served to dramatize one of Ontario's finest natural resources—as far as trout fishermen are concerned—and I'm sure the exposure helped to launch Albert's new Sutton River camp into a successful business venture. I haven't been back to the area since, but I hope they recognized the importance of sound conservation practices and have been able to protect such a magnificent cold-water fishery.

The trip just described was the first of many I have since made with Red Fisher. With the growing interest in fly fishing and sensing that an increasing number of his viewers wanted to see fly fishing content in the show format, he arranged at least one show each season to include a fly-fishing setting—and I was fortunate enough to have been involved in most of them. We went to the Big River in the far north of Labrador for Atlantic salmon and sea-run brook trout with veteran Toronto Maple Leaf hockey goalie John Bower—and taught John how to catch fish on flies. There was another memorable week on the famous Miramichi River in New Brunswick with baseball-great Ted Williams, who shared with us his expertise on Atlantic salmon. Many believe Ted Williams to be the best salmon angler in Canada, and he very well could be—because he approaches salmon fishing with the same intensity that made him the last .400 hitter in major league baseball and gave him admittance into the Baseball Hall of Fame. He knows the Miramichi like the back of his hand; he knows the habits of the salmon; and he knows tackle and how to use it. He is a remarkable man.

We shot footage for a couple of shows during a trip to the Yukon with pro football player and TV personality Merlin Olsen and veteran western movie actor Ben Johnson. Merlin and Ben were there to make a show on lake trout—while my role was to get footage on the Arctic grayling with the fly rod. The Arctic grayling is one of my favorite fish—they take dry flies readily and, because they are found only in the far north, a trip to grayling country is always an exciting and memorable experience.

Always a practical joker, Red pulled a dandy on me in the Yukon. One morning we were trolling for lake trout on Wellsley Lake, located about 200 miles northwest of Whitehorse. He had rigged and was using one of the ugliest, heaviest, bulkiest, strongest, trolling rods I have ever seen—and installed on the end of his line was a Dardevle about half the size of a frying pan. As we moved along a drop-off, with the camera boat running alongside, he handed the rod to me, saying "Here, hold this for a minute." Just at that moment, a small laker took the spoon and I winched him in—not realizing that the cameraman was shooting away—full frame. Sure enough, when the edited program appeared on the air, there, for all of Canada to see—was Leon Chandler, noted for promoting delicate fishing with a wand-like fly rod, pulling in a small fish with a rod more suited for tuna or marlin! I'm still waiting for a chance to even the score!

But perhaps the most fascinating trip we ever made occurred during the summer of 1982. The Austrian Tourist Bureau had expressed interest in having a couple of shows made in the westernmost Austrian province of Vorarlberg. Vorarlberg is an extremely scenic alpine district tucked in an area surrounded by Italy, Switzerland, Liechtenstein, and Bavaria. A popular European winter resort with dozens of ski areas to entertain hordes of visitors during the cold months, the tourist bureau wanted to show how attractive Vorarlberg can be in the summer—and a Red Fisher Show had promise of enticing Canadian tourists during the off-season. The focus was to be on the magnificent scenery in the Tyrolian Alps—and the trout fishing. Knowing that I had fished for trout in Austria a couple of times, Red asked if I would go along and take my fly rod. The invitation was accepted quickly with enthusiasm.

Red's wife Lois joined us for the trip and we departed from Toronto on a Lufthansa jumbo jet bound for Munich, West Germany. The Austrian Tourist Bureau representative met us on arrival in Munich and quickly loaded our luggage, fishing gear and camera equipment into a Volkswagen van for the four-hour drive to the small picturesque Austrian town of Schrun where our adventure was to begin.

Driving through Bavaria is impressive; neat, prosperous looking farms stretch mile after mile along the main thoroughfare leading to the Austrian border. Crossing the border into Austria and moving through deep valleys dominated by high mountain peaks, we were awe-struck by the quaint orderliness of the neat little villages we passed through. Each of the distinctive wood frame chalets had window boxes filled with flowers in full blossom. Small chalets perched on the steep mountain slopes reminded us of calendar photographs. And my angling instincts rose to a high pitch as we passed over clean, clear rivers and smaller streams winding through the valley floor.

Our first day dawned bright and cloudless. In the thin mountain air the blue sky seemed to stretch forever above the snow-capped mountain peaks. During breakfast, our host-guide determined that because of favorable weather conditions we should spend the day filming in the high country. The Volkswagen van motor struggled as we slowly followed the winding gravel logging road past dense forests and an occasional landslide—up, and up, and up—until suddenly we broke out into a beautiful miniature alpine valley just below the tree line. Our guide explained that the valley was used for summer pasture by the low-land dairy farmers. Because of the difficulty of making the trip down the mountain, the farmers stayed up there all summer and converted milk from their dairy herd into cheese and butter, which could be stored for several days or weeks until it was convenient to make the transfer down the mountain to the market.

The valley was so pretty in the bright sunlight, with lush green grass sprinkled with brightly colored wild flowers that seem to grow profusely in all alpine meadows. A herd of 50 or so sturdy brown Swiss dairy cows spread out over the meadow. Each wore a bell secured with a heavy leather neck strap. Each bell had a different pitch, and as the cows swing their heads to graze they echoed an orchestration of melodious sounds that can be found only in a similar alpine setting. And to remind us of the real reason we were there, was a stream winding through the bottom of our little valley that served as the headwater of one of the rivers we had crossed miles before as we started up the mountain. Quickly breaking out and assembling our rods, we had about four hours of fishing for small, brightly spotted wild brown trout. Nymphs and wet flies were effective in the pocket water created by water swirling around the boulders, and Red abandoned his spinning rod for a fly rod to get in on the fun.

We have both had more spectacular fishing for larger fish in various parts of the world, but we agreed that for pure pleasure, few of our fishing experiences can compare with the tranquility and uniqueness we found in that peaceful little alpine meadow tucked in below the lofty peaks of the Austrian Alps.

Another day we fished the gin-clear waters of the Lech River, a few miles upstream from where it flows through the town of Lech, an important winter resort. The Lech is a medium-size stream laid out ideally for fly fishing—with long slow pools, deep-cut banks, and meandering shallows. There we found a good population of rainbow trout in the nine to 14-inch range—very active fish because of the cold water draining out of the surrounding mountains. Insect activity was minimal, but we teased up a few trout using Adams dry flies rigged with a long leader tippet to minimize drag. Fished down and across stream, the deer hair muddler streamer pattern worked well—as it does on almost any trout stream in the world. The Lech River offered the type of trout fishing I find very appealing—and we shot some good film footage to show the folks back home that first-class stream rainbow fishing is available in Austria.

The unique experience of the entire trip occurred on the last full day of our stay. Our hosts wanted to show fishing scenes on a high mountain lake and arrangements were made for us to travel to a small high-altitude lake in a most unusual manner—on a ski chair lift! For the benefit of the camera, we donned waders and fishing vests and rigged our rods at the base of the lift. And up we went, holding our rods carefully to keep the tips from the supporting cable—perhaps the only time two fishermen have been transported to a fishing spot by chair lift! The lift is normally closed during the summer season. As we topped the last rise and disembarked from the chair, our eyes took in a scene that will be etched forever in our memories. Lying below us was a lake I judge to be about 100 acres in size. The color was aqua blue and the perfectly calm surface mirrored the peaks of the surrounding snowcapped mountains. Just like a picture postcard. And in the shallow coves we could see dimpled circles made by feeding fish.

Little time was lost in scurrying down to the shoreline about 300 yards below us. With my fly rod already strung up, I quickly tied on a Gold Ribbed Hare's Ear nymph, dropped it into one of the widening rise circles, and was promptly into a nice fish—first cast! It was a rainbow trout of about 15 inches, deep and fat from gorging on aquatic insects all summer. We had a fine afternoon. I found that either nymphs or streamer flies cast to the rises and worked slowly would take fish consistently—while Red was equally effective in casting flashing spoons just beyond the drop-off and allowing them to settle into the deeper water before retrieving. All the trout were carefully released. They are probably still there, considering the degree of difficulty in getting to the lake without the aid of an operating chair lift.

The next time Red Fisher and I get together, we will undoubtedly continue the old argument about the respective merits of the fly rod versus the spinning rod. But we both know neither of us can win—because no single type of equipment is best for all fishing situations. Both spinning and fly rods have a place in the scheme of angling and consistently successful fishermen will use the one that best fits the situation that confronts them.

Gardner L. Grant

The Salmon That May Live Forever

November 13, 1984

TO: Fellow Salmon Anglers
FROM: Gardner Grant
RE: Sequel to the 1984 season on Grimsa

On July 21, 1984 I caught and placed in our salmon hatchery on Grimsa the largest salmon I have ever taken on that river. I was quite proud of that fish.

The very next week fellow-angler and friend, Nathaniel Reed, caught a 28-pound male and placed him in the same hatchery along with my fish. Later Nathaniel prepared a log of his salmon fishing experiences in 1984 and sent copies of it to a number of his friends. Perhaps you received a copy.

The attached is my rebuttal.

Gardner

October 31, 1984

Dear Nathaniel,

I was delighted to receive your 1984 salmon log and found it most interesting and enjoyable reading until I came to an entry under "Iceland—Field Notes," Thursday, July 26, 1984. The last sentence of the entry under that date reads: "He made Gardner Grant's 24-pounder, also in the hatchery, look emaciated."

Please note, Nathaniel, that my salmon survived battle with a far more formidable adversary than yours, and when my salmon entered the fray, he weighed 35 pounds.

Best regards,
Gardner

December 12, 1984

Dear Nathaniel,

I was in Iceland last week and had an opportunity to visit, on December 5, the Grimsa, its hatchery, and its hatchery manager. You will be pleased to know that all brood stock, including your 28-pound male, survived spawning and were tagged and released into the estuary. The manager noted that the eggs fertilized by your male appeared substandard, and he believes this indicates a low sperm count. This may explain why this salmon was subdued in 14 minutes—just thought you would like to know.

Best wishes.

Sincerely,
Gardner

December 19, 1984

My Dear Gardner,

I am delighted to learn that my supreme Grimsa cock performed as expected. I suggest your manager is inexperienced in identifying genetically superior eggs among all those little competitors. The real test will be in five to seven years when Grimsa anglers will be broken left and right by a new race of "Reed Super Salmon!"

As for the 14-minute duration of the fight, remember that the combination of a truly frantic fight by a great salmon combined with superior angling technique usually ends up in a short fight.

Enough said!

Special best wishes and a Merry Christmas,

Nathaniel

Herb Beattie

A computer and telecommunications expert who just loves to fish with a fly. Vienna, Virginia.

The Day I Died

It was on the fourth of July, 1977, and I was in my forty-third year when I had a strange and frightening experience while fly fishing. It happened the first time I saw what we now call the "Fourth of July Light Cahill hatch" on Arkansas' Norfork River. I had been fishing the White River since 1974 and discovered in 1976 that the Norfork had more big fish than the White. Up to now, fishing on both rivers had always been almost exclusively with nymphs, streamers, and sculpins—virtually no dry flies. July Fourth was to be a three-day weekend and minimal power generation was scheduled in this productive tailwater. I left my wife in the middle of the night and hit the Norfork with high expectations.

After walking about a mile to get away from other anglers, I came to a shoal where I could see some mayflies hatching and some fish feeding on the surface. I put on a dry fly I thought might work, cast, and immediately tied onto a 17-inch rainbow. As the two of us performed our ritual, I started looking around for another candidate to be my next playmate. I saw one, then another, another, and another. There, within easy casting distance were eight, 10, 12—I don't know how many—*big rainbows rising to a mayfly hatch*! It was something I had never seen in 30-some years of trout fishing. I was really excited and felt like I had died and gone to heaven.

I finally landed the fish, released it, and cast to my next target that readily took. I set the hook, but popped the leader. After an appropriate profanity, I told myself to cool it, "You're too excited! You have no business breaking a 5X leader." But I needed a new tippet and so prepared to knot one on, which I knew would take precious time as the fish continued breakfast all around me. But I could not tie the damned tippet on. I tried again. Another failure! When I get nervous, I sweat. When I am in waders and the sun is shining and it's the fourth of July, I really sweat. I was wringing wet!

Thinking to myself, I said, "To hell with it—forget the tippet and just tie on a new fly." But I could not do it. In near panic, I waded to the shore to sit down, relax, and make my hands stop shaking. I tried, but now my hands were shaking violently and the sweat was profuse. Suddenly, my mind left my body—like being two different entities. I was "spaced out," as the younger generation says.

I realized I was very ill—I swore off the tobacco I was chewing and vowed I would never wear waders in the heat of the summer again. Maybe I should have slept longer last night. I started the long walk back to the car. My hands were shaking so badly I could barely hold the rod.

Then it happened: I died, or at least I thought I did. I was dead and there were spirits around me. It was not a bad feeling—being dead—just kind of curious and "spaced." And there were these spirits around me, and as a new awareness came over me, they came into focus. There were the wonderful volunteers of the Norfork Rescue Squad. I was in their ambulance on the way to the Mountain Home Hospital.

In my 50 years I have "died" or hyperventilated only the once; my brain became independent of my body only the once—Independence Day, 1977, and it all had to do with bright skies, bright waters, big rainbows, and the dance of the mayflies.

Russell W. Hardy, Jr., M. D.

An avid fly fisherman and tennis player, and a practicing neurosurgeon at the Cleveland Clinic. Fortunately, he says, his talents as a surgeon exceed those he displays in fishing and tennis. Cleveland, Ohio.

Three to Make Ready

Let me begin with an immediate disclaimer that this vignette is in any way intended to be sexist. There are many excellent female fly fishers. In fact, my own skills as a fly fisher (which are admittedly limited) were taught to me by a charming lady of my acquaintance, who is now in her 80s.

While it may be true that there are many gifted female piscators, however, none of them unfortunately are in my family. At least yet. I discovered this one hot day last July when the four of us, wife Judy, and daughters Jennifer and Caroline, and I went fishing on the Millbrook, a stream in the western Catskills.

That day began when Caroline, age 9, asked me to show her how to fish. I offered to take her and also her teenage sister. Jennifer, however, announced that she was bored by the whole proceedings and had no interest in anything as dull as fishing or as slimy as a trout. She then retired to her Walkman and a Bruce Springsteen tape. The musical preferences of teenagers being what they are, I could not compete with Mr. Springsteen.

284

Following this rebuff, Caroline and I set off to fish by ourselves. I began with a short casting demonstration, figuring I'd catch one or two before she scared off the trout. Naturally, I did not catch anything.

After 45 minutes of fruitless "demonstration," I decided to let Caroline have a go at it. We had an old glass rod and antique reel, and I attached the largest, most gauche fly I could find, I think a Neversink Skater[1], and let her try a roll-cast. Before the cast, I warned her not to expect any fish. Wouldn't you know, her first cast was followed by an immediate strike, and with some help she landed a 12-inch brown. After I dispatched the unfortunate trout, Caroline carried it with great glee back to the cabin and waved it at her older sister.

Jennifer affected boredom and continued to listen to her tape. However, after lunch, which included Caroline's fish, Jennifer announced that she had developed a sudden interest in learning to cast.

So, that afternoon, the four of us set off on another expedition to the brook. This time Jennifer went with me to a section with a small waterfall and pool, while Judy set off for a pond lower down the brook. After a lesson on roll casting, I turned the rod over to Jennifer. A number of unproductive casts followed; Jennifer announced she was bored again, and returned to her Walkman. I took the rod back and continued, using, I think, an Adams. Soon afterward, I got a strike and called to Jennifer to come and play the fish. She was up like a flash, and came running along the bank in oversize hip boots, but unfortunately slipped and slid off the bank, rear-end first, into three feet of water. Nothing daunted, she surfaced, kept going, and I handed her the rod.

If this were a fairy tale, she would have landed the trout, but it's real life and, unfortunately, she gave a great yank on the rod and lost the trout, Adams, and some leader. She then threw down the rod, announced that fishing was a ridiculous sport, and stomped back to her Walkman.

While all of this was going on, Judy was playing out a drama with a trout down at the pond. The particular water in question is part of the stream, and is crossed by an old and picturesque covered bridge. Beneath the bridge is a small waterfall and a deep hole that contains several monster trout, which are readily seen but rarely caught. Now I should say that my wife is really a splendid caster, having been taught by Joan Wulff herself. Judy's casting ability far exceeds my own but, alas, she has never landed a fish.

She had spent the afternoon casting at a lower end of the pond. Superb casts, but no fish. After a while, she got hot and bored, and wandered onto the bridge, looking for shade. While there, she looked down through the side slats of the bridge and saw a large trout in the pool 10 feet below the bridge. She then let out some line into the pool. Judy claims there was a dry fly on the end, but I still suspect it was a piece of salami. Whatever, the fish struck, and now was securely hooded. But what a dilemma! Here was this fish, 10 feet below the covered bridge, on a 6X leader, and no way to land it. The rod was poking through the slats on the bridge, so she couldn't walk off and

[1]Caroline claims it was a Woolly Worm

beach the fish. And there was no one to whom she could pass the rod. So she had to try to reel in through 10 feet of air. Almost made it, too, but halfway up, the leader snapped and that was the end of what I was told was the largest trout ever seen in the Millbrook.

We're going to try again this year. Daughter Caroline has shown some progress and is actually learning to cast. Jennifer has progressed to Prince[2] and has abandoned Bruce Springsteen; whether she will be back on the water is problematical. And wife Judy, now equipped with a new eight-foot for six-weight graphite rod, has vowed to catch a fish this year and not to fish off covered bridges.

---

[2]Jennifer proofread this story and claims she would *never* have been listening to Bruce Springsteen, since *no one* listens to him anymore. She says it was actually Billy Joel. For my readers, the difference is probably academic.

Charles M. Loveless

One of the top career men in the United States Department of Agriculture's Forest Service and the Department of Interior's Fish and Wildlife Service. He is an enthusiastic fly fisherman, fly tyer, and wingshot. Fort Collins, Colorado.

An Extraordinary Day

It was one of those typical winter days in our nation's capital, a gray, heavy overcast lay like a veil of doom over the city, chilly and mind soaking wet. The whole East Coast had been socked-in for nearly a week with predictable outcomes: reduced air travel and suppression of otherwise bright outlooks.

The underpowered bus struggled up the steep incline. Its cargo of listless humans homeward bound after surviving another day of ubiquitous challenge and opportunity. Perhaps more of the former than the latter. Most were totally absorbed in their own thoughts, or staring straight ahead (we used to call this the "1,000-yard stare"), or straining to see detail through the rain-spattered windows. The windshield wiper beat a steady, rhythmic *put-a-ta, put-a-ta* that kept reminding me of Walter Mitty. The atmosphere was anything but electric and vital.

It occurred to me that I was nearly 2,000 miles from my favorite place on earth, which happens to be a trout stream. And, there seemed to be little likelihood of getting very much nearer in the foreseeable future. Overall, a most dismal circumstance. One solace, however. It was Friday, and within 30 minutes or so I would be home in the suburbs in front of a blazing, crackling hearth fire with a dry, chilled martini.

"Hold his head up, son, keep his head up now or you'll lose him for sure," my uncle shouted above the wind and driving rain. The old Shakespeare reel whined and clanked as the big trout made yet another run for the deepening channel. The short, little bamboo casting rod had a good feel to it as it throbbed in response to the desperate thrashings of the largest fish I had ever hooked. As my arms tired the rod tip would go down and I would hear, "Get his head up, son! You must learn to keep that rod high when you're playing a big fish!"

He was my uncle by marriage, no blood kin, yet I felt a closer kinship with him than with any man I knew, blood relative or not. He was tall, broad shouldered, athletic with large arms and wrists and had played professional baseball, been a boxer, and was an excellent swimmer and tennis player. My uncle didn't exactly keep his eye on the ball, though. Among other things, he had been an auto mechanic, stevedore, tractor driver, farmer, and I suspect had an eye for the ladies. I guess he decided that it's more important to live like you want to, quite contentedly, than to live more profitably but less happily. His later years were spent as the celery man for one of the big truck farms in the Glades near Lake Okeechobee. That's the last I heard of him after he and my aunt parted ways. To my regret I lost track of him. But, he was a man's man and especially to me. He never knew that, though.

My grandmother thought he was a rascal. She may have been right. Above all, though, he was totally dedicated to angling. And so was his wife, my aunt, who was very bright, had a bachelor's degree in business and was a successful insurance salesman (nowadays we say "salesperson"). They were both more than enthusiastic saltwater fishermen and always took me along on their weekend trips. They would pick me up before daylight and we rarely ever got back to the boat dock before sundown. As they say in the South, we fished from "can't-see to can't-see," a long day for a 10-year old but I loved it all. But I guess I didn't know it. At least at the time.

We fished the Inland Waterway year-round, in all kinds of weather, trolling mostly from a 12-foot dingy powered with a 10-h.p. kicker. Once in a while, my uncle would pull into a quiet cove, unlimber a long thin, custom-made bamboo rod and cast for snook with huge wooden plugs. Mostly though we caught lady fish, jack crevalle, snapper, blues, mackerel, and occasionally a sand shark near the inlet. On days when the "real" fishing was slow my uncle would anchor the boat near the pilings of the old abandoned railroad bridge and let me catch dogfish, mangrove snapper, and toadfish.

In the spring, when the big schools of pompano ran in the ocean, we had wonderful fishing with big 10-foot bamboo surf rods, large levelwind reels, and hemp line. For bait we used "sandfleas" that we scooped out of the surf as the waves rolled back from the shore. I remember many a croaker sack filled with four and five-pound pompano caught surf-fishing. But, Christmas Day was always *the* day to go for blue fish near the Palm Beach inlet. We'd "chum 'em" with meat scraps using an old grinder off the stern plate. We often stayed in one spot and filled the boat with three to five-pound blue fish literally snatched out of the water with hand lines as fast as we could work them. We always kept a few to eat and to give to friends, and a few we planted in the vegetable garden or flower beds for fertilizer. Most, however, we sold at the boat dock to the wholesale fish dealers. Ten bucks for a boat load of blues. Lots of money for having fun!

Well, anyway, I did land the big fish after what to me was a monumental struggle. An eight-pound eight-ounce sea trout. I was 10-years-old that Sunday afternoon in 1937 and this "huge" trout won the Palm Beach County juvenile-division fishing contest. I don't remember the prize but I sure remember the fish.

I had never heard of a fly rod in those days, or fishing with artificial flies. All this came later after moving out West. But, I had heard about trout. Not that I had ever seen one. I hadn't. I didn't even know anyone who had ever seen one. All I'd seen were pictures in outdoor magazines. But I did know about them and what I knew I liked. I guess it wasn't the trout so much as the vision I had of where they lived: high mountains, evergreen forests, and clean streams you could drink out of. Anyway, this is where it all began, and these are many of the angling memories my heart holds dear.

It had been unseasonably warm for the park. I had rolled and tossed most of the night in my second-story room at Mammoth Motor Inn. This was partly due to the heat and partly (maybe mostly) thinking about those big trout I was going to fish for the following day. I had been a long time getting back to Yellowstone and I was pretty anxious. I was underway early the next morning heading up the Lamar Valley just as it was getting good daylight. This valley is one of the most beautiful and most pristine pieces of country anywhere and looks today essentially as Osborn Russel first saw it in the 1830s as he described in his book, *Journal of a Trapper*. The only part that's changed is the meadow in front of the old ranger station that was planted with grass to feed the buffalo back in the '20s.

It was late October. The cottonwoods and aspen were their usual glorious golden, the sky such a deep blue it made tears come to your eyes, and the streams low and sparkling. The "shining trails" the Indians called them.

When I turned off onto the dusty service road and drove down through the tall sagebrush to the stream, I remembered the first time I had come here. It had been many years before with a close friend who fished it often. He had decided to share this secret place and its big fish with me.

I rolled up to the pool at the old bridge crossing and stopped the car. From this moment throughout this marvelous day, my fly fishing would be a very private affair. Most fly fishing is, I guess, but this was an especially private moment. The stream flowed smooth and clear as I had always remembered it. I was the only person for hundreds of miles in every direction. Or so it seemed. The wind gently stirred the tall June grass and some ravens quacked in the distance. I had been to this place many times over the years but each time was always like the first. Hardwired into the memory bank. The cathedral quiet, the great, overwhelming heights and distances, and, of course, the trout. As George Sand wrote, "Nature possesses the secret to happiness and no one has been able to steal it from her."

"*Slurp*." That got my attention! I took my eyes from the fresh snow on the far peaks and focused on the water. Fish were quietly and steadily rising.

Back to reality and one of the reasons for coming here. I anxiously rigged up my fly rod and struggled to get my waders on. The intensity of the rise increased. My intensity also increased and with it the inclination to screw things up. Like missing a line guide on my fly rod or putting my waders on the wrong foot.

Once a very close fishing buddy of mine did that when we were trying to get organized to fish a heavy hatch and before he noticed it he had also laced up both boots causing a slight delay. I kept telling myself, "relax, slow down, you've got all day: can't-see to can't-see." Ultimately, I got it all together and walked down to the pool. It looked like a small mayfly (*Ephemerella*?) dun on the water. I tied on a Blue Winged Olive, a #16 with a long 6X tippet. The water is gin clear. I waited for the wind to pick up and put a rip on the surface. Finally it came. I started stripping line and false casting. A large fish was taking the duns in a rhythmic cadence fairly tight up against the opposite bank near the overhanging willows. I put out a quartering upstream cast and the fly dropped about four feet ahead of his feeding lane. A good float—closer, close, there! Nothing. He refused. I tried again. Nothing. Again. Zilch! OK. Rest him. He's a big fish. Worth waiting for. Other smaller fish are now rising all up and down the pool. I'm tempted. Maybe there's something not quite right with the Blue Winged Olive. I tie on an #18 Adams. I moved upstream about eight or 10 feet hoping I could control the cast a little better and get the fly to him ahead of the line. He was still taking the duns and I put the little Adams right on his nose. Refusal again while my heart really got up in my throat. This sport is not for the fainthearted! Or the pious either. It's best for philosophers and near-drunks. My fly floated another three or four feet drag free. Something distracted me and I look away for a split second. I hear a *pop* and instinctively raise the rod. I was onto a nice fish—the first of the day. It wasn't the one I'd been working on but I'll take 'em anyway I can get 'em. I netted a beautiful 15-inch rainbow and gingerly released him enjoying the sense of well-being from having assisted life rather than destroying it. Conscience again triumphs over the palate!

Rainbows are not the dominant species in this stream but there are a few and, interestingly, most of those I've caught have been big ones. In fact, my largest stream rainbow, outside of Alaska, was taken on a Caddis Pupa about 100 yards upstream from where I stood. He measured a substantial 23 inches, jumped nine times, and fought like a demon. I was fishing alone, no one in sight, the way I like it, usually. But this time I somehow desperately wanted someone to see me catch that fish—someone to share the experience with. I didn't even have a camera. Never mind. I'll always remember.

Three or four more fish took my Adams, cutthroats this time. I missed some and got quite a few refusals. The Adams wasn't exactly right either. Well, I didn't want to kill myself having fun! The wine was chilled in the cooler and the turkey sandwich I had made up at the little restaurant in Gardiner the previous night was getting staler.

I found a soft spot to sit where I can see the water and savor my glass of Stags Leap 1982 Chenin Blanc (a great wine to fish by, to make love by, or to do anything by!) and turkey sandwich. Another glass of wine and I became drowsy in the warm October sunshine. I was tempted to take a little snooze. But I could see the trout beginning to rise again and reject the temptation of a nap out of hand. There was all winter to sleep.

I moved back to the pool, but farther down this time, and stand on the bank in the grass and begin to fish. The rest of that spectacular afternoon I never moved more than 10 feet in any direction from that spot and got in the water only once. I caught one cutthroat after another—over 20—on an #18 Henryville Special. All were taken on dries that I had tied. My "thing" is fishing with dry flies to rising fish. Why? Because there's some sort of exceptional visual pleasure when a trout takes your dry, especially if you've tied it yourself. As Nick Lyons says, ". . . I enjoy the incomparable rise, the abrupt opening of the stream, and the dramatic splash, the electricity from stream to eye to hand." Exactly!

Just before it got too dark to see the fly on the water, I took the trout I had worried over earlier in the day. With a very quiet gentle sip he inhaled my little Henryville, exploded as I set the hook, and with his crisscrossing runs put down every fish for 30 yards in all directions. He went into my backing three times and twice almost made it to the fast pocket-water below the pool. At last, as my arm tired and the rod tip dropped—"hold his head up, son, keep his head up now"—the ancient fish gave it up. I eased him in toward the bank as he wallowed and turned on his side. It's then that I saw him for the first time—not only the largest cutthroat I had ever caught but the largest I had ever seen!

As I nervously reached for him with the net he recovered briefly and made one last short, frantic run. But it was all over and he knew it. I waded into the shallow water near the tail of the pool and coaxed the great fish into my net. My legs were trembling. I had to sit down on the overhanging bank. I was exhausted and so was my aquatic friend. The hook came out easily and, after rendering some "artificial respiration" (I needed some, too), he finally stayed upright and swam slowly and majestically back into the depths of the pool. As he went I wondered, "If he had known that after the fight he would be released, would he have struggled so long and valiantly"? I think so. It was a matter of principle.

Well, I *did* "hold his head up" and wished my old rascal of an uncle could have seen this great trout, too. Perhaps he did. He would have been pleased and proud. Guess I finally closed the loop.

That day on my secret nameless trout stream was perhaps the most thrilling, ecstatic day of angling I ever experienced. It was truly an extraordinary day. An extraordinary day, indeed!

George D. Kirkham

An investment banker when not on fishing safaris throughout North America, the results of which, he says, have been remarkably mediocre. (The fishing, not the banking!) Willoughby, Ohio.

Two for the Show

For several years, beginning when she was 10-years-old, my daughter, Samantha, had not only shown a distinct lack of interest in trout fishing, but claimed to find it repugnant (otherwise known as "gross"). At the age of 12, perhaps inured to violence by television fare, Sam allowed as how she and her alter ego, Pixie Taylor, would permit me to escort them up to the Castalia Club for the weekend. I was informed, however, that if they deigned actually to fish, I would be required to remove the fly and dispose of the slimy things, if any happened to be caught.

The almost two-hour drive to Castalia was consumed by expressions of misgivings, queries about the food ("Why do they serve dinner at 4:30?") and about the sleeping quarters. The separate building for women was deemed a fine idea by the two 12-year-olds.

The serenity pervading Castalia did not appear to have any effect on Sam and Pixie, in fact it was somewhat the reverse. Quickly taking over the choicest room in the ladies cottage, changing outfits at least twice and decimating the soft drink cupboard, they made themselves at home in very short order. Several members headed for the most remote sections of the stream, seeking peace and quiet.

The room in which members store their tackle is off limits to women, hence outfitting Sam and Pixie with fly rods not only took some walking back and forth but subjected me to comments about being a male chauvanist pig. Gratitude is rare at their age.

Pixie had never seen a fly rod before, and Sam had thrashed one around once in our back yard. While my thoughts on the proper method of fly casting were not particularly welcome, both girls did grant me a brief audience, while making certain that I would follow them around with net, creel, and priest in hand. Nothing like a little optimism.

There is a pool in front of the club house at Castalia where anyone fishing will be observed by members and guests on the porch who are taking a respite. Therefore, when Pixie's third cast, and I use that term as charitably as possible, hooked a three-pound rainbow, the ensuing bedlam was watched by a small crowd. Considering the assorted, not to say conflicting, instructions shouted at Pixie while this large trout jumped five or six times and then tore up and down and around the pool, it was a miracle that the fish did not rid itself of the fly. After a great deal of excitement, the fish tired, and I netted it and administered the *coup de grace* with my priest.

A little while later, Samantha hooked a large trout (later weighing in at just under three pounds) and, without my assistance, landed it, after which I again performed my duties. Score so far: girls two, Dad zero.

Samantha and Pixie then decided that netting and killing trout was not "gross," but might add to their whole fishing experience. Therefore, I was relieved of my net, creel, and priest, and the girls moved upstream.

During the remainder of the day the peacefulness of Castalia was interrupted from time to time by squeals, shrieks, sounds of fish splashing, and sounds of fish being beaten to a pulp. I could see through the shrubbery a tree branch being wielded instead of my small priest. One hapless trout was grabbed by the tail and swung home-run style against a nearby tree. Score at the finish: girls seven, Dad three. Exit two girls thinking trout fishing at Castalia is really cool.

Last May (1984) Samantha, Pixie, and I went back for a return bout with the trout. The weather was particularly balmy. As is usually the case, serious fishing was interspersed with serious resting on the large club house porch, accompanied by a variety of liquid refreshments.

The girls favorite post in front of the club house was occupied by John Bernard, the club's senior member (46 years). John knew every inch of the serpentine Castalia stream, particularly the areas that were the most productive, and consistently filled out his limit, even on dog days. Something was amiss this day, however, and after a half hour of trying every trick he knew from one end of the pool to the other, John gave up in disgust and retired to the nearby porch, a lounge chair and a cool drink.

Enter Samantha and Pixie, stage left, who prance down to the edge of the pool where every trout in the place can see them, and then beat the pool's surface to a froth with their patented casting techniques.

Result? Six trout in 10 minutes. I had a feeling that the results would have been the same with sticks, string, and safety pins. Somebody was watching out for the girls.

Several members offered John advice of assorted degrees of helpfulness on how he might improve his skills by watching Samantha and Pixie. In return some suggestions were made as to what could be done with the advice.

Once again we left Castalia to return home with two very excited and enthusiastic young ladies talking about next year.

Author's note: During the time that I was struggling with this little tale, John Bernard died. Samantha expressed considerable sorrow over the fact that the man who taught her how to fish would no longer be at Castalia when she goes up there. I'm sorry, too.

Elmer L. Lindseth

Elmer spent 50 years in the electric utility industry. He is a self-styled novice at fly fishing, although he has fished in New Zealand, Iceland, Scotland, Ireland, Mexico, New Brunswick, and elsewhere and is a life member of Trout Unlimited. Shaker Heights, Ohio.

Hooked

This is a sort of sequel to Robert Ruark's *Old Man and the Boy*. Only I am the old man, not the boy. The boy was my son Jon, then just turned 12. He's now 50. I was with him and my wife Anne on a Quebec canoe trip in 1947. For his birthday a few weeks earlier we had given him a fly rod and rudimentary tackle. It is not easy to recreate the excitement of a 12-year-old who is packing a duffle for a canoe trip, especially his first fly-fishing trip, and to do this 38 years after the fact.

Our neighbor Charlie Farran, who was then and is now a good fisherman, had suggested an area west of Lake St. John in the Treuche River country where he and Harry Grinton had fished the year before. After Charlie had regaled us with stories of the fine speckled trout fishing they had, we made a deal with their outfitter in Roherval to take us on a canoe trip with a couple of guides.

My son had been on canoe trips with us in the bush since he was five or six but always into bass and pickerel country where it was trolling June Bug spinners, or Dardevles. But this time it was to be fabled speckled trout. The kid was to become a fly fisherman.

We went by train, of course—this in itself was enough to excite a young boy. No jets in those days! We went by sleeper to Montreal arriving at noon in time to look in at a tackle shop—I think it was Eaton's—to check out flies and gear. Doesn't a young fly fisherman have to learn to visit a tackle shop en route? I remember buying a reel—a Hardy St. George it was. What fly fisherman doesn't need yet another reel? Or some more flies? Better start the lad out properly.

Then the evening train—the old-time dining car—to Quebec City where we lay over a day at the Chateau Frontenac. Kids in those days found that event in itself an important experience, especially kids learning to be trout fishermen. Besides he was studying French in school and this was to be his first laboratory. He could try his French on the bus drivers and the waiters. Maybe he'd even fish France some day. A kid can't learn too young!

The sleeper north from Quebec to Lake St. John was routine—routine that is for old folks but pretty exciting for a budding fisherman on his first quest. Remember those old Pullman cars, and those upper berths? Jon was in my upper.

We were called at 4:45 a.m. And soon off the train at Chambord Junction. Even father and mother could sense adventure at dawn in the north country. Here our outfitter picked us up for the run to Rokuval where we met our guides, two brothers, Robertson by name although there was nothing Scottish about them. Actually, one of them could speak no English at all, his brother a smattering. Some Scottish Robertson ancestor must have come over with the Hudson's Bay Company generations ago. Maybe an Indian squaw was somewhere in the background as well.

Our gear and canoes were promptly loaded into a truck and we took off over a lumber road for our launch point. It turned out that the country had been badly burned over a few years before in a fire that took 38 days to burn itself out. Not unnaturally the country was not only desolate looking but pretty dirty as well; not an auspicious start for the neophyte. And then there was the language barrier. We did have a French-English dictionary along as well as a Berlitz. But who in the bush needs to ask Mr. Berlitz "Where is the hotel dining room" or "Where can I get a taxi?"

Up to this point we had scarcely seen any water, let alone trout water, but, in due course after lunch at an abandoned lumber camp site, we transferred our gear and grub, launched our canoes, and were off. It was but a small lake and after a 15 or 20-minute paddle we were at a portage, the first of what we later thought were dozens and dozens of them.

The first portage took an hour because we had to make three trips. Then another short paddle and another one-hour portage. "When do we fish"? the young fisherman was heard to ask his mother. That first day we didn't fish, but after we made camp and had supper we were glad to crawl into our sleeping bags.

Then there was the fly situation. Not the trout flies we took along but the black flies and mosquitos. These were so plentiful that we had to dope ourselves up every 20 or 30 minutes. And, to get to sleep, we had to spray the tent. Flit was the standard bug spray in those days but, as some of you remember, inhaling it kept a person awake. So if we did not spray, the bugs kept us awake. If we did spray, the Flit did the same. Sort of "damned if you do and damned if you don't." A delightful experience for a young fisherman. And no fishing yet.

After two days of this and a dozen portages we got into decent country with good trees, lakes, and rivers. The evening before we made camp we stopped at a spot where the guides had obviously taken fish before. It was at the mouth of a spring-fed creek which emptied into the lake we were crossing.

Jon excitedly put his rod together and in 30 or 40 minutes had taken a dozen brookies, the largest maybe 13 or 14 inches long. "Nice fish," our so-called English-speaking guide said. This should have been the tip-off that we weren't going to get into any four- or five-pound fish on the trip. Maybe not any three-pounders or even two-pounders. But it was obviously a great start for a youngster on his first trip with a fly rod. As I remember, he fished wet flies in the current where the creek emptied into the lake, not unlike the way others have done before and since.

The going that second day had been routine, paddle 15 minutes or so, then portage for an hour. Then another paddle and another portage. And so on. But now life began to change. Now that we were fishing and had caught fish. That evening we had broiled trout for dinner with fixings. And a good campsite. And no rain. A little gin rummy and early to bed maybe would wake us healthy, yes, but wealthy? Not likely there at least.

The next morning the young hero was up early and had half a dozen trout before breakfast. Trout and pancakes—how can you have it any better? And this was only the third day out? Jon was definitely hooked! That day we had trout chowder for supper. One of our guides was an excellent cook, having cooked in a lumber camp. No one lived any better than we did.

The next day it was another dozen trout among us in an hour's fishing, even though we were still traveling. And then the day after, Jon went off with a guide to a nearby lake for an afternoon. Returning, he announced that he had "taken" (not "caught," mind you) 54 trout. A tough act to repeat.

The following day dawned warm and sunny, but the guides didn't like the looks of the weather. Too much of a good thing had also worn brook-trout fishing a little thin for Jon. "Can we do anything else besides trout fishing?" he was heard to ask.

One of the guides understood more English than he pretended. He must have thought, I'll show you. "Tomorrow we'll go lake trout fishing," he announced at supper. By now we had been out seven or eight days, making camp at a new site almost every night. "How about our stopping at the Forest Ranger's cabin for a few days?" I asked. Moreover the weather didn't look very promising.

It turned out to be a fine deal, especially since the weather did turn bad and by the time we had our air mattresses and sleeping bags spread out on the floor it began to rain. The guides had pitched their tent outside. But we had a decent roof and a good cook stove and the guides were happy not to have to cook in the rain. Pie for supper that night, lumber-camp pie with a jar of strawberry jam for filling. The good life—and rain on the roof to lull us to sleep!

Early in the trip Jon had taken to wearing my A&F bug hood, one I had first learned to use in Labrador where the bugs were so bad one couldn't see his cast hit the water. Most of you remember those hoods, to fit over a wide brimmed hat, a hole for your pipe if you smoked and a drawstring around your neck. Jon didn't like to fuss with bug dope and so had adopted the hood.

This was to be our day for lake-trout fishing. But none of us had anything but our trout rods. "No trouble," said our guide. "I'll show you how." First we caught eight or ten chubs for bait right off our campsite. Then we were off for lake-trout water.

The technique was to use only the two butt sections of a three-piece rod and troll a chub or a Ouananiche fly. We let out 25 or 30 yards of HCH line (as it was rated then) and a substantial sinker to get it down.

Anne hooked the first fish fairly promptly. And it was a good fish, too, that required 30 minutes or so to land with the crude rig she was using, for obviously she couldn't put much pressure on the fish. We didn't have a De-liar but the guides estimated it at 12 pounds. And on part of a trout rod? Jon had his sights raised somewhat. A new world, this so-called fly fishing. These were the legendary "Lake trout at the surface just after the ice goes out." But this was mid-July!

During the next couple of days we took 15 or 20 lake trout weighing from two to 10 pounds, and were eating lake trout baked, broiled, boiled, and name it. Said Jon, "So, what's next?" He had conquered brook and lake trout, and needed a new adventure.

It was time to head back. Up to that point, we had been in moose country on and off, marshy shores of lakes and swampy portage. Moose sign was plentiful. One morning one of the guides said "Let's go easy—we might see a moose." And promptly we did—too promptly in fact because Jon didn't have his camera ready before the moose—actually Mrs. Moose—was gone into the bush. But from then on it was "Let's find some more moose." And we did. Our guides guided hunting parties in the fall and they knew the likely areas.

When shortly after Jon was able to get a picture of a moose at fairly close range he was more a moose fan than a trout fisherman. In all he photographed three or four moose as we pushed our way back to our starting point. But all adventures have an end. The last night out Jon talked some in his sleep. The next morning his mother, suspecting that he had been fighting a big brookie, asked him what he had dreamed about. It turned out he had dreamed moose all night.

Thus ends the saga of a 12-year-old's maiden trout fishing adventure. From brookies to lakers to moose in two weeks! Strictly downhill all the way.

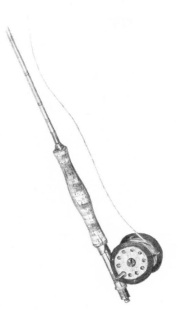

James E. Gavacs

Jim graduated from tom cod and bullhead catfish in the Hudson River to bluegills and rock bass in Shawnee Lake and the Juiniata River to trout across the continent. Cleveland, Ohio.

Emerger

It was our third trip to the Beaverkill. My Dad and I spent our Memorial Day weekends camping and trout fishing along the river. We arrived late Friday night and pitched camp in a vacant lot just below the Junction Pool. Somehow it was different that year. The rushing roar of the river was a mere gurgle. The smells of a summer evening were intense. Three itching welts on my neck made me acutely aware of I'd forgotten the insect repellent. It was late, so gurgle, smell and itching not withstanding, I went to sleep immediately thinking of the fishing in the morning.

Saturday morning was crystal clear and warm with just a light mist over the river. It seemed such a waste of time to build a fire and make breakfast. All I had on my mind was that telltale tugging on the line that meant a trout was at the other end.

Formalities out of the way, we were finally ready to catch fish! I left my Dad in the dust on the way to the riffles above the Junction Pool. The water was clear as liquid glass and the fish seemed suspended in air. The only problem was that our squirming worms just kept floating by the fish without a hint of interest.

This mockery of our offerings had to stop! After two hours of my best presentations I gave up to watch from the bank. I became interested in several fishermen at the other end of the pool. They were fly casting and catching fish! This held my attention very well. I also soon became aware of the fish in front of me eating flies on the surface.

Being a fan of *Field & Stream*, thoughts of Al McClane's articles danced through my head. I recalled the account of his fishing a particularly tough situation. Al was on a rock-strewn stretch of an unnamed Catskill stream with three 16-inch browns lying behind two boulders. Being Al McClane, he could be gutsy, so he made a pact with himself. If he didn't catch all three he would release the ones he did catch. Somehow with exact casting, line mending, and drag-free floats Al overcame the situation and creeled all three. What a fisherman! But here I was 14 and fishless and looking at what appeared to be a long, tedious, and fishless weekend.

Fly fishing was something I had only read and dreamt about. I had a fly casting outfit. I also tied flies as a hobby. In my collection were lemon yellow mayflies, bright blue caddis and even some candy apple red nymphs. But I had never fished a fly. Noontime came and it seemed a relief to leave the river.

Over lunch I noticed the fly fishermen from the pool were also camping in the lot. I went over to meet and talk with them. During the conversation one of the men asked to see my collection. He said they were tied well but probably not the appropriate colors. He spent some time with me, helping me tie several appropriate patterns and giving me practical advice and encouragement. The encouragement was what I needed. Tying flies and believing you could actually catch fish on them were two different things. That afternoon, my enthrallment with fly fishing began.

With my new found enthusiasm I set out. I returned to "my" spot above the pool only to find it with many more people than when I had left. I thought for a minute of just stepping right in and fishing, but thought the better of it. After seeing my casting ability, they might think I was actually fishing *for* flies.

It was a short hike up the river and around the bend to a spot devoid of others. There was a long flat stretch with large rocks poking their tops through the surface. The sun and trees made a patchwork of shadows shimmering and everchanging on the water. The leaves were that light spring green that gives an intensity of freshness and being. Looking back on the scene I don't see how I could not have realized that something rare and transforming was happening. Even though it took place over a quarter century ago, my eyes still squint from the sunlight and I get that smell of summer whenever I think about it.

What amazed me most about this scene were the fish. It seemed there were trout rising everywhere to feed on surface insects. Remembering my mentor's advice I thrashed about in the water trying to catch an insect so I could match the hatch. Today, I would think, it's a mayfly, light brown in color, probably best imitated with a #16 Light Cahill. That day it was a small tan bug. I searched my collection of flies. The closest I could come was a gray-bodied fly with a dun hackle that wasn't really very close. The morning's doldrums began to settle back into my thoughts and the sun was not as intense, the river and trees not as vivid.

Halfheartedly I began flailing my fly on the water. Then it happened. A trout rose to my fly from out of the depths only to turn off at the last second as the drag of the line pulled the fly away from its mouth. Suddenly the sun was bright again and the colors vivid. I cast again, and again, and then, wonders, a fish once more rose to my offering, but this time my float was true and dragless. The fish took, I set the hook and off he went upstream and so did I. Four runs upstream and three runs down, four slips, and three dunkings later, I brought him to net. It was a brown with brilliant red and blue spots and bright red gills. I carried the fish at least 30 feet from the edge of the river before removing it from the net because I didn't want it jumping back into the water.

At the end of the day I had two creelmates for my brown. I also had a new way of life!

I still look forward to that stream that leads away from the road. It changes constantly from visit to visit and from hour to hour. It fills me with smells and sounds and visions. Visions of trout rising under a branch, from behind a rock, or scooting away when they sense my presence. Visions of a brown trout jumping in a net with such red gills and vivid red and blue spots, the like of which I have never seen again. Visions of a 14-year-old's emergence of many years ago and visions of my four-year-old son, whose emergence is yet to come. . . .

Birgir Karlsson

Competent chief steward of Iceland Air, he is in charge of ministering to the needs of all Iceland-bound Atlantic salmon fishermen from North America. Birgir also is a highly proficient salmon angler in his own right. Reykjavik, Iceland.

Leifur's Heppni[1]

On a flight from Chicago to Reykjavik in July, 1982, I started to talk to Mr. Marshall Field, a great fly fishermen from that city. He was on his way to fish one of the better rivers in Iceland named Vididalsa. After chatting together about Atlantic salmon and fishing for a while Marshall invited me to come fishing with him for a day or two in Vididalsa and that's how it happened.

Two days later I drove up to the river and met Marshall about 10 that morning. He had already caught three salmon. We started to fish and that night I came home to the lodge with three beautiful salmon and three three to four-pound char. I could not complain after such a wonderful day nor could Marshall, who caught three that morning and a 15-pounder and a 10-pounder (both of which he let go back into the river) that afternoon.

The next day was a nice day for fishing at Vididalsa, a bright but cloudy

[1]Icelandic for good fortune.

sky and a light wind. Before breakfast Marshall tied a fly, a Roger's Fancy on a #6 hook, gave it to me and told me to enjoy it.

Well, breakfast was over and everybody gathered outside to get ready, putting on waders and other fishing gear, to go out there to catch salmon. Oh brother, I tell you, what a sight: about 10 fishermen dressed like that, armed with rods, flies, tailers, and everything you can think of. It would be enough to scare any salmon right out of the river and never come back, so it was a good thing the salmon didn't see us.

Now we drove off with our guides in their Jeeps to our sections on the river. Marshall pointed out to me an area of good, strong current where I threw my fly for a few minutes but nothing happened, but I knew there was a salmon. So I said to my partner to try next, because I knew if anybody could catch it, that would be Marshall. Sure enough in five to six casts the fish was on and in 10 or 15 minutes the fish was out of the river and on the bank.

After an hour, we moved to another place on the river. This was a very wide pool, 25 to 30 yards across, and in one spot there was a large rock about 10 feet long, sticking maybe three feet out of the water. The water came down the river in strong current about 25 yards above the rock forming a deep pool alongside. I was supposed to try this pool first so the Roger's Fancy was the fly on my list. I walked onto the sand bar and made my cast a little above and outside the rock, letting the fly sink with the current into the rock-pool where I thought a fish would be. So few casts later the fly was stuck when I was getting ready for the next cast and quick thoughts ran through my mind. Oh hell, did I let the fly sink down to hook into my dearest country or was it a — ? I just stopped thinking because now I saw some waves start on the surface and then *wham* and some giant fish jumped high out of the water away from us preventing us from clearly seeing the exact size. My partner shouted to me, "Be careful now, Birgir, you have a beautiful salmon on the fly, possibly bigger than mine yesterday." So I thought, yes, I'd better be careful and then the fish took off downriver. Seeing the line go out of the reel at this speed, making this singing sound and the cracking sound in the reel, I dared not touch the line because it might burn my fingers; and out went the line, 30 yards fly line and almost the same of the backing and me running after it. Also I was pulling much on the rod. I wanted to feel first how the salmon had taken the fly and I had only a 12-pound-test leader and it could snap.

Finally the fish stopped and turned around and back up the river. So now it was all in reverse, me backing up on the bank trying to reel in the line as fast as I possibly could to keep the slack out of it. The salmon came up to the rock and dived into the deep pool where he had taken the fly, trying its utmost to tangle the line around the rock, giving me a hard time to wade in three feet of water to get to the sand bar where I could lift the line over the rock with my rod.

One time, after the usual 40 to 60 yards of quick sprint downriver, the salmon turned and dashed up again with me reeling in the line and backing up. I just barely managed from the bank to lift the line up over the top of the rock when the fish stopped in the deep pool and now the line was over the top of the rock. I decided to halt right there on the bank, and see in which direction the fish would pull the line next and it was good to catch a little breath before next action began.

Now I tightened the line to pull the fish into action again hoping it would go downstream, but it took off up the river and the line slid off the rock, the fish pulling line out of the reel. I knew the salmon would turn around in a few seconds and so it did, heading the same path through the deep pool downriver. I was hoping to be able to get the slack out of the line and lift it over the rock again but no, I was too late. The line got tangled under the rock so now the next quick action was to dash through the three feet of water to the sand bar with the water splashing away from my breast (as from the bow of a battleship going into action), the fish speeding downriver. I was shaking because the line was like a guitar string under the rock. Would I be too late to reach the sand bar to lift the line before it would play its last *snapp-pinnng* note, and *bon voyage* to my beautiful fish? No, I made it, lifted the line over, turned around and played a battleship again to the river bank, running like mad after the fish on its way down and with the backing line way out.

By now, I knew the fish had taken the fly well, most likely in back of the mouth through the skin around the bone in the upper jaw, not giving the hook a chance to scratch into the bone structure and irritating the fish very much, which usually causes fish to jump more out of the water. And this fish really didn't jump but once, just when taking the fly.

At this point we were getting to know each other after being together for 20 to 30 minutes with the #6 fly, 12-pound-test leader, line, and single handed (no ended butt) 3¼-ounce 9½-foot rod tying us together.

So the fish took off once again like it wanted to get this over with and show me who is the winner, and it kept on pulling farther down the river. But now my fingers were holding tighter on the line causing a heavy pull for the fish which was slowing down a little bit. But it turned around again upriver, same path, and same work began for me running, reeling in line but, now, not taking any chances on the rock but always dashing over to the sand bar to avoid another tangling. This went on, but with shorter sprints, for some 15 minutes more and both of us getting worn out causing me to trip down and allowing the line to get tangled in back of the reel, which gave me a little scare while getting it unhooked but fortunately I was quick enough.

At this time, after about 45 or 50 minutes, the fish was getting tired and I was able to pull the fish on the inside of the rock to shallower water. I still was not able to really see how big it was because now the shallow water was so muddy from my wading plus the fish stirring up the mud. But I was sure the weight had gone a little higher than 15 pounds. Finally the fish was giving in and turning on its side and I pulled it into the shallows. Marshall now waded into the river and, only armed with his hand (no tailer was available), tried to pull it out with one hand by its tail. He quickly realized both hands had to be used and brought it to the bank and declared "This beauty must be about a 28 or maybe 30-pounder." I could only answer,

"Thank you. It would be nice if it is so." I was thinking about early on, when the fish acted like it wanted to get the fight over with to see who would be the winner, so this time it came out on my side.

A few minutes later, while I was resting on the bank admiring this beautiful fish which had given me so much fight for almost an hour, our guide came over and stared at the fish, took the scale and hooked it in the gills, looked at the scale, ran to the car, picked up the microphone of his CB radio and shouted into it that he had one 27-pound hen fish.

William E. MacDonald

Concluding a life-long career with Ma Bell, Bill retired as chairman and CEO of Ohio Bell Telephone in 1983. He retained, however, another, almost as important post, as president of the widely known and venerable Castalia Trout Club. Bill puts first things first. Shaker Heights, Ohio.

Confession

The stream at the Castalia Trout Club is stocked with rainbow and brook trout and a few browns. We raise our own fish at the club and have only put a few browns in the water because as they grow big they enjoy nothing more than feeding on the smaller rainbow and brooks.

Over the years, some pretty big browns have survived and roam the stream. They are well fed and difficult to catch. While they add excitement to the fisherman's quest, we like to get them out whenever we can.

A couple of years ago, I quietly approached a favorite pool which often finds good-sized trout present because a large drainpipe empties into this pool from a nursery section where fingerlings are raised. Some of the food fed to the smaller trout thus finds its way into the pool.

As I drew near, I spotted the largest brown trout I have ever seen at the club. Using every skill I possessed—along with every fly imaginable—I failed to get even a hint of interest. All of a sudden he swam into the drainpipe with just the tip of his tail showing. Now I carry a big net and so I carefully got down on my belly, leaned over the bank and covered the pipe opening with my net. Mr. Brown backed up and what do you know, I had him. A 6½-pound lunker.

If confession is truly good for the soul, mine is now vastly improved for this is my first public admission of how the Big One was really landed.

Russell A. Olson

An attorney, law director, father, hiker, camper, bird hunter, white-water rafter, soarer, and fresh and saltwater fly fisherman. Lakewood, Ohio.

Zero Defects

A huge rainbow appeared and, as quickly, disappeared.

I continued fishing my Light Cahill dry fly at a bend in the stream in front of the clubhouse at the century old Rockwell Springs Trout Club, near Castalia,Ohio. It was late in the afternoon of a resplendent September day and, although I had only been fishing for about an hour, I already had two fish in the creel.

Suddenly there he was again. The autumn sun at my back was creating vivid shadows so I stepped into the shade of a nearby tree. The big trout held in front of me, but he was near the stream's bottom, about eight feet down. Don't scare him was my first thought. No quick movements. Just an easy cast with the Light Cahill to see if he'll come off the bottom. Three times, without a budge. It's clear I'll have to go after him.

Stepping back from the stream slowly and cautiously, I reviewed what to throw. Moving quickly I cut off the dry fly and went to a #10 Black Woolly

Bugger. Why the Black Woolly Bugger? I don't know. I tied it onto the nine-foot 3X leader at the end of the weight-forward sinking line.

Believing that the large rainbow would likely be gone when I stepped back to the stream, or if he was still there would decline my offering or if he accepted it would probably snap it off, I decided to try to do everything right. I clinched the hook with extra care and then sharpened it. Directly ahead of the fly I attached a small piece of lead twist-on and removed a blade of grass from the leader.

Finally I stepped slowly and softly back to the stream, my shadow blending with that of the tree. He was still there. But so also were two or three average-size fish. What if one of the others grabbed the hook? A chance I would have to take.

I was ready. No mistakes. No false casts. Probably only one shot.

I flipped the Bugger about 24 inches upstream from the fish. In spite of the size of the hook and the twist-on, it was a good cast with little disturbance to the calm clear water. As the Bugger started to settle its long marabou tail began to pulsate and breathe.

Suddenly the fly stopped. "He's on!" raced through my head. Fortunately I didn't overreact. My first instinct was to keep the line tight—and I did. Then quickly, but gently, I raised the tip of my favorite seven-foot six-inch bamboo rod, glad that the hook was sharpened.

The fish immediately made a strong downstream run and I put him on the reel at once. Turning about, he charged directly back at me making it almost impossible to bring line in fast enough to keep it tight. After turning about once more, the rainbow headed straight into the bank where the line became entangled with weeds and when he bolted back out to midstream the line remained entangled. Here's where I lose him, I thought. But the line broke free and he was still on. Maybe, it's my day.

After a couple more runs and reverse runs, my quarry surfaced and tried some serious rolling and thrashing, all without success. The hook was still in; the line was holding. I was giving it my best shot.

With yet another burst, the large trout ran downstream passing clean under a footbridge about 50 feet away. Carefully I worked him back. He was in charge yet under control—a strange feeling.

By this time several other fishermen, including my son, Craig, and fellow Woods and Waters Adviser, Bill Dean, had gathered about, attracted by the commotion. Some offered advice, others just watched. All were surprised by the size of the fish, including club manager Jeff Smith and his two small children.

Probably 45 minutes had elapsed since I had set the hook. The sun was getting low but I was holding up. I hadn't made a mistake yet and I felt growing confidence.

The fish had one more trick—to the bottom and into the mud. No way could I "horse" him off. The only possible way to break a sulk, of which I was aware, was to keep the line tight and steadily apply pressure while gently tapping the handle or reel. It worked! Craig and Bill, after about 15 minutes of struggle, manning the largest net they could find, got it under him and brought him to the bank.

It was immediately clear that my fish was a giant. When we put him on the scale at the fish house he weighed 11 pounds 11 ounces—a club record. I couldn't believe it then and, in a way, I still can't.

That night after drinks for all in the bar I slept well. The next night, however, I woke up several times, tossed and turned and thought of all the things that could have gone wrong. I was glad they hadn't.

Records are made to be broken, and mine will be too. Perhaps it will be you. Until you do catch your record-buster, however, here's a wish!

"May care's nets ne'er entangle
nor poverty depress
A brother of the angle"

—Thomas Stoddard, 1866

Werner D. Mueller

A Cleveland barrister, he was taught as a child to love nature and the out-of-doors by his father, Omar Mueller, who was an admirer and spiritual twin of Teddy Roosevelt. Werner has been trouting, birding, waterfowling, trained by Labs, and trying to raise bluebirds ever since. Novelty, Ohio.

The Saga of Old Werner and Old Fighter

"Look at those salmon in the main run! Three good ones! Can you see them?"

John Jonssonn, my twentiesh, red-haired Icelandic guide, was perched next to me overlooking a deep canyon. He pointed down toward three dark shapes undulating just above the river bottom, then gazed inquiringly into my untrained eyes. After a two-minute lesson in how to tell the difference between a mossy rock and a salmon lying on the river bottom, I, known as Old Werner after attaining the dignity of my sixtieth year, was able to grunt "Uh, yes, I see two. They are near the middle of the pool. Lying on the bottom, barely moving their tails. 10-pounders?"

"Look downstream from them, just 30 feet in front of the island—there's one at least half again as big. Maybe 15 or 18 pounds. That's about as big as they come in this river. Twenty-one pounds was our top fish last year."

"I see him."

"Good. I'll go down with you to show you how to get to the bottom of the canyon in one piece. Then I'll meet you downstream in about an hour." Jon spoke English like an American. He had studied in the States.

He guided me down the least treacherous draw of the canyon to stream-side, handed me a #10 black wet fly with the undignified but well-known appellation Black Rat, wished me luck, climbed back up the canyon to his Jeep, and bounced away down the dirt road that paralleled the river.

I decided to test my equipment and casting ability on one of the smaller salmon, on the theory that I could lead him away from the others without frightening them. After a careful stalk, I cast the Black Rat above the first fish, and the wet fly quartered downstream clearly in its line of vision. No action. I repeated the tactic a dozen times, then moved to the second fish. No action. I then gave the big fellow a chance at it. No response. Disappointed, my right hand reached mechanically for my fly box in the right outer pocket of my fishing vest. My well-trained right hand groped for but did not find the right outer pocket of my fishing vest. I was not wearing a fishing vest! It was still in the Jeep, now parked one-mile downstream!

During the 45 minutes that it took to climb the canyon wall, hike down to the car, retrieve my fishing vest, hike back up the canyon rim, relocate the salmon from above, descend to streamside, tie on a new fly, and stalk the salmon, I had plenty of time to reflect on how I happened to be there in the first place. A Cleveland duck-hunting friend, Willard Brown, had called me at my law office to advise me that my second career of fishing and hunting, which had taken me from Alaska to Spain to Columbia and other parts in between, was seriously flawed: he had heard, on the best of authority, that I had never caught an Atlantic salmon. Ten-pound Alaskan rainbows and five-pound brookies, let alone two or three-pound cutthroat trout, were not in the same category. This blot on my record could be cured, however, as he had an opening for one rod on Iceland's Laxa i Kjos, one of the top salmon rivers in Iceland, based at least on numbers of fish landed the past several seasons; and this prime July slot was to be mine, if I still claimed to have any spirit of adventure.

It had taken a full five seconds to make up my mind.

The trip had started out well. Of the nine fishermen who made up the party, I had known only Willard, but we all seemed basically compatible. After a short one-hour drive from Reykjavik, north, we were treated to a splendid smorgasbord of herring, salmon, shrimp, fork tender Icelandic lamb, and various vegetable dishes vinaigrette. Furthermore, during the first day and a half of fishing, most of us had landed one or more scrappy, fresh run, Atlantic salmon.

Now back at streamside, I focused on the problem at hand. The fish were there, the first stalk and fly presentations had not spooked the fish, but they had totally ignored my small Black Rat. What to do? A lifetime of trouting had not prepared me to make a selection from a box full of mysterious salmon flies with equally mysterious names such as Hairy Mary, Rusty Rat, Blue Charm, Collie Dog, and so forth. On the theory that veterans of the area usually know best, I finally tied on a fly that the most experienced of our group, Hal Haskell, of Wilmington, Delaware, had invented and swore by: his version of the locally celebrated Collie Dog tube fly, in #10, double hook.

Old Werner then ignored the two 10-pounders, and began a patient stalk toward Old Fighter, trying to imitate a hungry lynx stalking a fat bighorn sheep. When I reached a point properly above a huge mid-stream boulder, which I had picked out as a marker of the big salmon's position, I carefully dropped the tube fly upstream of the long, dark shadow, so that the fly would quarter downstream and cross his line of vision only slightly above his lie. One second, two seconds, three seconds, and the fly disappeared in a silvery flash. I tightened up until I felt the fish, and Old Fighter set the hook himself as he bolted upstream to the music of a screaming reel. He half-jumped, half-thrashed the surface; and then, reversing course, raced downstream on the far side of a rock-strewn island! I raised my rod tip, but not fast enough or high enough; the fly line caught on a tall rock, and the heavy fish was about to get deep into the backing, not only downstream, but with leverage. Disaster!

Without a thought in my mind other than the need to get the line off that rock so that I would have a direct connection to the fish, I charged into the near channel through three feet of water churning over algae covered boulders towards the island. Ten feet from the island I slipped, upended, banged my right knee against a submerged boulder, and tumbled downstream in a wheel of waders, head, feet, and fly rod.

During one split second when my head was above water and one foot had a brief grip on the river bottom, I hurled the fly rod well up onto the island, and then grabbed with both hands for a rock in order to arrest my downstream excursion. The rock dislodged and splashed into the water next to me. I glanced downstream and glimpsed 300 yards of white water roaring down the canyon. I had neglected to fasten my wader belt, and the waders were full of water. The prospect of tumbling and bobbing down that chute with over 50 pounds of water in my waders was an energizer. I squeegeed both feet into the river bottom and jumped as hard as I could for a huge boulder perched on opportunity Last Chance: the end of a reef that ran downstream from the lower tip of the island. Each hand gripped a separate side of the rock, but both hands could not meet in a bear hug. My hands held—but would this rock hold? It felt solidly anchored. I heaved with all my strength and hurled my soggy self onto the reef; then crawled like a moulting crayfish onto the island.

Water spurting from my waders, and blood from my hands, I ran to my new nine-foot Orvis graphite fly rod, which had survived its landing, grabbed it, waddled over to the line which was still wrapped around the rock, lifted the line, and felt no fish. But wait. I didn't feel a line extended 100 feet downstream, either. Dawn! Light! The salmon, feeling a pull downstream from the bend in the fly line, had again reversed directions and was holding still, facing upstream against the current and pull of the fly line, only about 20 yards from the island!

But strategy? I could not land this fish on the island; he was too strong and heavy to bully; and he would very likely choose to dash downstream again, which would leave me stranded on the island watching the last of my backing peel off. I couldn't cross to the far bank; the water was too deep and fast. And finally I had just found out the hard way that it was not exactly a snap to recross back to my original position.

But now our intrepid fisherman's visage assumed a crafty look. His gray eyes sparkled. He would sneak to the upstream riffle end of the island, neutralize hazardous rocks on the way, cross back for the island by quartering slowly downstream this time in an *upright* position, and then, solidly positioned on the riverbank, and line running directly to fish, tighten up, raise the rod tip, let forth a Saxon cry, and give battle again, free to slog downstream after Old Fighter!

As my war cry echoed down the canyon, I retrieved line with my left hand until it was tight and I could feel every movement of the fish's head. I turned his head toward me and then slightly downstream, and he did what I now wanted him to do: the outsized salmon again rushed downstream into the white water rapids, huge tail surfacing from time to time as the combination of the current, rocks, and pull of the fly line affected his equilibrium.

Twenty minutes later he was rolling, and I started his head toward shore by walking steadily backward until his head rested quietly in six inches of water between boulders of a rocky, steep streamside. I tightened the line as hard as I dared, ready to let go if he snapped his head, and stepped forward undecisively, even timidly, hoping that Old Fighter would wait for a grizzly bear scoop. How nice it would have been to have had guide or ghillie, net or tailer in hand, to help out at this moment!

Hope vanished. Old Fighter flopped mightily, tore the fly line screeching from the reel, was well into my backing and was about to turn a corner of the canyon before I started gaining on him, jogging over boulders in the most unpromising track shoes invented by man: a pair of waders still full of water.

Upon turning the corner, I saw a rainbow of hope 300 yards downstream: a gravelly beach, and quieter water. I thumped downstream after the now-tired salmon, hoping the hook would not tear out, and when we reached the beach, we both decided to slug things out to a conclusion.

By this time, we had walked, run, and swum downstream to within sight of the Jeep. I looked up, hoping to see Jon's touseled head. But no Jon was in sight. He must have been helping Earl Groves, the other fisherman assigned to him, and the only member of the group other than myself who had never salmon fished before.

Seeing no sign of Jon, I focused once again upon the water and the job to be done. Old Fighter lunged gamely but weakly toward midstream. Old Werner turned his head, pumped line in, bent the fly rod sideway, and walked backward slowly but steadily until Old Fighter's head rested at stream's edge in only one or two inches of water, the rest of his body almost beached because of the gentle slope of the gravel bar. Holding rod in left hand, with a slack line this time, Old Werner conquered the indecision and timidity of the novice that had helped Old Fighter escape the last attempt at landing him, dashed to the midstream side of the big fish, grabbed one gill plate, and heaved him upon the bank: three feet and 16 pounds of hook-jawed, male, Atlantic salmon. Forty-five minutes had elapsed since the take, each minute charged with excitement and doubt about the outcome.

Just then Jon's silhouette appeared at the top of the canyon next to the Jeep, net in hand. He waved. Ha! My Viking helper! Perfect timing.

After winning the battle, I suddenly suffered a sharp pang of regret that the hook-jawed battler that had survived any number of hazardous spawning runs would never again leap from the water with sea lice clinging to his silver sides. However, Jon reassured me that the fish would never have survived after the ordeal of that battle, and that in any event his fellow Icelanders were protecting their fishery well enough to justify keeping all the salmon we caught sportfishing.

Jon immortalized Old Fighter with a photograph, while I poured water from my waders. I was wet from head to foot, blue-faced, and shivering. Both salmon blood and Werner blood oozed from my left hand; the ligaments of my long-injured wrestler's knee had been twisted and they throbbed; and one knee cap smarted and had turned black and blue where it had banged against a rock. But, a hot shower, a strong scotch and soda, and some jolly conversation with the other eight fishermen healed all hurts.

Old Fighter added to the pleasure of the trip long after he was landed. The seven fishermen who I had not met before this trip, but who knew each other intimately, apparently decided that second evening that anyone eccentric and single-minded enough to roll downriver like a wheel in pursuit of a salmon must be the right sort, even if he did live hundreds of miles west of Wilmington; and we all laughed and shared wide-ranging conversations without a hint of inhibitions for the rest of the trip.

James W. Knox

A southern gentleman who married a beauti-
ful southern gentlewoman, Miss Kitty. They
together live the Southern good life. This
includes Atlantic salmon fishing which they
both enjoy. Greenville, South Carolina.

Carrying the Male

This is a story of two deliveries, the first a baby, and the second an Atlantic salmon on the River Vididalsa in Iceland. The key people in this tale were Thurster Lydursson and his sweet new wife. The others involved were Doctor Robert Ahearn, his wife Rita, and my own wife who, for the purpose of this story we shall call Miss Kitty. Bob Ahearn was a practicing obstetrician in New York State while his lovely Rita had been a nurse prior to Bob's successful courtship.

The fishing had been pretty good during the week. As the weekend approached, Thurster, our young guide and Land Rover driver, was more and more filled with anticipation. His young wife lived in Reykjavik which was over five hours away, and she planned to come up for the weekend to visit him. Thurster told us how excited he was, particularly in view of the fact that she was pregnant and expecting a child in about six weeks.

We came in from fishing about 11 p.m. on Friday, July 19. While I cannot be 100 percent sure, I am reasonably certain that it was the year 1973. At

316

any rate, there was considerable commotion at our lodge where all of the people fishing the river were headquartered. It seemed that Thurster's wife had arrived in mid-afternoon, and was not feeling too well. Dr. Bob Ahearn was called to her room. After a brief examination he came to the lounge where we were having before dinner drinks and gave us some exciting news. He announced that our young lady was having labor pains and needed to get to a hospital for the delivery of her child.

Blondous, in the very northern part of Iceland, was over two hours from the lodge by Land Rover, which was our only means of transportation. The next few minutes were busy ones. Cans of hot water along with blankets and other possible necessities were loaded into the Rover. About midnight, Thurster and Bob Ahearn escorted Thurster's wife into the Rover. Rita went along to fill in as nurse in the event that the baby arrived en route to Blondous.

Luck was with them. They were able to get the mother-to-be to the hospital before the baby put in its appearance. At about 3 a.m. Thurster's first child, a son, was born without difficulty and by 8 on Saturday morning he, together with the Ahearns, arrived back at our lodge.

After breakfast Thurster took his people the few miles to their salmon pools. This was Miss Kitty's first year of fly fishing for Atlantic salmon. She was prepared for it, having attended the Orvis fly-fishing school at Islamorada in the Florida Keys during the prior winter while we were visiting Billy and Laura Pate at their place at Pen Key Club. She was taught to cast by a pro—none other than Ted Williams who had shown up to watch the students at work. I was sitting on a bench also watching when I heard him say, "That gal in the mini skirt is going to make it!" and he jumped from his seat to give her his personal tutelage. And he stayed there each day, until the three-day school had ended, to prepare Miss Kitty for her future as a fly fisherman.

In any case, that Saturday morning, a very happy Thurster put us on the Armot Pool near the middle section of the Vididalsa which had a long history of being quite productive. The first hour or so went by uneventfully, and about 11 a.m. Thurster left us to check the other group of fishermen he had put on the river. Not many minutes later, Miss Kitty got her first Atlantic salmon to eat a #8 Blue Charm. He was a nice fish, and I went to her side to help her get him to the bank. The Blue Charm was tied on a single hook. We've always heard that you get more fish to take with a single hook, but that you also lose more fish. After 25 or 35 minutes (I really don't know *how* many), the fish seemed ready to be beached.

Neither of us carried a tailer, and our guide was not nearby to tail a fish, so we tried to find a suitable place to beach him. Miss Kitty did this with professional skill, leading the salmon into a narrow canal not over two feet wide. At just about this same instant, Thurster drove up in the Rover and realized what was happening. The fish also, decided to make *his* last effort, and the fly slipped out of his mouth. As Thurster arrived at our side, *salar* made a leap for the main stream. As he disappeared into the river, Thurster went in after him complete with waders and also disappeared. In a moment he reappeared shouting with a big laugh, "Miss Kitty, I hope I got the right salmon!" He proudly held forth a 12-pound cock salmon by the tail. Can you imagine!

When all of this excitement was over we returned to the lodge for lunch. Miss Kitty had a well-earned Bloody Mary; and while I had little to do with the action, I enjoyed mine also. From that day to this, I have no doubt our friends still laugh about Thurster's comment as he came up out of that river with the fish by the tail.

While I haven't seen him in some years, we still go each summer in July to Iceland for a week or so of salmon fishing. Thurster is now the father of three children, and his dad keeps him busy at their office in Reykjavik. However, last July we did spend three or four very enjoyable days with Lydur, the father, on the Vatnsdalsa River, only 20 or 30 minutes from the scene of this story.

Clinton W. Stallard, Jr., M. D.

A retired surgeon, anecdote collector, fly-rod builder (who made the usual transition from bamboo to fiberglass, to graphite, to boron, and back to bamboo), and active member of a little known but widely fished group called "Bullpasture Enterprises." Newport News, Virginia.

English Fly-Fishing Idyll

Having accepted an invitation to attend a conference at Brittanic House in London on a Wednesday, realizing that it would take Tuesday for travel, I asked for, and was granted, a day of vacation on Monday, thus beginning my journey on Friday evening, leaving a meeting at Old Ben Coal main offices in Chicago and taking a TWA non-stop to London. The trip was quite comfortable, and I was able to sleep throughout a major portion of the night, awakening with considerable anticipation of my jaunt into the English countryside.

Ginny, my wife, had investigated the possibilities of a weekend's fishing on a stream within reach of London and was able to billet me at The Greyhound Inn in Stockbridge, Hampshire. She had done her usual thorough job of inquiry and planning, having called Hardy's in London, asking them for the most feasible location for some good fly fishing. Stockbridge turned out to be about seven miles from Winchester, so as I cleared customs (incidentally, carrying a fly rod seems to expedite that!), I caught the underground to

319

Leichester Square, then changed, and arrived at Waterloo Station some fifteen minutes before the departure of the 12:10 train for Winchester. I was able to obtain a first-class compartment which was shared with a solicitor, Harry Lawford. When he learned of my excursion, he referred me to Ian Hay at the Rod Box on St. Georges Street in Winchester, who, he said, would kindly supply me with advice as to flies and local stream conditions.

When I got off the train, I placed a call to the Greyhound Inn and finding them ready to receive me, summoned a taxi which delivered me to the door, first stopping at the Rod Box for a dozen flies. The Greyhound Inn was actually a pub "with accommodations." Immediately on entering, one sees shadow boxes on the walls with large trout, well-designed fireplaces with copper appurtenences, and harness brass as decorations. My room was quite comfortable with a clothes press, lavatory, double bed and easy chair. Having unpacked, I immediately made for the stream which ran nearly underneath the inn. Mr.Norman St. Paul, the publican at the Greyhound, controlled one bank of the Test for 350 yards immediately adjacent to the backyard of the Greyhound Inn; consequently, my first visit to the river was not delayed.

The Test looks like a Montana spring creek, or a meadow stream, finding its way across the downs, clear, with a great deal of green growth rising from the bed of the stream, and dense rushes lining the banks on both sides. The area where I fished was approximately 40 feet wide, and I would guess that in most places was no more than waist deep.

I rigged up an eight-foot Orvis graphite rod (of which I had recently broken the tip) and seated a Hardy Princess reel with a forward-tapered Cortland 444 floating line. I still had the 15-foot leaders that I had been using in Montana streams with a 6X tippit, breaking strength approximately 1.9 pounds. The tip of this rod immediately broke again for no apparent reason; however, having fortunately brought along an eight-foot. Fenwick 1⅞-ounce glass rod, I retired the out-of-commission Orvis and began to cast, this time with a Marquis Hardy #5 reel, again with a Cortland 444 forward-taper floating line and the aforementioned 15-foot leader with the 1.9 tippit.

I then walked the length of the stream without seeing rising fish, making a few tentative casts along the way to no avail. The wind came up, and the combination of tall reeds behind, a fair stand of reeds at the water's edge, and a long leader, all contributed to making fly casting somewhat unpleasant. Soon tiring of this, I retired to my quarters and immediately fell asleep, sleeping through the late afternoon and the shank of the evening, waking about 20 minutes past 8. Not wishing to give up the day entirely, I returned to the stream. The wind had subsided somewhat, so casting was easier, however, with approaching dusk, I could not see the small flies which I was using. These flies had been supplied to me by the Rod Box on my visit there and included a Royal Wulff, Orange Sedge, Blue Sedge, Black Sedge, Iron Blue Dun, Pale Evening Dun, Little Marryat, and one or two others whose names I have now forgotten. These were all dark flies in #16 and #18. Not being able to see them and faced with the evening rise, I decided that I needed a fly I could see. Tying on the reliable Royal Wulff, I began to cast to rising fish.

The first fish to strike was missed entirely, simply struck too soon and too hard, and the fly pulled out of the fish's mouth. It was obviously a good fish, so a certain excitement began to mount. Other rising fish failed to be attracted to the Wulff, and darkness approached. Walking down toward the cabin and seeing one last rising fish, I drifted the fly downstream over the rise. It was immediately taken by a large, strong fish which, feeling the hook, broke the leader immediately. Obviously, there would be no more action from the fish that evening, so I decided to pack it in and start again in the morning.

I slept a bit late but was on stream by about 9. No fish were moving; however, the sun was in favorable position, so that I was able to visualize the bottom of the stream and here and there pick up a silhouette of trout at their feeding stations. This again was very much like a Montana spring creek and made it easy to drift flies over the fish. Again, they were not interested in the English patterns, nor in my remaining Wulff patterns as they were #12s. A number of flies were in the air and there was a little bit of activity up and down the stream. I did not recognize any of them but finally decided that most of them would resemble a #16 Adams as well or better than any other fly I could find in my box. Very simply, that was the answer! The first fish weighed about four pounds and was a beautiful brown which I released. By now two young visitors, ages 11 and 13, were at my heels. The next fish, also a brown, weighed three pounds four ounces. The boys retrieved a net for me so we killed that fish, the boys taking it back to the inn to be prepared for their later consumption. The next fish was of similar size, perhaps larger, and was lost when almost ready for the net because the clinch knot came undone. After that, a succession of mishaps occurred, larger fish were lost, and I became hungry and a little tired.

After an excellent breakfast, I decided to rest a bit before returning to the stream. The rest turned into a five-hour nap, so it was late afternoon when I reappeared streamside. Another fisherman was there with two companions. He was fishing a large glass rod, I would guess at 9½ feet, weighing in the neighborhood of five ounces. This was rigged with a level line and a short leader, not tapered, about 5½ to six feet long. He was a River Warden on the Test, much nearer the ocean, on salmon beats. I moved above and killed a three-pound rainbow, then below, losing a fish of similar size. At this point, my host had set up a picnic meal in the backyard and invited me to join them. I did, eating lamb cutlets with curry sauce, an excellent salad and a pint of the estimable Courage beer.

Another night and another return to the stream. To my surprise I caught a 12-inch grayling as a result of casting to a rise in the middle of the stream. When asking the River Warden about the fishing, he told me that there were also, here and there, a cannibal pike and that it would be advantageous if I were able to hook one of those. Pike are said to eat at least two reasonably large trout per week. I didn't try, even though I had streamers which readily took pike in Labrador.

No more fish came to the net; however, some exciting action with broken leaders ensued, and I am sure that at least one of the fish I lost would have exceeded five pounds. Again in the late evening, I returned to the pool immediately above the inn to look for the big fish of the first night. He was there and rising. A repetition of the previous evening followed. I now had a 4X leader and a #12 Royal Wulff rather than the 6X tippet and the #14 Wulff, which he had taken before. Drifting the fly downstream as before, I found again a very cooperative and very large fish which I was entirely unable to land. He made a strong upstream run, went into the reeds at the opposite side of the stream, came back out, having circled a patch of reeds and sulked somewhere in the middle of the stream. The vibrations indicated that he was still hooked, but I was unable to make any progress in the fight. Finally, by moving upstream, somehow or other the line came free and again the fish was in the middle of the river. We stood, more or less at bay, I with the rod arched but unable to gain line, the fish sullen, holding in midstream. Tapping the rod a few times finally induced another strong run, another trip into the reeds, another fouling of the line, and this time there was no vibration. The fish was gone with the broken leader.

At this point, I felt that the Test had given me all that a fisherman could reasonably require and looked forward to another time when, with my recently acquired knowledge of the stream, I felt that I would be on to more large fish.

The next day dawned extremely cold and blustery; worse, I also learned I did not have the stream for that day. My host instead took me to a lake called "John O'Gaunts" where he indicated that larger fish were to be had. When we arrived, the weather was fairly moderate, the lake was quite attractive and was surrounded by fishermen. There was some time before we were able to find the owner and obtain his permission (with the exchange of £4 sterling) to fish in the lake that day. I began to walk the edge of the lake and cast to rises with no success. For the first time, I realized why the English trout fisherman dressed as he did, for example knee-high boots, heavy jackets or coats, or heavy fishing vests, which were considerably more garment than any American fisherman wears. The temperature now dipped into the 40s, the wind rose and a cold and miserable rain began falling. I sat in a fishing shelter for awhile watching three spirited horses, in an adjacent field, play for the better part of an hour. That, in itself, was interesting as there appeared to be definite structure to their game. Two would gang up on one, and after that one had been chased and nipped, he became a chaser, and one of the chasers became the chasee. This went on for awhile and was quite amusing.

Eventually I became quite cold and decided to try to find transportation back to town as my host had agreed to pick me up at 7, some two or three hours in the future. I, therefore, walked to the nearest farmhouse and attempted to get a taxicab. None would be available for some time, which would mean that my host would have an unnecessary trip. Finally, the farmer himself was kind enough to drop me off at Stockbridge. I volunteered my name, he did not supply his, so to this day, I do not know whom I should thank. Nevertheless, his assistance was most appreciated, and I was glad to get back to the pub.

Venturing back to the stream where the two fishermen, who had the stream for the day, were still active, I found one was a Mr. Robinson, the local butcher, the other a Mr. Timm, whom I think was a businessman and perhaps a solicitor as well. They had had no luck at all, neither of them having a fish and only one having struck a fish. The weather continued windy, fish were rising, however, and I walked back to the stream to watch Mr. Timm casting. Having seen a fish rising on the way up, I pointed out what his feeding lane must be. Mr. Timm was fishing with an Orange Sedge, which he promptly cast into the exact position, and drifted it over the fish. A quick take occurred, but the fish spit out the fly before he could be struck. I watched for a few more minutes but became chilled again and returned to my room.

The rest of the evening was spent enjoying the company of the pub's guests and the fishermen who remained to have a few. All of the guests were very convivial and quite pleasant to the American visitor.

I would love to spend a great deal more time on English chalk streams, which I feel offer as much action to the fly fisherman as he could desire. The Itchen is a very good stream, and I also learned that the Wye and the Avon were well-known trout streams in the area. I only wish I had been better prepared from the standpoint of clothing. One of the things that would have been quite useful was a pair of knee boots. Since these are quite clumsy to pack, rivaling waders in difficulty, I would suggest that the overshoe made by Totes, which comes in several heights, would do quite well. Further, they roll up to pack in a small space. I also recommend that foul-weather gear, including jacket, which I had, and trousers which I did not, would be useful in the English spring and no doubt during the summer as well.

John C. Harkness

John claims his unbounded enthusiasm and voracious appetite for sporting literature make up for what he lacks in skill and opportunity to pursue his chosen outdoor activities. He occasionally resorts to the practice of metallurgy to raise additional funds for more fly tackle and shotguns. Lakewood, Ohio.

When You're Not, You're Not

When my brother-in-law George Izso invited me to join him on a fly-fishing trip to Oil Creek State Park in western Pennsylvania one May, prefacing the invitation with mouth-watering tales of trout caught and released on a similar trip the year before, I jumped at the chance to go.

To fully appreciate the ensuing turn of events you have to bear in mind that I'm pretty much a weekend outdoorsman, sneaking in a duck or grouse hunt or fishing trip here and there as my hectic schedule permits. This is not always conducive to success, and I look forward to the Cleveland Museum of Natural History Trout Club's annual outing at Rockwell Springs Trout Club in Castalia, Ohio to restore my faith in fly tackle.

On the other hand, George is a true sportsman. He's successfully hunted big game and fished in Alaska, shot deer in Pennsylvania, gunned for waterfowl in the Sandusky Bay area, bagged upland game throughout Ohio, and fly fished the Yellowstone. George introduced me to fly fishing and helped me buy my first fly rod, for which I will forever be in his debt.

What's more, George is meticulous. He plans everything to the last detail—food, campsites, maps, proper tackle, the works. He even ferrets out local experts and gets their advice on the choicest fishing spots and hottest fly patterns for a given area. With such experience on your side, who wouldn't expect a fantastic fishing trip?

There was an ulterior motive to this trek. George owned a camper, a heavy, substantially "bear proof," rigid-wall design that telescoped to car trunk height for trailering, which had done yeoman service on a trip to Yellowstone National Park. It was parked in a camp ground at Oil Creek, where his wife (they were about to be separated) and nephew had left it the week before. The camper had to be removed to make room for the Memorial Day holiday crowd the following weekend, and his wife had planned another trip with it.

George phoned me with the itinerary—he'd arrive at my house Friday evening. We'd pack his pickup truck that night and depart early Saturday morning, arriving well before lunch. The early afternoon would be spent making minor repairs to the camper. We'd then hike into the park and fish the expected hatch of Light Cahills. Sunday we would get in a few casts in the morning, but would break camp early and head for home with the camper. As fate would have it, these well-laid plans were not quite to be.

George arrived on schedule Friday night, and after a few beers the business of packing his pickup with sleeping bags, fly rods, waders, vests, spare clothing and fly-tying gear was accomplished. A camp cooler laden with steaks, other staples, beer and a bottle of 101-proof Wild Turkey completed the burden. We turned in, eager for the morrow.

We awoke at sunrise on Saturday, had a quick breakfast, and mounted the cab of the pickup, anxious to get on the road. The truck had other ideas, however, and proceeded to balk and stall every few seconds, refusing to idle. It had run perfectly up to now, and there had been no hint of trouble. With his usual foresight, George even had a tune-up just to assure its roadworthiness for this trip.

It was absolutely necessary that we take a vehicle with a heavy duty trailer hitch. The camper was much too heavy for my Toyota with its bumper hitch. We lost precious time trying to troubleshoot the problem ourselves, then trying to find a garage that could fix it on a Saturday morning. Finally, we were forced to leave the truck at a dealership and seek alternate transportation.

The only viable solution was for George to borrow from his (soon to be "ex") father-in-law an old Buick Electra equipped with the requisite hitch.

I waited at home while my wife drove George to Strongsville for the car. He returned about 1½ hours later with the Buick, its odometer well into the second 100,000 miles and the former dark blue paint job weathering purple on the hood and trunk lid, amid splotches of rust. George was told it "ran a little rough," since the retired father-in-law only drove it back and forth to the local market, and all it needed was a good long run on the open road to "blow the carbon out of it."

Well, there must have been a lot of carbon, because that old car ran in surges, coughed, and occasionally backfired.But it got us to the camp ground in midafternoon, after a brief stop in Oil City to purchase non-resident fishing licenses at a sporting-goods store that had seen better days. Business must have been pretty slow, because a name-brand rifle scope I casually admired got cheaper by the minute as George completed his license application. We left the scope, took our licenses and moved on.

We arrived at the camp grounds shortly thereafter and set about the chores: erecting the top of the camper, tidying up its interior, repairing a plumbing leak and fixing a broken window canopy.

While George prepared a hearty steak dinner, I proceeded to tie up a few Light Cahills for use that evening. Since I had just completed my basic fly tying course at the Museum of Natural History, these artificials were somewhat lacking in delicacy, and might better have been called "Medium Cahills." But we both were confident they'd do the trick.

At last we headed for the stream to meet the anticipated hatch. We drove the back roads to a park entrance, along the way passing woodlots and cornfields while George gave me an impromptu lesson in deer-stand site selection. A steep, winding and rutted road took us to the floor of a picturesque valley through which snaked Oil Creek.

We parked the car at the site of the historic Miller Farm near where Wolfkill Run enters Oil Creek, then proceeded to suit-up and hike the black-topped bike path on the western bank of the creek about 1½ miles upstream to a hole George had selected on his last trip, known locally as Night Cap Pool. Rain had fallen heavily for the past few days and the creek was high and fast. Too fast, in fact to wade in most places. Our intended destination proved to be one of the few wadable areas.

Something was wrong, however. No hatch came off—not as we arrived, nor while daylight lasted. And there were apparently no fish. Nothing rose as we scanned the slick surface of the pool. For a while we succumbed to Halfordian logic and fished the water with our Light Cahills. Having no luck in "pounding them up" with last year's best producer, we began to experiment—attractor dries, nymphs, even streamers. Absolutely nothing caught the attention of a fish.

At one point I resorted to my pocket insect net to try and scoop a natural from the current to "match the hatch." The small tan spinner-like objects floating past the legs of my waders proved to be size 14 to 16-seed pods, much to our chagrin.

About this time three young boys, not more than 10-years-old, rode up on their banana-seated bikes, each kid displaying a discount store rod with a closed-face spincasting reel. They stood on the high bank for awhile, watching the two of us with our graphite rods, English reels and vests dripping with small fortunes worth of fly boxes, tools and nets. And then one of the boys displayed something else—a trout, a *big* trout that looked to be over 18 inches long. "Hey mister!" he hailed. "We got this one on a worm back there around the bend! D'ja catch anything?"

We continued to pound the water until dusk closed in on us, then reluctantly headed back to the car, fishless. Along the way a park ranger passed us in his patrol car and asked how we did. When we informed him we'd been skunked he seemed surprised. "That sure is hard to understand," he said. "We stocked that stretch just this Thursday with over 1,000 trout!" The only explanation he could offer was that the fast water from the heavy runoff of the last few days must have washed most of the fish downstream.

We arrived back at camp bushed and dejected. It then started to rain, softly at first but building steadily to a first-rate shower. We broke out the Wild Turkey and tried to talk of other things besides fishing as the raindrops pattered on the camper roof. I turned in for the night, but George decided to go into town to console himself with some country-western music at a local night spot. When he returned about 2 a.m. it was still raining.

We slept until about 8 a.m. on Sunday, and awoke to a faint drizzle that let up as we dressed and shaved. My clothes had been tossed on the camper floor the night before, under the kitchen table that had converted to my bunk. As I dressed, wetness alerted me to the fact that not all the leaks in the camper had been repaired.

George cooked a camp breakfast while I packed up our gear and tried to get used to my damp clothes. We then dropped the camper top and George backed the car into position to hitch up.

The rain resumed as we started to pull out of our campsite, and it was then that we first became aware of a slight incline from our location to the camp road. Try as we might, the Buick's old tires would not bite on the wet grassy slope, and we succeeded only in spinning a deep rut. After several futile attempts to budge the car, the owner of a four-wheel-drive vehicle from the next campsite drove over and tossed us a tow line with which he proceeded to pull us up onto the road. We thanked him, and set out for home.

We weren't on the road long when George announced we needed gas. Simultaneously, it started to rain in sheets, one of the hardest downpours I can remember. We found a run-down discount gas station that fortuitously had a canopy over its pumps and we pulled in. That was when George started to swear.

"What's wrong now?", I asked.

"They gave me the ignition keys for this car, but forgot to give me the key to the gas cap!" he sputtered.

Well, let me tell you, those locking filler caps may look cheap, but they are effective! It took three of us—George, me, and the station attendant—half an hour to pry that thing off in a spray of rain that slanted under the canopy. Of course, all we had were a screw driver, a pair of pliers and a beer can opener. When the last shards of cap were finally wrenched away we filled up and begged a spare non-locking cap that came close to fitting from the attendant, one some other unfortunate had driven off without.

Back on the highway we drove along Oil Creek as it flowed into Oil City and looked longingly on as an angler hooked and played a fish in a broad curve of pocket water—in the heart of an industrial area. Then the rain let up again.

A bit farther on we came to a long, steep winding uphill grade. The old Buick coughed, bucked and ran slower and slower as we groped for the top of the hill. The best we could do was three miles per hour and stalled several times so we began actively looking for a place to abandon the camper until we could get the car checked out. George persevered, however, and we made it over the top, but it had taken nearly a half hour to go less than a mile.

The road was easy going from there to the Ohio Turnpike interchange at Warren. But all was not well with the Buick. The car continued to shudder and surge as we drove on, and dropped dead in its tracks just as we nosed into the toll booth and stopped for our ticket. There was no starting it this time.

With a long line of horn-honking traffic behind us, we were obliged by the toll booth attendant to summon a tow truck. It arrived in about 45 minutes and towed us through the toll booth, where we dropped the camper by the roadside, and then it took us off the turnpike to a garage. Since it was Sunday and the garage was closed, we had to leave the car.

I called my wife to report the situation, but there was little she could do except sympathize. We simply had to find a way to pull that camper back home. Reluctantly, George telephoned his (not yet "ex") wife who graciously consented to drive down with her hitch-equipped station wagon from 40 miles south of Cleveland and collect us.

The wait was a long one, after the tow-truck driver returned us to our camper. But there were consolations. First, it wasn't raining any more. Second, I remembered the Wild Turkey in the cooler. Third, we had some junk food left. And as we sipped bourbon, munched potato chips and paced back and forth in the uncut grass at the roadside, George bent down with a shout and came up with a $20 bill! It must have blown out of a driver's hand at the toll booth. With nothing better to do, and rationalizing that someone unlucky enough to lose one $20 could just as well have lost several, we scoured the area looking for more loot. We found all sorts of unimaginable junk, and drew curious stares from passers-by, but unfortunately located no more money.

Our driver finally arrived about two hours after George had called her. We hitched up the camper and headed for home. It was a quiet, uneventful return trip—partly because there wasn't much to say except that we got miserably skunked, and mainly because we were both dead on our feet. I fell asleep in the back seat almost immediately and so can't vouch for the conversation up front.

It took me several weeks to work up enough enthusiasm to pick up a fly rod again. And George had to work out the logistics of recovering the Buick the next week. But we can now look back on this fly-fishing fiasco and laugh.

Fortunately, our fishing trips since then have been more productive and filled with happier memories.

Anthony J. Obara, Jr.

"Buddy" is one of the most exciting and highly regarded wildlife sculptors in America. His work has been displayed in the Oval Office of The White House and received acclaim in exhibitions at prestigious galleries on both coasts of the United States and in England. He also comes on to fly fishing! Unionville, Pennsylvania.

Who's Counting?

Reuben Armstrong, who sometimes works for me as a carpenter in my sculpture studio in the rolling hills of Chester County, Pennsylvania, and I were eagerly awaiting the opening day of trout season. We had already decided to head for the Octarara River and fight the multitudes of wormers who would be following the release truck. None of this nonsense for us, however, but rather split bamboo and flies.

Now in Pennsylvania trout always opens on the second Saturday of April, whatever the date, and I know this. I really do. Anyway, Reuben told me that this year's opening was April 13th so off we went that morning expecting to find elbow to elbow fishing except on the fly section. When we arrived it was obvious something was missing, namely a thousand cars parked bumper to bumper along the country road. Hurray! we thought, everyone is at work and would not be there till evening. We had the whole stream to ourselves.

Parking the car and gearing up in minutes, we decided to fish a little run that no one ever bothered with, a feeder stream called Stewart's Run.

Twenty feet from the bridge I cast a muddler minnow and, first crack, *bang*! A nice 12-inch brookie, fat as could be! Carefully releasing him, I cast again and, second crack, *whammo*!! A 15-inch brook.

Reuben, across the stream maybe 10 feet wide, was taking all this in without a word. I fished another 20 feet upstream and caught four more fish. Now we are both incredulous. Sure this stream had a few fish in it, but never anything like this! Had we found brook trout heaven? Had this little run been wrongly written off because of its size? Whatever the reason, we didn't much care because, boy, was it producing fish now. Reuben, who had not yet taken a fish, asked what I was using? I told him a maribou muddler with tinsel. He asked for one but at this point I was reeling in my eighth fish to his great disbelief. Then I tossed a fly over to him, sat down for a smoke and let him take over.

A short cast and bingo! A carniverous brookie took it and a smile that only a fisherman knows came over Reuben's face. After he netted about six more fish we decided to work our way upstream, hopping from boulder to boulder to where no one ever fished, while our good fortune continued for about another 2½ hours. Our talley at the top of the stream was 38 fish, all brookies, all between 12 and 15½ inches, and all fat! All we could think of was getting back to tell a friend or two of our newly discovered "Brookie Heaven"!

The grins on our faces as we neared the bridge were almost a glow. While Reuben went to the Jeep for sandwiches and beer, I plunked my fly in right below the bridge and immediately another marauding brookie hit. We could do no wrong today, every cast was magic! Two more casts and two more fish. Would it ever stop?

On top of the bridge was a father and his son of about seven who had come to watch. Casting again and hooking up again, I turned to the little boy and asked if he would like to reel in the fish. His eyes lit up and his father nodded approvingly. The little tyke played this fish as if it were Moby Dick himself. Rod now back in my hand, the father asked what fly I was using and I told him it was a maribou muddler. He then inquired how we had done and I nonchalantly answered, "Thirty-eight, all released, of course," and mentioned the absence of fishermen on opening day, having never seen it like this before. Old Dad then dropped the bombshell, "Why, the season doesn't open till tomorrow, guys. I was wondering why you were fishing and I thought maybe you were with the fish and game department." With this I looked at Reuben, he looked at me, and we both got that same sinking feeling.

Well, the season did open the next day on the second Saturday in April as always. No major harm was done. We had released everything and we didn't get caught. But boy, were we lucky. Two ways. Thanks, Reuben. It *was* one magic morning.

J. Steven Renkert

*As do his Brothers and Sisters of the Angle
herein represented, Steve displays an uncommon passion for his pursuit of the trout
of Potter County and the salmon of Iceland.
Canton, Ohio.*

Return to the River

It had stopped raining as Buck eased down the steep slope to the river far
below. The soggy hummocks and ankle-deep moss made his progress pain-
fully slow. Volcanic boulders and loose rock forced him to move sideways as
much as downward. Occasional gusts of wind swirled through the canyon
and up the slope. It was over 200 feet down to the river. He could understand
now why some fishermen declined to fish this stretch of water. His ghillie
had said the way down and back was difficult, but still he wanted to fish it
himself. He wasn't sure how much longer he could fish for salmon and he
wanted to gather in as much of the experience as he could.

It had finally been agreed that the ghillie would take Buck's fishing partner to the lower water. He would meet Buck at the Climbing Rope Pool
where the Icelanders had set a line of posts up the canyon side and had
attached a rope to assist those making the long climb back to the top. "If I
move slowly, I'll get down all right," he said to himself. "Even if my legs
ache, I can still move. I just wish my fingers weren't so swollen. If I ever

could cast well, I surely can't now—and if it gets much worse, I won't be able to cast at all. Then it will be over, but I have this trip—at least this one last time. If I can take one good salmon, then I can stop."

The loose rock slid away under foot and Buck fell heavily, breaking only part of the fall by rolling to his side as he hit the slope. His first thought was for his fly rod. He saw it was undamaged. He stretched his legs. "I guess I'm OK, but I'm going to be sore this afternoon and worse tomorrow," he worried. "Maybe I shouldn't have tried it after all. I could have fished the 'home water' and left the canyon to the younger men." He sat there and watched the river below him, cold and gray, swirling through deep pockets moving out again into long riffles and on to large pools. "The river is there, the salmon must be there too. They have survived the deep sea trawlers, the nets, and all of the other obstacles. If they can do that, I can," Buck reassured himself as he slowly stood up. His waders were scraped but there were no tears. "They're tougher than I am. Old age is hell!" he continued his one-way conversation and grimaced as he took his first step. "But there will be plenty of time to take it easy after this trip," he thought, as he carefulled his way over the loose rock. He cut diagonally across the hill, and watched every step.

Twenty minutes later Buck reached the river. Above him a 30-foot falls roared down, cutting off the salmon from further travel upriver. He worked out his line. The #8 Blue Charm dropped into the foam at the base of the falls and was swept deep by the currents and the belly in the line. "I'll never hook anything that way," he speculated, as he tried his second cast at the edge of the cascading waters. Again the line bellied and ripped the fly through the water. The third cast fell off target and it too was swept up by the swirling water. "I can't fish here," he fretted. "I'd need a sinking line and a better sense of the water. I can't even see some of these currents."

He moved downstream. The water widened into a big riffle. There were several good-looking pockets and Buck covered them as best he could. He didn't see a sign of salmon as he worked on downriver to a bend where a larger boulder smoothed the water and had formed a big backwashed pool. He eased into the water and found he could wade easily—out of the main rush of the river. He began to work the pool slowly and carefully with lengthening casts. "I can handle this," he thought.

He was pleased, as he began to work the edge of the current flow just to the side of the boulder. He watched the fly sweep downriver. Suddenly, the line began to move steadily upstream. There was no strike, no sign of a fish, just an irresistible pull that quickly had the line slicing through the water. Buck struck once, but he was sure the drag from the line would drive the hook into the salmon's jaw.

"He must be a good fish," he reflected as he moved toward the shallows in a better position to play the fish. The line continued to stream off the reel for over 75 yards. Then, well upstream, Buck saw a large salmon broach the surface and then hold in deep water.

Buck slowly worked his way to shore, keeping the tension on the line. He moved upstream nearer the salmon. He could see it now—a truly large fish holding in the current behind a boulder. The salmon had lost his brilliant black and silvery ocean coloration and was taking on the dark tones of the river. "He is enormous! He must have come in with the first run of fish this spring," Buck exulted as he approached, sweating from the exertion and the excitement. As he got to within 10 yards of the salmon, it turned and headed downriver with increasing speed. The reel whined as the line sped out, and Buck could see he was deep into the backing before the salmon stopped in another pool well below the boulder where he had been hooked.

Buck stumbled on a loose rock as he turned. He caught himself just before he lost his balance. "I've got to be more careful," he admonished. "If I fall here, I could have real trouble."

He splashed downstream and awkwardly crossed through a long riffle. Again he approached the salmon and again it simply went back into the main flow and headed downstream. Buck watched the line melt off his reel again. "This is tiring me more than the salmon," thought Buck. He tried to apply some pressure to the line, but found it was impossible to slow the salmon's progress. "I'll have to keep moving," Buck inwardly stated, as he began to follow the fish. "At least I'm not losing as much line." Finally, the salmon stopped once more and held. He was able to regain all the backing and was well into the line when the salmon took off again downstream. Buck marveled as he saw the wake of the salmon as it angled across and then down the river. "It's an enormous fish! It must be bigger than the 21-pounder I caught years ago. If I can only catch this last salmon—then I can quit and no regrets."

As he neared, the salmon made a move upstream. "Now he has to battle the river, too," thought Buck. He found he could apply pressure to the salmon as it reached a stretch of heavy current. Eventually, the pressure became too much and the salmon turned and swung downriver past Buck. He seemed never to stop. Almost all the backing was gone. Buck moved as fast as he could through the shallows after the salmon. It finally held near the river's edge. Buck's knees trembled and he was nearly out of breath as he slowed his own race downriver. He kept the rod tip high as he worked down towards the salmon. He came to within 15 yards of the fish when it swept back into the flow downstream. Buck tried putting some pressure on the line and found he could. "He's tiring," Buck confessed. "But I can't take much more of this either." The two of them fought on down the river. Finally, Buck saw the sheer canyon walls by the Climbing Rope Pool where his guide would be waiting.

The salmon held, and then ran once more, and then held in a shallow pocket. Buck closed in as carefully as he could. His hands hurt and all of his body ached. He could see the salmon hanging in the flow and scarcely moving. "Maybe I can tail him," he conjured. "That would be perfect. To have hooked him and fought him alone all the way down the river and to land him myself." He reached into the water and attempted to tail the salmon. As he touched it, the salmon exploded forward and then downstream. "I can't chase him," thought Buck, "not again." He applied all the pressure he could to the salmon. It swept on downriver. Buck saw his guide waving and heard the shout of encouragement. "I can't quit now," he muttered, and he slowly began to move downstream, recovering some line and losing some, too. Finally, the salmon came to rest in a pool at the canyon's edge. He saw the guide turn and begin climbing up the canyon wall. "That's all right," Buck thought. "I want to do this alone. I can land him without the guide." He stumbled once and nearly fell into the river. "Not now, not here!" he cursed. A surge of adrenalin seemed to wipe away the exhaustion. He stumbled again, but made his way downriver.

He could see the salmon holding in the current. "It's worn out, too," he thought. He approached and slowly bent to tail the fish. He brushed the tail as he grasped ahead of it with all of the force he could muster. The salmon shuddered, but didn't move. "I've got him!" cried Buck. "He's tremendous! He's wonderful!"

As he held the salmon, he saw his guide reappear coming down the steep slope with a large green cage. "That was it," thought Buck. "They want to keep him for the fisheries program." The guide approached and exclaimed at the size of the salmon. "It will go over 25 pounds. That's what they want for stocking the river." For an instant, Buck wanted to keep the salmon forever. Then he heard himself say, "That's fine. Take him."

The guide placed the cage ahead of the salmon. "Wait, I want the fly," said Buck. He watched the guide take hold of the fly. With scarcely a tug, it came free. "You wouldn't have held him much longer," the guide said. "That's only fair," admitted Buck. "I couldn't have held much longer either." Then he eased the salmon into the cage and secured the door.

The guide anchored the cage near the edge of the pool. "The fisheries people will be here tomorrow. They'll move the salmon downriver to a point where they can transport him out to the fisheries station."

Buck watched the giant fish holding steady in the wire mesh cage. "May you return to the river," he said quietly. Then he slowly began putting away his tackle.